DATE

D0583922

OFFICIAL
LEADERSHIP
IN THE CITY

OFFICIAL LEADERSHIP IN THE CITY

Patterns of Conflict and Cooperation

JAMES H. SVARA

New York   Oxford
OXFORD UNIVERSITY PRESS
1990

Riverside Community College
Library
4800 Magnolia Avenue
Riverside, CA 92506

MAR '02

JS 331 .S87 1990

Svara, James H.

Official leadership in the
  city

ty Press

Toronto
Madras   Karachi
Petaling Jaya   Singapore   Hong Kong   Tokyo
Nairobi   Dar es Salaam   Cape Town
Melbourne   Auckland

and associated companies in
Berlin   Ibadan

Copyright © 1990 by Oxford University Press, Inc.

Published by Oxford University Press, Inc.,
200 Madison Avenue, New York, New York 10016

Oxford is a registered trademark of Oxford University Press

All rights reserved. No part of this publication may be reproduced,
stored in a retrieval system, or transmitted, in any form or by any means,
electronic, mechanical, photocopying, recording, or otherwise,
without prior permission of Oxford University Press.

Library of Congress Cataloging-in-Publication Data
Svara, James H.
Official leadership in the city : patterns of conflict
and cooperation / James H. Svara.
p.   cm.
Bibliography: p
Includes index.
ISBN 0-19-505762-7
1. Municipal government—United States.   I. Title.
JS331.S87   1990
352'.0072'0973—dc20   89–3398   CIP

2 4 6 8 9 7 5 3 1

Printed in the United States of America
on acid-free paper

To Claudia

Preface

This book is the product of several years of focused research, but it draws on observations and participation in local politics that extend back to the late sixties. As I learned more about city politics, I was increasingly struck with the diversity among specific cities and between classes of cities, on the one hand, and the inadequacy of the scholarly literature on urban politics in dealing with this diversity, on the other. Bigger, multiethnic industrialized cities with executive mayors have loomed large in writings on city politics. Other kinds of cities have been overshadowed, and their distinct qualities have not always been evident to researchers. In my writing and teaching, I have tried to fashion a framework for appreciating how cities and the officials who run them are different in positive ways.

In my exchanges with public officials, the gaps in what we know and the limitations in our research are evident. This is not the disjuncture between theory and practice. Rather, the gaps reflect a failure to develop theory that pertains to the challenges and conditions city leaders face in handling the tasks of their offices. Modest theory—in the form of models, typologies, and concepts for key phenomena—with supporting analysis is needed to bring to academic discourse a better grasp of the complex circumstances city officials face.

This discussion is an effort to correct these shortcomings and other deficiencies in the literature on city government officials. Some are patently obvious. We know far more about mayors than we do about council members, for example, and what we know about mayors applies to roughly half of our cities if we divide municipalities by the form of government they use. We have too often treated urban administrators as if they were power-hungry bureaucrats by not looking closely enough at their attitudes and behavior in different institutional settings. Because of these limitations, academics drawing on the urban politics literature have little to offer to council members, to mayors in council-manager cities, or to department heads trying to deliver services in a political environment that is not always conducive to fairness, effectiveness, or efficiency.

In some respects, this is a book about some specific cities. They do not receive special treatment in these pages, but New Haven, Connecticut, and Greensboro—along with other North Carolina cities—have been important places in my life and in my thinking about cities. Having lived, studied, and politicked in New Haven from 1966 to 1972 and received "inside" information from my wife and friends who worked in city government during the Lee administration, I had a good grasp of the fascinating politics of this city, which has figured so prominently in writings on urban politics. After moving to Greensboro in 1972, I in time came to develop a similar grasp of the political and governmental life of that city. In the eighties, I have had many contacts with officials in Charlotte, Durham, Raleigh, and Winston-Salem and have lived in Chapel Hill.

Familiarity with the politics of New Haven did little to help me understand the politics of the North Carolina cities, and vice versa. This was a startling realization. There is not just a difference in region and political culture. Indeed, the differences had less to do with these factors than with the governmental institutions used. Similar differences are present between cities within any region or cities that share other characteristics but have organized the governmental process along contrasting structural lines. To be sure, cities of the same "type" are far from identical among themselves. These five large North Carolina cities, all of which use the council-manager form, diverge in interesting ways. A single city may experience change over time even though the formal structure of government remains the same, as New Haven and Greensboro have experienced with turnover among officials and the emergence of new issues. Still, analysis of governmental affairs in the types of cities that New Haven and Greensboro represent is more productive when it is guided by different conceptual models. Developing a better understanding of the way officials behave in different governmental contexts is the purpose of this book.

I have come to appreciate that there are distinct opportunities and constraints for officials in cities with mayor-council and council-manager government. Too often there is a sense that some kinds of cities are better and the officials in these cities are the exemplars of their office. The biases run both ways. Mayors in the mayor-council cities are the "real" mayors in the common perception, whereas their counterparts in council-manager cities are ersatz versions of the position—mere figureheads. Some consider all administrators to be narrowly self-interested; to others, however, city managers in council-manager cities are public-spirited, competent administrators whereas administrators in mayor-council cities are bureaucrats or hacks. Council members in both types of cities are often regarded as fifth wheels. The negative stereotypes are inaccurate and unfair to officials who are trying to serve their cities. We need to take a fresh look at the strengths and weaknesses of mayors, council members, and administrators in both types of cities.

Many people have helped me to be able to write this book, some of whom I can acknowledge here. Comments and suggestions regarding my research on relationships among city officials have come from many colleagues in political science and public administration. These include Lee Bernick, Charles Goodsell, Robert Gump, Donald Hayman, Lawrence Keller, Timothy Mead, John Nalbandian, Chester Newland, David Olson, Richard Stillman, Gordon Whitaker, and Deil Wright. Practitioners and those who work in organizations of local officials have provided invaluable assistance as research subjects and interpreters of local government. They have read my work and listened to my comments in panels, offering advice that helped me know when I was on or off track. E. S. (Jim) Melvin and Thomas Osborne, former mayor and city manager respectively of Greensboro, and John Witherspoon, Guilford County Manager, have patiently explained over the years their perspectives on how local government works. City managers Wendell White in Charlotte and Bryce Stuart in Winston-Salem shared their thoughtful observations on many occasions. Valuable insights have been offered by William Cassella from the National Civic League and Terrell Blodgett from the League and the University of Texas at Austin, William Hansell of the International City Management Association, and Leigh Wilson and David Reynolds of the North Carolina League of Municipalities. Finally, elected officials and administrators in cities where field research was conducted between 1984 and 1986—Akron, Charlotte, Dayton, Greensboro, Hartford, Kansas City, Knoxville, Lincoln, Memphis, Minneapolis, New Haven, and Raleigh—deserve special thanks for their cooperation in completing interviews and questionnaires.

In the Political Science Department at the University of North Carolina at Greensboro, Maggie Davis, departmental secretary, and Virginia Hoover, former graduate program secretary, kept things running smoothly when my attention to departmental matters was diverted by research and writing. Undergraduate and graduate assistants have contributed to the research over the years, including Cheryl Allee, James Bohmbach, Jeffrey Colbert, Cheryl Coller, Joseph Koury, and Dona McNeill. The Research Council provided grants and support for a research leave in the fall semester of 1984.

At home, John and Kevin have been encouraging or tolerant but always supportive as the book progressed and helped in many ways to get it done. Claudia has been my constant companion and strongest supporter. Her contributions have been more extensive than I can recount and greater than she can know.

Greensboro, N.C.   J.H.S.
September 1988

Contents

OFFICIAL
LEADERSHIP
IN THE CITY

1

Introduction: The Governmental Process in Cities

Cities in the United States are under increasing pressure to find effective ways to meet their problems and respond to the needs of citizens. With diminishing outside assistance, officials in city government are challenged to determine the purpose and direction of their government and to generate the resources to carry out their mission. They must not only find more revenues locally to address their problems, they must also discover the resources within themselves to give leadership to their city, provide quality services, and manage shrinking budgets with greater efficiency. In an era of fend-for-yourself federalism, cities and their leaders are on their own.[1]

This book examines the roles of mayors, council members, and administrators in the urban governmental process and seeks to identify ways to improve performance. In this sense, the discussion is oriented toward practitioners and those preparing to assume positions in government, yet it makes no claim to being a handbook of techniques for practitioners. In another sense, because this book also addresses important theoretical issues about the study of politics and administration in the city—an area unduly neglected in recent years—it holds interest for academicians and scholars. Throughout its discussions I have made a conscious effort to speak as directly to the practitioner as to the scholar.

We need better theory to understand city politics. H. L. Mencken reportedly opined that "a professor must have a theory as a dog must have fleas,"[2] but in this case the itch to build theory is not simply an inescapable nuisance. If one is to understand fully how officials perform in city government, there are three conceptual issues that must be clarified. First, it is necessary to distinguish the *governmental process* from the *political process* in cities. The latter encompasses such a broad spectrum of topics that it is easy to lose track of the part that officials play. The nature of the governmental process—the decisions made and actions taken by governmental officials—is explored in this chapter.

The second problem is understanding how officials divide up the work of government among themselves. The long-standing "dichotomy model" that is based on a clear separation of responsibility for "policy" and "administration" has fallen into disfavor for good reason. An alternative approach is needed, one that recognizes both the separation and sharing of responsibilities. (This "dichotomy-duality" model is discussed later in this chapter.)

The final problem is to conceptualize basic patterns of interaction among officials within the governmental process. We have tended to view city governments as being dominated by conflict, but this is not always the case. The next chapter identifies two models for explaining interactions within the governmental process—one pattern based on "conflict" and the second on "cooperation."

These issues may be translated into the everyday concerns of practitioners. For each issue, several questions can be identified.

First, what is the work of government? Where does one draw the line between the politics of city government and the rest of city politics? Does city government try to intervene in every political dispute and problem in the city? To turn that question around, does every political dispute spill over into the workings of city government?

Second, what are the distinct and overlapping contributions of mayors, council members, and administrators to the work of government? How can positive contributions be expanded and negative ones reduced?

Third, are officials locked in a struggle with each other for dominance and control of resources? How does conflict arise in city government? Can it be managed? Is it possible for officials to sustain a different pattern of relationships based on cooperation?

The Governmental Process

The governmental process refers to the way that officials make public policy decisions, implement them, and manage resources and ongoing operations. Put simply, it concerns what happens in and emanates from "city hall." Examination of the governmental process is a more narrow perspective than is the study of the total political process, which would include all the factors and forces that shape the politics of the community and shape public policy. The governmental process may be viewed as that part of the political process that occurs within government itself.

A point of clarification is needed about "politics," a word used in many different ways. There is a gap between the connotation of "politics" when used as a social science concept and its usage in ordinary conversation and the media. The definition that political scientists typically have in mind when they refer to politics is the "authoritative allocation of resources and values."[3] The *concept* refers to the authoritative character of decisions backed by the coercive power of the state. Allocation of resources encompasses the distribution of all sorts of goods, services, and resources—job-training programs, police services, and cable television franchises—and deciding who shall bear the tax burdens to pay for government programs. Allocation of values includes decision about rules governing behavior (e.g., is use of marijuana legal?), recognition of values (e.g., should discrimination be permitted?), and symbolic rewards (e.g., should Martin Luther King's birthday be a holiday?) These decisions are political whether made on the grounds of pure rationality, noble vision, crass patronage, or mindless logrolling. As a concept, then, politics refers to nature of the allocation rather than the method of arriving at decisions. A site for a community center may be chosen as a payoff in exchange for a council member's support of the mayor or on the basis of a needs assessment study, but it is a "political" decision because it determines the distribution of a resource by government. Thus, when scholars examine "politics" in administration, they are analyzing the bases for allocation, not suggesting that there is (necessarily) patronage or corruption.

The study of the governmental process in this book is not intended to be a comprehensive investigation that encompasses all phenomena in the political sphere of urban life. Topics included in the political process that are excluded from the governmental process include political actors in the population (e.g., interest groups, business elites, the media, or neighborhood organizations,) other institutions, higher levels of government, economic and natural resources and constraints in the city, and so on. This is not to say that officials act independently of these forces or factors. If one visualizes a simple input/output systems model of the political (or policy-making) process, presented graphically in Figure 1–1, the emphasis here is on the "black box" in the middle in which

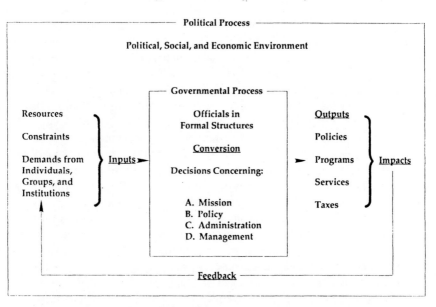

Types of Structures: election systems; form of government and assignment of authority among mayors, council members, and administrators; and administrative organization.

Types of Decisions: Dimensions of the Governmental Process

A. Mission: Determine "purpose," nature of development, scope of services, tax level, and "constitutional" issues, e.g., charter revision and annexation.

B. Policy: Approve projects and programs, develop budget, determine formulae for service distribution.

C. Administration: Establish practices and procedures and make specific decisions for implementing policies.

D. Management: Control and coordination of human, material and informational resources to accomplish the purposes of the organization.

Figure 1-1. The Governmental Process in the Political Process

inputs are "converted" into outputs. The boundaries of the box and its internal architecture are formed by structures such as electoral system, form of government (e.g., mayor-council or council-manager), and administrative organization. The occupants of this box are the officials of city government—elected executives and legislators, appointed board members, and appointed administrative staff, both short-term

"political appointees" and the permanent staff. *The behavior of officials within a structure defined by the city charter—particularly the form of government—and the administrative organization is the governmental process.*
The "conversion" occurs through the choices officials make. The decisions are usefully divided into four types, which represent dimensions of the governmental process—formulating mission, making policy, administration, and management. These dimensions are found at all levels of government and in any organization—public or private. Although government and business organizations differ in how the dimensions relate to each other and who is responsible for each dimension, any organization must decide (1) its goals and purpose, (2) the policies needed to accomplish goals, (3) the methods for implementing policy, and (4) how to control and coordinate resources in order to accomplish the goals of the organization.

This four-dimensional approach is superior to the distinction that is often made in government between determining and executing policy or, to use more common terminology, between "policy" and "administration." Each of these categories has been subdivided into two parts to create the four dimensions. The determination of policy involves defining a purpose and setting broad goals—the formulation of *mission* —as well as specifying detailed middle-range *policy,* such as the content of the budget or the formulae for delivering services. Executing, or implementing, policy is the translation of policies into operating programs and the delivery of services, which shall be referred to as *administration.* It also requires creating and maintaining personnel, budgeting, informational, and other operational systems, which sustain but are independent of policy and administration. These latter activities are *management.*

To illustrate the dimensions with a simple example, when a city decides for the first time to meet the recreational needs of its citizens, it has altered its mission by expanding the scope of services it provides. To establish a playground program in neighborhoods with lots of children is a policy choice that meets part of the broad goal. Deciding where to locate (within the program criteria) and how to equip the playground are administrative decisions that have obvious policy consequences and are probably made by staff. Other persons may influence the decision informally—a council member applies pressure to locate a playground in his neighborhood or a community group stages a demonstration—or formally, as through an advisory committee of neighborhood residents.

Technical aspects of the playground—writing specifications for bids or deciding how high a basketball rim should be—are administrative decisions that are probably made by staff experts alone. Selecting a contractor, purchasing equipment, and training and supervising staff are management decisions.

The distinctions are important in dividing responsibilities in city government, in determining what are the "proper" roles of elected officials and administrators. For government to be democratic, elected officials must control policy. If an administrator, however, makes a "policy" decision that is consistent with a "mission" goal determined by elected officials, then there is democratic control even though an appointed official is "making policy."[4] There has been a long debate about what role elected officials should play, if any, in the execution of policy. The consequences for the governing process are far different if elected officials only influence the "administrative" decision concerning the overall allocation of services, but stay out of specific administrative decisions and management. The council will probably approve the eligibility criteria for participating in a housing rehabilitation program (administration), but council members may or may not also influence the determination of individuals who are eligible to receive grants (also administration) or select the contractors to do the rehab work (management). The four dimensions are discussed in more detail in the next section of this chapter.

Thus, in studying the governmental process one examines how elected and appointed officials interact which each other within differing structural arrangements to make decisions concerning mission, policy, administration, and management. External factors will not be ignored. The inputs, particularly pressures from elements of the city population, are crucial to understanding the behavior of officials. The consequences of outputs—the impact of official actions—must be considered as well. The emphasis, however, is on what officials do.

At first glance, this may appear to be a reasonable topic to pursue. The attention of political scientists, however, has been turned elsewhere until recently. Between 1960 and 1974, there were many studies of city government leaders. Mayoral leadership was a popular topic during this period, as researchers sought to identify the crucial qualities of urban leadership that would enable the city to respond to the urban crisis.[5] The "Urban Governors Series," based on research in the Bay Area and studies of nonpartisan elections in California, greatly enriched our knowledge of city councils.[6] Finally, important studies of city administrators appeared.[7] In contrast to that period, no book-length treatment of city officials was published between 1974 and 1984.[8] A major exception to the declining attention given to the determinants of performance internal to government has been the research on patterns of service delivery.[9] Even this research, however, further diminished the influence attributed to elected officials. If any officials are important, it is the administrators, a conclusion which reinforces earlier arguments that urban "bureaucracies" dominate city government and elected officials are helpless to control them.[10] There was reason to wonder whether examining the internal dynamics of government and the behavior of all officials—elected and administrative—was worth the effort.

Studying the governmental process separate from the more inclusive political process, however, is important for several reasons. First, the public is interested in assessing how officials are doing. They have to make specific choices such as deciding whom to call about a problem with services, whether it will make any difference to report a crime to the police, whether to participate in public programs, and whom to support in elections. More generally, they confer or deny legitimacy to incumbents and institutions and exercise options of voice or exit in response to the performance of city officials and agencies.[11]

Second, the performance of officials and the institutional arrangements of local government make an important difference, at least at the margins, in the quantity and quality of city programs, costs, and services. The socioeconomic, demographic, ethnic, and racial characteristics of a city will affect the level of expenditures on municipal functions. These factors do not, however, determine specific characteristics, for example, the locations, level of maintenance, and cleanliness of parks in a city or the recreational and cultural programs provided therein. The content and the quality of programs and services is shaped by the decisions and performance of government officials.[12] Furthermore, city governments do not respond to change or meet new problems except as officials take on the hard task of deciding what their government should—or should not—do. Shifts of program responsibilities from the federal to state and local governments and the decline in federal financial assistance increase the pressures on local officials to make critical decisions about purposes, programs, and resources. Consequently, more attention should be given to how officials can be effective in the performance of their responsibilities and how they can work together better.

A third argument for this study is that the available literature has important shortcomings. Some may be attributed to the passage of time. Much has changed on the urban scene in the past decade, but new studies have not caught up.[13] There are long-standing gaps, both specific and general, as well. The office of mayor in council-manager systems has never been adequately understood. Comparative studies of officials in mayor-council and council-manager cities are rare. There is no comprehensive framework for examining all official leadership roles across differing formal structures.

Fourth, there has been a gulf between much of the work for practitioners published by associations of officials, such as the National League of Cities and the International City Management Association, and the writings of mainline urban scholars in political science.[14] The former has addressed "applied" concerns and is often prescriptive with neither a clear conceptual foundation nor adequate empirical support. Typically, these publications have been partial to reform institutions and have conceptualized government in ways that emphasize the technical aspects of government and ignore or denigrate "politics."

The empirical work of political scientists, on the other hand, has analyzed data to test theories, but the behavior of officials has been measured in gross aggregate decisions, such as total expenditures of city government, which may have little applicability to the problems that practitioners encounter. There has been more attention given to the characteristics of council members than to the behavior of council members. Political scientists have tended to view the governmental process in terms of a conflict model and to be suspicious of reformism as a mask for the expansion of business interests and bureaucratic power. For these reasons, officials and urban administration scholars and political scientists have sometimes had difficulty talking to each other.

Fifth, there appear to be common pre- and misconceptions about city government structures among partisans of one form or the other. Such attitudes impede understanding of other forms much less the interchange of practices across cities with different structures. One may encounter among proponents of the mayor-council form the notion that professional city managers "don't feel any responsibility to the public," as an otherwise well-informed aide to the mayor in a large Tennessee city argued in an interview. Council-manager supporters, on the other hand, may dismiss the strong executive systems as corrupt and ineffective because mayors appoint some nonprofessional political supporters to offices.[15] Better understanding is needed of the relationship between structure and performance. How are patterns of interaction among officials, governmental outcomes, and official roles associated with differ-ent forms of government?

This question is linked to a larger one about the impact of the munici-pal reform movement. Although this book will not try to settle that complex issue, much of the discussion will have a bearing on the suppositions that have been made about the advantages of one set of institutions or another. Furthermore, there will be frequent references to "reformed" and "unreformed" cities and "reform" and "traditional" institutions. Consequently, a brief digression to examine the municipal reform movement and major interpretations of it is in order.

The reform movement promoted institutional changes intended to make the operation of government more efficient and economical, and more oriented to promoting the good of the community as a whole. Recommended institutions included the council-manager form of gov-ernment, selection of the mayor by the council, at-large elections, non-partisan elections, merit systems in personnel, and city planning. These institutions were packaged in the Model City Charter, first adopted in 1900 but changed to include the institutions just listed in the second edition, which was adopted in 1915.[16] The Charter was promoted by the National Municipal League (now the National Civil League) and other reform groups, which advocated accepting all the changes together rather than picking and choosing among them. Two reinforcing impacts of these changes were to concentrate authority in the hands of elected officials and to produce integrated administrative control under the city manager. The proponents felt that the institutions they proposed would democratize city government by weakening the power of political ma-chines—seen as unaccountable aggregations of power—and eliminat-ing the corrupting influence of money and privileged access to govern-mental outcomes. There was the hope that the needs of the entire city would be addressed more fully if the special interests of particular neighborhoods represented in ward elections were eliminated. The ward was also seen as the basic unit of the party organization. In contrast to the democratic rhetoric, critics have charged that these changes pro-duced undemocratic consequences—reduced participation and lack of representation—and contributed to centralization of city government.

An unreformed government (perhaps better labeled traditional) is one with institutions that preceded the reform movement of the early twen-tieth century or one that has been modernized but retains separation of powers between the mayor and the council. The institutions include the mayor-council form of government, ward or district elections, and partisan elections. To muddy the waters a bit, *strong* mayors in whom most powers in city government are centralized were also proposed by the reform movement in its early stages. This option was dropped from the Model Charter in the second edition, and most observers of city government do not interpret the strong mayor as a reform institution.[17] To add more confusion, in recent years activists, calling themselves "new reformers," have campaigned for the return to district elections in order to increase the representativeness of city councils.[18] In addition, the Model Charter has been revised in an edition completed in 1989 to recognize district elections and direct election of the mayor as acceptable alternatives to the original reform institutions. Many cities have already chosen to mix and match institutions associated with reform and traditional approaches.

Powerful images have developed about the intentions of the reformers and the virtues and ills of the reform movement. In contrast to historical research on the Progressive era, which demonstrates the complexity of the period and the diverse and often inconsistent ideas that contributed to it,[19] political scientists have tended to interpret the purpose of the reform movement narrowly. The movement is commonly seen as anti-immigrant and elitist with a commitment to structural rather than social reform.[20] Given these origins, political scientists have expected reform cities to be dominated by upper-class groups and professional administrators and have commonly characterized reform governments in this way.

Historians have observed that the genteel, "old-line" reformers who supported the nativist cause "sloughed off [their] former xenophobia" after 1900 and blamed the ills of the city on the alliance between urban bosses and business interests rather than immigrant voters.[21] To be sure, the reformers in the National Municipal League concentrated on structural remedies as opposed to emphasizing social and economic reform.[22] Although structural changes were dismissed by some as superficial, Pease argues that the reformers believed that institutions and practices had to be thoroughly modernized "if urban government were to move effectively into the field of social welfare and were to ride herd on economic interests."[23] Thelen indicates that the ranks of structural reformers included social reformers as well.[24]

In contrast to the mainline reformers, the supporters of the new commission plan—a novel form in which elected commissioners act as department heads—were predominantly businessmen, and they were also likely to be elected as commissioners. This form, which appeared on the scene after the first Model Charter, was given only lukewarm support by the National Municipal League.[25] Even in the more WASP, conservative cities that adopted the new forms early, the reform impetus to rationalize government and provide necessary services economically "led [officials], perhaps unknowingly in some instances, in the direction of municipal ownership, of increased planning, and even of social reform."[26] Rather than being a "closed" system, the council-manager form (as opposed to the electoral reforms) improved access to power and expanded services for minorities and the working class and, thus, may have enhanced "the advancement of pluralism."[27]

Thus, although nonpartisan and at-large elections have overrepresented elites and underrepresented minorities, the total package of reforms—most importantly the council-manager form of government itself—has had effects that may be positive on the governance of cities and the performance of city government. These issues have not, however, been systematically studied. In the present study, we shall at least seek to move beyond stereotypes about how governments with different forms operate and how the officials within them behave.

In conclusion, the focus of this study is the governmental process—an examination of how official leaders make decisions within the formal structures of government. In order to have a common framework for studying mayor-council and council-manager forms of government, official actions in the four dimensions of the governmental process are examined. Fuller elaboration of these dimensions is necessary.

Four Dimensions of the Governmental Process

Governing the community requires that officials decide on goals, translate those goals into programs and services, and then implement the programs and deliver the services. Mission, policy, and administration, therefore, are facets of governance. (See Figure 1–2.) Underlying these decisions and essential for smooth operation is management, the foundation of governance. In discussing these dimensions, some comparisons will be made to private, profit-oriented organizations. The similarities and contrasts not only help to clarify the meaning of the concepts, but also show that the business model has little applicability to local government organizations.

The term *mission* refers to the organization's purpose and its scope of activities. Any organization—large city, small town, service agency, or

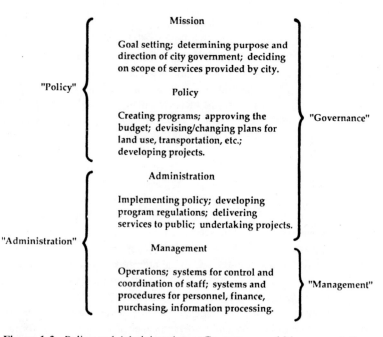

Figure 1-2. Policy and Administration or Governance and Management: Four Dimensions of the Governmental Process

business corporation—needs to have clear goals toward which it strives in order to be successful. This point has been made repeatedly in handbooks for officials. For example, the first question in a checklist of policy-making activities developed by the International City Management Association for council members is "Does the governing body determine the overall mission of the organization?"[28] Still, mission decisions often get lost in the shuffle of more pressing tasks and immediate decisions.

The formulation of mission is particularly difficult in local government. Cities and counties have a wide range of purposes and potentially conflicting priorities. Broad intergovernmental, social, and economic changes are forcing local governments to rethink their goals and purpose. Because the future is unknown, however, it is natural that officials will sometimes focus on continuing to do what they have always done and respond to crises when they occur. A new mayor or city council does not sit down before a clean slate to decide "what should the purpose of our city government be?" Rather, local officials usually reconfirm and only occasionally change their goals.

The concept of mission refers to a collection of broad decisions and approaches that determine purpose, direction, and organization for the city, and thereby create the framework within which other more specific choices are made. These include the range of services provided, philosophy of taxing and spending, and policy orientation, for example, pro-growth versus limited growth. Thus, mission may be thought of as super-policy or mega-policy, because it determines the content of other more focused policies. In business, it is called strategy, business policy, and purpose, as well as mission, but decisions made in this dimension serve the same purpose—they define the purpose and goals for the organization.[29]

There are two important differences in the nature of mission between the public and private sectors that are germane to understanding the local official's role. First, a local government's mission, even in small cities, is far more complex with more numerous and diverse goals than in the typical corporation.[30] A second difference is that the private organization's mission is more likely to reflect conscious choice by officials currently involved in the organization.[31] In cities, on the other hand, some goals are imposed from outside rather than being chosen by local officials. In addition, at any given time, the local government's mission may include some clearly articulated strategies intentionally chosen and other notions about what the city does and whom it serves which, though generally accepted, have not been assessed for many years. The challenge to officials is to make the city's mission coherent and meaningful in light of current conditions.

Policy can be understood as the actual programs undertaken within the parameters shaped by mission. These decisions fill in the details of purpose, create programs, and specify plans. Examples are the budget, the land-use plan, and a project proposal. This distinction between mission and policy has been identified at the national level as the difference between the "agenda" and the "alternatives" and between the "high game" and "middle game."[32] The broader decisions, which I refer to as mission, determine "what government should or should not address at the broadest level," as Ripley and Franklin put it,[33] whereas policy choices refer to decisions of narrower range.

A unique feature of government in contrast to private sector organizations is that deciding on mission and goals only takes officials part way toward deciding what to do; they must still make a host of difficult policy decisions. It is usually obvious what a corporate manager needs to do to carry out a company's mission, although being successful at it can be difficult to be sure. When a city, on the other hand, decides on a strategy of controlled growth, it faces many policy choices concerning zoning, transportation, utility extension, commercial expansion, housing, parking, and so on. Keep in mind that this city may simultaneously be pursuing other strategies, such as crime reduction and attacking discrimination in employment, with their own array of choices. Deciding what to do is made more difficult by uncertain impacts and long lag times between policy making and feedback of results. Furthermore, in government, there may be programs that serve no current purpose, that is, they cannot be linked to a general goal that is part of the government's mission, but survive because of inertia or constituency support.

When programs have been defined, there is another major point of translation. Most policies are not self-implementing. Additional decisions are required to fill in more details and determine who gets services at what level. This is *administration,* or implementation, the final dimension of governing, and includes all the arrangements required for operating specific programs and delivering services. Such administrative decisions as eligibility criteria and application procedures have policy implications and must be consistent with the spirit of the policy decision if the intended purpose is to be accomplished. Policy and administration are intertwined in these decisions. Still, administration is different from policy: the purpose of programs does not originate in administration although purpose is shaped by it.

Implementation is a special concern in the public sector, although Peters and Waterman note that it does not receive the attention it deserves in businesses because of the emphasis on rational decision making in American companies.[34] There is great potential for slippage between decision and action, Graham Allison has observed, because "after a decision, the game expands, bringing in more players with more diverse preferences and more independent power."[35] The executive's ability to control subordinates in the process of implementation may be limited. Generally, the public manager has far less bureaucratic clout than the business manager. Unlike administration in business, which entails the rather straightforward execution by staff of simple policies, administration in government involves the tasks performed by elected officials, staff, and sometimes citizens to implement complex policies.

Distinct from implementation is *management.*[36] This dimension is not less important than the others, nor is it confined to narrow operational concerns. Management—defined in the typical textbook way as the coordination and control of resources to accomplish the purposes of the organization—includes the internal organization and assignment of authority; methods for hiring, developing, motivating, and appraising staff; systems for budgeting and fiscal control; procedures for purchasing and contracting; systems for information processing and decision making; organizational development and planning; and the technical details of performing tasks. Performance in the management dimension determines whether it is possible to meet a goal by marshaling resources and controlling their use toward that end.

The four dimensions—mission, policy, administration, and management—are common in public and private organizations. There is a great divergence, however, in the complexities associated with each dimension found in government, as we have noted. There are two other important sectorial differences. First, the dimensions are disconnected in government whereas they flow together in business. Bower has observed that a "business executive carries out the corporation's purpose by building and modifying organization structures, systems, and relationships through the efforts of the men and women whom he (or she) recruits."[37] Indeed, new business strategies may first be evident in reorganization and shifts in recruitment with the change in mission only revealed at the time when the initiative is announced. In government, the need for democratic control and accountability require that public initiatives proceed in a stepwise fashion through each of the dimensions. The public manager is severely constrained in anticipating or inducing change through management decisions prior to official program approval.

Second, in government there is far greater external control over mission than in business, and in local government higher levels of government impose positive and negative requirements that affect mission formulation. "Outsiders"—elected officials, advisory boards, and citizens—play a greater or lessor role in all four dimensions, whereas in business, there may be no real external control, for example, when the owner and manager are the same person, or external control exerted through the board of directors is typically limited to certain mission decisions.[38]

These differences between the public and private sector are important because the idea has been advanced that reform institutions—certainly influenced by business practices—are an attempt to transfer a business structural form to local government.[39] The identification of common dimensions of decisions is not another way to promote the idea that local governments can be operated like (or by) the private sector. City governments, whether they use reform or traditional institutions, are fundamentally unlike businesses in the complexity of decisions in each dimension, the relationship of the dimensions to each other, and the degree of external control over decisions in each dimension. The management functions will be most similar, but even these are filled in widely divergent contexts under different constraints.

In conclusion, city officials determine the goals and purpose—the mission—of their government; the policies, plans, programs, and services needed to accomplish goals; the methods and processes involved in implementing policy and delivering services; and finally, the structure, systems, and procedures for the control and coordination of the human and material resources of the organization. These dimensions will be helpful in sorting out the contributions from different kinds of officials to the governmental process.

Division of Leadership Responsibilities

The relative contributions of officials are identified by examining how mayors, council members, and administrators divide responsibility for decisions in the four dimensions of the governmental process—mission, policy, administration, and management. The simplistic notion of a dichotomy of responsibility between elected officials and administrators for policy and administration has not been adequate.

An "ideal" and workable division of responsibility must make sense in theory and in practice if it is to be a useful conceptual construct. The practical consideration is an empirical test: Do officials in the real world behave in ways stipulated in the model? For a prescribed division of functional responsibilities among officials to have theoretical staying power, it must be consistent with democratic and administrative principles. Of the former, the most important are democratic control of government—political supremacy—and the rule of law. Unless one can trace the thread of control from electorate through representative to administrator as suggested in Redford's concept of overhead democracy,[40] one has not only a division of responsibility that is normatively deficient but also one that is subject to challenge and change in a putatively democratic society. Respect for and adherence to the rule of law reinforces but is no substitute for democratic control reflected in discretionary choices by administrators that are consistent with the public will.[41] This is the distinction between an action that is legal and one that is right.

The central administrative principle is that chain of command is essential to control. A necessary but not sufficient condition for chain of command is insulation of administrative staff from external interference. When interference occurs, lines of accountability and control are blurred. Staff who are accountable to elected officials (and perhaps to both the mayor and council) in addition to their accountability to administrative superiors may be subject to contradictory commands and/or may avoid control by playing authorities off against each other. Unity of command clarifies staff responsibility.

These normative conditions may appear to be the theoretical grounds for the thoroughly discredited "policy / administration dichotomy" concept for dividing functional responsibilities between elected officials and staff. This is not the case, however, because that concept, as we shall see momentarily, does not meet the empirical test. The normative conditions for dividing responsibilities do preclude acceptance of some other implicit models of division that can be derived from the literature of political science and public administration. Approaches that assign too much authority to administrators for policy, such as the "new Public Administration," violate democratic principles, whereas a political machine or a legislative-dominance model would violate the administrative ones.[42]

A division which passes these tests is one that recognizes the pre-eminence of elected officials over the formulation of mission for the government, on the one hand, and the nearly exclusive (but not total) control of the chief executive officer for management of the organization, on the other. Thus, there is essentially a dichotomy of responsibility for these two functions. In between, however, there is extensive sharing between elected officials and administrators. This cannot be otherwise because policy and administration are a duality, composed of two interrelated parts that, though distinct, cannot be separated. Democratic principles are satisfied if policy, when made by staff, is consistent with mission and if administration is faithful to policy. As long as mission is determined by elected officials, then it is less important which group of officials is entrusted with the tasks of policy making and administration, provided clear linkages among mission, policy, and administration are maintained. Operational details and the creation and maintenance of management systems are best handled, according to the principle of administrative insulation, by appointed staff. The normative case, then, can be made for a "dichotomy-duality" model for dividing functional responsibilities.

This model was first identified in council-manager cities and has been empirically validated in several studies.[43] It is applicable, with modifications to be discussed in Chapter 3, to mayor-council cities as well.

The dichotomy-duality model is presented in Figure 1–3. Elected officials dominate mission formulation, although administrators play an advisory role in developing proposals and analyzing conditions and trends. Planning studies and analyses of emerging conditions by staff yield a host of issues and choices that are of concern to the council as it

Elected Official's Sphere

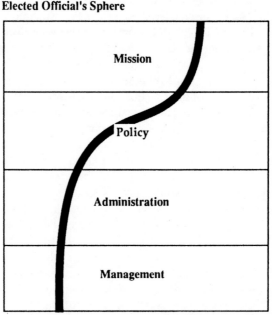

Mission

Policy

Administration

Management

Administrator's Sphere

Source: Adapted from Svara (1985a) reprinted with permission from *Public Administration Review* © 1985 by The American Society for Public Administration, 1120 G Street, NW, Suite 500, Washington, D.C. All rights reserved.

Figure 1-3. The Dichotomy–Duality Model

determines the overall direction of the organization.[44] In policy, the staff have a slightly larger space than the council because of the extensive policy advising and policy setting by administrators, but the larger "quantity" of administrative policy making does not alter ultimate responsibility of elected officials for all policy. The common impression that councils are bodies that simply rubber stamp staff proposals is not correct when both elected and administrative officials are highly involved in policy making. This is the case insofar as mayors or managers seek guidance about council preferences before making proposals; councils thoroughly dissect, alter, and request revisions of proposals that are made; and councils make proposals to which the executive reacts.

The budgetary process in council-manager cities is a good example of this give-and-take process. Council members are not very involved in the formulation of the budget. This is important because once the budget has been constructed, the extent of change by the council is small. Although reviewed and approved by the council, the size and complexity of the budget and the time pressure to approve it give considerable influence to the manager who prepares the document. Thus, budgeting appears to be essentially a bureaucratic process.[45] Councils, however, exercise control over the budget in several respects. First, most councils set budget limits, particularly a mandated tax rate, which serves as a powerful constraint for administrators in preparing the budget. Second, approval of new or expanded revenue sources has to come from councils who usually give an indication about their response to such changes early in the budget process. Third, some councils set goals for the year which provide a framework of current priorities for staff in preparing the budget. In addition to specific directions, the shape of the budget is largely determined by prior programs in particular and the city's mission in general. Thus, there is sharing of responsibility for this policy function, and neither council nor staff are dominant.

The staff has the much larger role in administration, although the council makes a substantial contribution to this sphere. The most common form of intervention in administration accompanies council-member handling of citizen complaints about services, and frequently councils make specific decisions that serve to implement general policies or programs or to obtain special benefits for constituents.[46] A potentially useful but weakly organized form of involvement is councilmanic oversight of administration, that is, examination of the results achieved through implementation. Councils often pay close attention, however, to the process of implementing policies, both by insisting on making specific decisions involved in implementation and through various checking procedures. The legislative veto may have been blocked by the Supreme Court as a congressional check on administration, but it is frequently used informally by councils. When elected officials are excluded from administration, they naturally become suspicious and seek to intervene. Their involvement in administration is not necessarily either good or bad. On the one hand, it can provide information and the opportunity to fine tune policies; on the other, it may serve to derail policy implementation and to undermine fairness in service delivery.

Management is the sphere of administrators. The council's role is limited to approving management "policy" (e.g., the nature of a new pay plan), suggestions on how management can be improved, and—in council-manager cities—appraisal of the manager. Unlike the details of administration, in which council members take an active interest, the details of management are usually determined by the administrators.[47] Council members despite a possible inclination to have a hand in contracts, hiring, promotions, and so on, usually restrain themselves from interfering or are prevented from doing so by strong mayors.

Thus, no officials are totally excluded from any of the dimensions, even though there tends to be a dichotomy of responsibility for mission and management along with the extensive sharing in policy and administration. There is give-and-take among officials in all aspects of the governmental process. The dichotomy-duality model is both a tool for use in studying the actions of officials and a normative guide to assessing appropriateness of roles and behavior.

Overview

In this chapter, the main supports for a new framework within which to study leadership in city government have been put in place. A distinction between the governmental process—the behavior of officials within a structure defined by the city charter and the administrative organization—and the larger political process has been established. It has been explained why the decisions within that process are grouped in four dimensions—mission, policy, administration, and management—rather than two, such as policy determination and execution or simply policy versus administration. The dimensions will be used to talk about who does what in city government.

In the next chapter, the conceptual framework for the discussion is further developed with an elaboration of the patterns of conflict and cooperation in the governmental process. City governments manifest varying levels of both. Although this variation might be viewed as differences along a single continuum, there are two patterns of interaction that will be identified. It is argued that each pattern has different characteristics and results from different conditions, one of which is the form of government. The characteristics of mayor-council and council-manager governments which make them prone to conflict and cooperation are described.

Chapter 3 examines further the differences in the impact of mayor-council and council-manager forms of government on the policy process and its outcomes in cities. Form of government has been linked in the political science studies with divergent representation, policy outcomes, service delivery, and levels of participation by officials. Therefore, it is necessary to consider whether the cooperative pattern, reformed governments, and unresponsive but efficient governments are linked in one cluster of attributes in contrast to a second cluster consisting of the conflictual pattern, traditional governmental structures, and responsiveness with inefficiency. A review of research studies indicates that responsiveness to citizen needs and equity of service delivery are largely independent of the form of government. Furthermore, the expectation of restricted involvement by elected officials and greater bureaucratic power in council-manager governments is not substantiated. Attention can be focused, therefore, on how the behavior of officials within each form differs, rather than assuming that governmental form determines the overall performance of government.

Those readers who have little interest in the fine points of debate regarding concepts and research in the political science discipline may skim the next two chapters and refer to a summary of the major points at the end of Chapter 3.

In Chapter 4, the conceptual framework elaborated in the first three chapters begins to be filled in with details about city officials. The remainder of the book examines the roles and behavior of the major city government officials—mayors, council members, and administrators. For each group of officials, the basic differences in governmental process associated with the form of government produce two distinct orientations that are developed as contrasting role types. Although the preview that follows stresses these differences, in each chapter there will also be consideration of characteristics and concerns which cut across different forms of government.

Chapter 4 deals with mayors. In mayor-council cities imbued with a conflictual pattern, the mayor is the central source of direction, control, and conflict management. Unless the mayor energizes city government, a committed, coherent source of leadership is likely to be absent from the government. The mayor is the driving force, and the performance of city government rises and falls depending on that of the mayor. In council-manager cities with a cooperative pattern, on the other hand, the mayor can make important contributions by coordinating the efforts of other officials and sharpening the sense of direction. Because there are other sources of leadership in this form, the city is not as dependent on the mayor. Still, the mayor remains the primary agent for improving and maintaining cooperation. As the guiding force in council-manager city government, the mayor can either enhance or detract from the quality of municipal performance.

Councils, discussed in Chapter 5, occupy dramatically different positions in the two forms by virtue of their relationship to an elected executive officer in the one and to a chief executive officer whom the members appoint in the other. Given the separation of powers and the prevalence of conflict in mayor-council cities, councils largely serve to check the executive by examining, correcting, and cautiously approving the mayor's proposals. They also link constituents and administrative agencies as citizen advocates. The council is thus largely confined to the mission and policy dimensions, although the council in a weak mayor-council city may play an active role in all dimensions. The council is labeled a counterweight to the executive and staff in the strong mayor-council setting. In council-manager cities, on the other hand, the council's role is that of senior partner. The council is senior because it is ultimately in charge, and it is more active than its strong mayor-council counterpart in all four dimensions of decision making. The council, potentially led by the mayor, is a partner with the city manager in handling the work of government. This partnership can break down if the level of cooperation is low, but conflict is rare because of the absence of separation of powers.

The perception of administrators and their roles varies as well, as explained in Chapter 6. With an elected executive and conflictual pattern, the administrator might be considered to be either controlled or autonomous—a servant or a knave. The "good" administrator is a loyal servant, following the dictates of the mayor and political appointees and pushing subordinates to reflect these priorities in their action. The typical administrator, however, is commonly viewed as a knave, one who avoids control by playing off the mayor and council to protect autonomy, but this image may not be deserved. To be sure, self-interested behavior is expected as part of the conflictual pattern in mayor-council cities. Whether an administrator is contained by the actions of the mayor and the council or exercises the self-restraint of a responsible professional will be examined. The manager and staff, on the other hand, can be expected to act responsibly, although they exert great influence on council decisions and have substantial freedom. They bring a unique perspective to the governmental process due to their training, experience, and value commitments, which predispose them to accept the direction of elected officials and to promote the public interest in a professional manner. The cooperative pattern of interaction permits more actions to be based on a combination of professionalism and political sensitivity and fewer to be motivated by the need to protect interests. Managers as junior partners in the relationship with the council, however, are constrained in the intensity of political leadership they can provide.

In the final chapter, commonalities, differences, and emerging areas of convergence are identified. Approaches to increasing the effectiveness of officials and improving the performance of city government as a whole are addressed. Methods of decreasing conflict and promoting cooperation and practices that might be transferred between mayor-council and council-manager governments are suggested. The concern is to improve the quality of urban governance and management. This is the ultimate reason for examining official leadership in the city.

2

Patterns of Conflict and Cooperation in Mayor-Council and Council-Manager Governments

"Politics," Banfield and Wilson assert at the beginning of *City Politics,* "arises out of conflict, and it consists of the activities . . . by which conflict is carried on."[1] This orientation colors their observation and interpretation of the phenomena of urban politics. Most political science research has shared this perspective. Attention has been given to those aspects of the political life of cities which conform to a pattern of conflict. Conflictual conditions, however, are not universal in the governmental process. To have a more complete view, one must look for a different pattern in the interactions that occur among officials. In some communities, there is not only an absence of conflict but the presence of cooperation. This cooperative pattern needs to be elaborated and understood as well as the one based on conflict.

The two patterns became apparent from informal and organized observations of city governments.[2] In some cities, the tendency for conflict to occur is obvious. Interviews with officials and reviews of the press reveal what battle is in progress, what just completed, and what anticipated in the near future. There is a rich history of conflict, and past events shape current alliances, opposing sides, and factions within them. Conflict need not be disabling and, indeed, leaders may be highly proficient at containing and resolving conflict. Yet in these cities, a given of governmental affairs is that conflict is always close to the surface. In other cities, one is struck by the absence of rancor and contention. This appearance is not simply a facade; indicators of cooperation are present—trust, sharing, and a reasonably full flow of information. These conditions limit the extent of disagreement, and "honest" differences of opinion are resolved by examining evidence and considering the merits of the case. Still other cities are a mixture of the two.

Politics within the governmental process in some cities apparently does not arise out of conflict. There have been explanations starting with Banfield and Wilson of the absence or suppression of overt conflict. We have not, however, recognized a true alternative pattern, explained why it occurs, or systematically described it.[3] That is the agenda for the first three sections of this chapter. The final section links the characteristics of mayor-council and council-manager government to these patterns. Survey responses from officials in twelve cities with different forms of government indicate that divergent patterns of interaction are produced by the governmental structure rather than other characteristics of the cities. These data shall be examined after an introduction of the conflictual and cooperative patterns.

Two Patterns of Interaction

The view of city government held by many citizens, which is also one reflected in much scholarly research, assumes a high level of conflict. From this perspective, officials in government interact essentially to promote their personal interests, those of their office, or those of their political or administrative organization. Since all strive to advance their own differing interests, conflict results, and the stuff of politics is working out these conflicts. The governmental process is marked by bargaining among competitors and mutual adjustment. Decisions reflect the balance among contending forces. Officials in city hall are competitors whose resources, liabilities, and skills at playing the game determine their relative advantage within the governmental process.

When a "model" is widely accepted, the questions it raises and the interpretations it offers seem self-evident. So it is with the conflictual orientation. It is necessary to examine this approach critically, however, to identify the nature of conflict and to question whether the governmental process in all cities manifests, in fact, the characteristics associated with it.

In some respects, any extended interaction in a common endeavor involves differences in perspective and preference and mutual adjustment among participants, whose actions are affected by the behavior of others. In this sense, there is always some degree of difference of opinion and competition when two or more people interact. This situation may be labeled "conflictual," but to be meaningful the term should be used in a more discriminating way. Conflict is qualitatively different from other forms of disjointed intentions or misaligned actions. For example, two persons may differ over what is the appropriate solution to a problem, but they are not in conflict unless other conditions are present. Zeigler, Kehoe, and Reisman conclude, based on their review of definitions in the literature, that "conflict is a situation in which two or more parties perceive that their goals are incompatible."[4] Furthermore, the participants in conflict take active measures to "achieve their own goals (at least in part) by blocking the goals of others." Disagreement becomes conflict, therefore, when incompatible goals cause some participants to seek to impose their preferences on others. It is not in their interests to do otherwise because they cannot trust the competitor to act in an altruistic way.

Conflict involves the use of power for offensive or defensive purposes, and it appears to be the paramount resource in urban politics. Other resources that might affect the resolution of issues—knowledge, reason, persuasion—are neglected.[5] Power is used in four ways: (1) to compel others to act or agree; (2) to block someone else from acting; (3) to resist the compulsion of others; and, by extension, (4) to maintain the freedom to act without being checked by someone else. Power need not be exercised directly or unilaterally; control is often gained in exchange for something else through bargaining.[6]

The study of the governmental process from the conflictual perspective involves measuring the formal and informal power of the competitors, how it is acquired, and how it is used. Formal resources are derived from the governmental structure. Informal resources draw upon the individual's personal characteristics and assets and organizations and networks outside of government. The common conclusions derived from this analysis may be briefly summarized. Mayors have only limited powers to compel or resist compulsion. By pyramiding resources, however, they may acquire leverage over other actors, an advantaged bargaining position, and freedom of action in certain areas.[7] Councils, in contrast, are weak in all respects. They have their greatest impact when exerting a negative checking force, as in blocking a mayoral initiative or derailing a program hatched in an administrative agency. The city "bureaucracies" lack the formal ability or legitimacy to compel, although they can be quite powerful in persuading elected officials to do what "must" be done. They have, moreover, extensive capacity to check elected officials through bureaucratic "vetoes," resist compulsion, and exercise discretion.[8]

Power is not equally divided among officials but it is widely dispersed. No one is clearly in charge. The cleavages among groups in the larger political process are translated into intragovernmental contests. As a consequence, government tends to be sluggish. When it does act, it reacts and shifts from one crisis to another. There is little capacity to plan and anticipate, programs and services are uneven in quality and poorly controlled, and resources are not used efficiently. City government, then, is weak in both governance and management.[9]

These views are commonplace, yet for many cities they are totally inappropriate. Opposing interests, incompatible goals, manipulation of power, and other aspects of the calculus of conflict need not be the dominant features of the local government process. Positive conditions in some cities indicate the need to question the basic premises of the conflictual orientation and to propose an alternative.

Interests may be shared among participants within a framework of common goals. When this condition is present, there may be high involvement of different kinds of officials without winners and losers. If conflict is *not* assumed, then power is less important, and other resources are also used in securing agreement. Leaders may share or give up resources rather than hoarding them. They may accept control, ask for advise, grant discretion, invite appraisal, and in other ways manifest a substantial degree of trust toward the other participants in the governmental process. Decision making can approximate a "best" solution rather than a compromise among antagonistic approaches. Under these conditions, policy makers can anticipate problems and develop plans. Policies can be faithfully translated into programs and services that reflect the intent of policy makers. These characteristics are consistent with a pattern of cooperation in the governmental process.

The predominance of cooperation assumes that elected and administrative officials have compatible goals and, therefore, do not actively seek to block the goals of others. Consequently, they may work in concert to make city government purposeful, responsive, effective, and efficient—each of which is a value held by at least one set of officials and not necessarily opposed by others. Although each set of officials has distinctive and potentially divergent responsibilities, they seek to discharge their responsibilities in ways that impede the other as little as possible. Thus, conflict for its own sake, or because it is inherent in the larger political process in cities, is not assumed to be the overriding feature of relations within the governmental process. Indeed, cooperation is sought, if not always achieved, in many city governments.

These characteristics conform to standard definitions of cooperation as observed in organizations and small groups. The most important elements in cooperative relationships are (1) common goals and goal-directed behavior; (2) sharing of rewards among participants; and (3) coordination of effort.[10] All participants are working toward common objectives, and they all derive at least some of the payoffs from the effort. These conditions may also be found in the relationships among officials in city government under certain circumstances. In these cities, one does not ask who has power and how is it used but, rather, what are the bases of common action.

The patterns can be viewed as two continua for analyzing the modes of interaction within the governmental process, rather than as a single continuum with conflict and cooperation as the opposing poles. Any given city may be placed on one of the continua based on the level of conflict or cooperation they experience. Cities can shift from one pattern to the other as conditions change. Although a hybrid that draws from both is possible, the patterns are—theoretically at least—distinct. A low level of conflict is not equivalent to a high degree of cooperation, just as the absence of cooperation is different from the presence of conflict. (The characteristics of the two continua are presented in Figure 2-1.)

In order to understand the patterns, it is useful first to define the "positive" pole on each continuum, where the pattern is expressed in pure form and then to describe deviations and combinations.

Ideal Types

"Total" conflict can be viewed as a process of interaction in which actors are motivated by self-interest—individual and suborganizational—alone. The city government is not completely atomized. For example, council members may work together as a group to improve their position vis-à-vis the mayor, as well as competing with other council members as individuals. Still, distrust is pervasive since goals are incompatible. The prevailing motto is "do it to them before they can do it to you." Contests are ultimately "zero-sum" in character: the gains of winners equal the losses of losers, or, to put it differently, your opponent gains at your expense. Interaction among officials is a con-

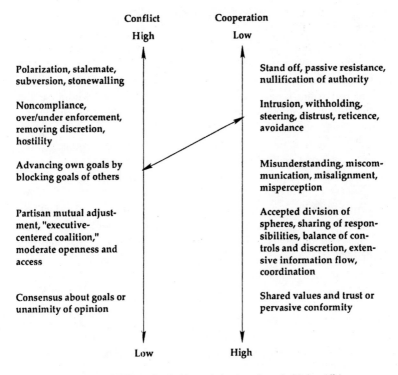

Source: Svara (1988b) reprinted with permission from *Journal of Urban Affairs.*

Figure 2-1. Patterns of Interaction in City Government

stant process of advancing and protecting one's interests. At any given point, however, this process may be, one, highly dynamic and visible, or, two, stable with either a single dominant force in charge (e.g., a Boss, or a division of power among fiefdoms that do not openly challenge each others' domains). A government marked by total conflict is inherently ungovernable since there are no goals or values that transcend the separate partial interests of the competitors.

The cooperative pattern, in contrast, is, in its purest form, shared values and consensus among participants. This does not mean agreement about the substantive ends of politics, necessarily, but rather a shared commitment to supportive interaction in the governmental process among elected officials and administrators. There is a common desire to determine and promote the public interest, since no narrower definition of interest would sustain consensus. There are goals that all participants share and that take precedence over separate interests. Mutuality rather than conflict of interests is stressed.

The "negative" poles on the continua are harder to relate to reality than the positive poles, although cities may move toward them. Ultimately, on each continuum one reaches a pure state of nonconflict or noncooperation. If ever larger coalitions can be formed within the conflictual pattern, ultimately there is total agreement about goals and the absence of conflict. In the complete absence of cooperation, actions to promote common interests are withheld, as in passive resistance carried to the point that one did only and exactly what one was told to do. It is hard to imagine how the point of complete noncooperation could be reached without active conflict having already occurred (i.e., the active promotion and protection of separate interests). It is assumed that conflict drives out cooperation: when one participant begins to act in terms of incompatible goals and blocks the efforts of another, that actor will respond in kind.

Intermediate Levels of Conflict and Cooperation

At intermediate points on the continua, the distinctions are less obvious and shifts between patterns can occur. In the middle range of the conflictual continuum, one finds interactions that might be termed "accommodation."[11] Trade-offs and compromise are common as a means of resolving conflict and reaching agreement. Settlements reached through a process of partisan mutual adjustment include some mixture of partial and larger interests. From the pluralist perspective, individuals and groups strive to advance their own separate interests but they also compromise to protect collective interests.[12] Astley and Van de Ven observe that the "working rules of collective action . . . embody an institutional order that defines limits within which individuals may exercise their own wills."[13] When self-interested conflict is restrained by concerns about preserving the relationship, accommodation emerges.

In the cooperative pattern, intermediate levels of cooperation result from a variety of factors that impede the participants from fully meshing their separate efforts toward common ends. Failure to coordinate activities is a common impediment to aligning contributions from several participants. Misunderstanding of goals or divergence in interpretation of how goals should be translated into actions can produce disagreement. Intrusion, such as telling someone else how to handle their part of a joint undertaking, excessively broad or narrow definitions of scope of responsibilities, or withholding contributions all interfere with cooperative action. Passive resistance, steering with slanted information, increased checks and controls, and nullification of authority signal the absence of cooperation in a setting that may still be essentially free of conflict. It is easy, however, for conflict to enter situations where cooperation is declining.

Shifts between patterns are common in the middle range. The perception of opposing interests and active steps to weaken the opponent and strengthen oneself signal the emergence of the conflictual pattern. On the other hand, a stable coalition may achieve conditions associated with moderately high levels of cooperation. Crossovers may also occur when a minority of participants play the game in terms of the ground rules of the alternative pattern. A city council may have a cooperative relationship with the manager as a collectivity, but some members of the council may seek to secure a position of special advantage over the manager to promote separate ends. Likewise, a mayor may have a strong affiliation with a majority of council members based on shared beliefs, but interact warily with the council as a whole in order to maintain his strength and weaken the council's position.

Why should these differences in the style and substance of the governmental process occur? One contributing factor already identified is the extent to which values are shared among officials. Further elaboration of the conditions associated with each pattern is needed to better understand them in theory. Then we shall examine the attributes of city government which foster conflict or cooperation in practice.

The Bases of Conflict and Cooperation

In *The Evolution of Cooperation*,[14] Robert Axelrod examines conflict and its moderation through a process of partisan mutual adjustment. Since he assumes competition among actors, the behavior he analyzes would be better labeled accommodation or "self-interested" cooperation to distinguish it from the "pure" cooperation of our ideal type. Still, his exploration of the foundations of cooperative action can be broadened to explain why patterns of conflict and cooperation occur and are sustained in city government.

Axelrod demonstrates that, under certain conditions, participants with opposing interests will do better by working together rather than by trying to take advantage of each other. Although selfish behavior may produce short-term gains, when the other side responds in kind all participants lose. The best strategy—whether in computer runs of the Prisoners' Dilemma game or in real life when the appropriate conditions are found—is "tit for tat." A participant starts by being "nice" (i.e., not taking advantage of the opponent) and then reciprocates whatever the opponent does. If the opponent cooperates, you cooperate. If he defects, you retaliate. If he stops opposing you, you forgive and cooperate once more. Thus following a tit-for-tat approach can lead either to endless recrimination or cooperation, but it results in higher payoffs than any strategy stressing either more altruism or more selfishness.

There are three conditions for situations in which "self-interested" cooperation can emerge. These deal with the structure of authority, continuity of interactions among participants, and the definitions of payoffs, shaped in part by the diversity of values among participants. By extension, these same conditions, with alterations, can be used to explain the bases for "pure" cooperation. The two sets of conditions are presented in Table 2-1. Whereas Axelrod explains why accommodation emerges within a conflictual pattern of interaction, the second set of conditions explains why a cooperative pattern occurs.

First, it is assumed that there is no central authority to "police the situation." This condition was important, in Axelrod's model, to demonstrate that accommodation can arise from the behavior of uncontrolled individuals.[15] The absence of a central authority is the condition of city governments with a separation of powers between the executive and legislature, and bureaucracies often have independent power resources. In the mayor-council system, although the balance of authority and resources is far from equal, no one actor can compel obedience. Therefore, if accommodation is to emerge it must be in the form described by the pluralists and explained by Axelrod's theory.

Table 2–1. Conditions Associated with Accommodation and Cooperation

Factor	Accommodation	Cooperation
Central authority	Absent, e.g., separation of powers	Present, e.g., concentration of authority
Continuity of interaction	Ongoing but limited in duration, e.g., fixed term for officials	Potentially endless, e.g., no fixed term
Nature of payoffs	Positive-sum, but competition for rewards	Collective rewards and distinct payoffs; no competition for rewards

Source: Conditions of accommodation adapted from Axelrod (1984).

There is no reason to think that having a central authority would deter cooperation, a situation not addressed by Axelrod. Indeed, the presence of such an authority makes cooperation even more likely. A central authority provides a structural basis for cooperation, and it will "naturally" be present, rather than emerging from competitive interaction. Conflict is contained by the imposition of authority: disputes between two parties can be resolved by an official with greater power. In terms of formal structure, council-manager governments have a central authority in the council and an appointed executive with integrated administrative authority over staff. It is expected, therefore, that cooperation will occur in the absence of disturbing forces.

The second condition is that the process is ongoing: "what makes it possible for cooperation to emerge is the fact that the players might meet again."[16] Thus, participants must take into account the future consequences of their actions. The importance of future encounters is illustrated by the reduced clout of a "lame duck" official. It is more likely that officials will refuse to follow the lead of mayors who are leaving office, because they will not have the opportunity to retaliate. By extension of this logic, officials who serve without term (e.g., city managers) have the potential for "endless" future encounters with their subordinates and presumably are more likely to receive cooperation from subordinates.

Third, there can be shared rewards rather than a single winner, that is, one side's winnings are not equal to the other side's losses. If, however, the situation is perceived to be a zero-sum conflict, then accommodation is not likely to occur and total conflict ensues. Levine, in his study of mayoral leadership in racially polarized cities, contrasts "pluralized" and "polarized" settings.[17] In the latter, conflict dominates all considerations and accommodation is not possible. There are no possible rewards for accommodation until participants' perception of the situation changes or until one side gains hegemony so that conflict can be limited to the extent that compromise is possible.[18] A strategy of tit for tat can then emerge, although the risk is always present that defection and mutual recrimination will reemerge and a condition of "zero-payoffs" will be created. If the situation is perceived in this way, then neither accommodation nor cooperation will occur regardless of the formal authority structure.

Just as "zero-payoffs" preclude accommodation, the circumstance of broadly shared rewards help to explain why a cooperative pattern is possible. If goals are compatible and officials have the same or complementary values, the issue of rewards is defused. Payoffs may be shared, or elected and appointed officials may each receive distinct rewards of little value to the other. For example, in a council-manager city, elected officials are more likely to seek support from voters and contributors. The manager, if a "cosmopolitan professional," seeks acclaim outside the city in order to enhance his or her professional reputation.[19] The manager also wants local support but need not struggle with the council for the spotlight. In the case of either shared or distinct rewards, agreement may be reached without direct competition for rewards.

We may, therefore, assert again the importance of a two-pattern interpretation of the governmental process rather than viewing city governments in one-dimensional terms. Accommodation—Axelrod's cooperation—is not the middle ground between opposing poles of conflict and cooperation. Rather, it is the expression of contained conflict that is created and sustained by reciprocity. Accommodation, however, can be undermined by reciprocity as well if one participant strikes out at others. Conflict is the underlying condition of situations without a central authority. When there will be continuing encounters, and differences are amenable to compromises with some sharing of rewards, then accommodation can replace the dissension and rancorous struggle that would characterize total conflict in the governmental process.

This situation, and the roles of officials within it, however, is conceptually distinct from that in which there is a central authority, potentially endless encounters, and collective rewards. Understanding why disagreement and conflict emerge and how they are contained in these cities is better done in terms of shifts along the cooperative continuum. The remedies to lack of cooperation are increased communication, clarification of roles, greater coordination, and reassertion of central authority. The character of interactions only shifts to the conflictual pattern when cooperation is absent to the extent that central authority is nullified, or when participants manifest self-protective blocking behaviors. Furthermore, if polarization in the community is carried over to relationships among elected officials, central authority is fractured and the conflictual pattern will obtain.

Thus, there are two major patterns of interaction—cooperation and conflict. The second in turn has two alternative forms—pluralized and polarized conflict. In the cooperative pattern, participants by and large trust each other because they do have not incompatible goals or opposing interests. Therefore, distinct roles can be viewed as complementary rather than competitive. When differences emerge, they can be resolved by reference to shared values. Conflict can be resolved by building compatible goals for the issue in question. Resolution can result from the reassertion of central control (e.g., firing the city manager as the resolution of conflict between the council and the manager), but participants probably prefer to avoid using sanctions in favor of approaches that build consensus or neutralize conflict. Officials may also avoid divisive issues to prevent disruption of cooperative relationships.

It is possible for the cooperative pattern to be "perverted" by an excess of agreement. There are cases of cities controlled by an appointed manager who cannot be challenged because of longevity or community support. The manager has become the master to whom the board defers out of respect and dependency. The dominant partner views questions or challenges to his or her recommendations as an affront. Differences are resolved by an insistence on having one's way by the stronger participant—the attitude of "support me or fire me"— and acquiescence by the weaker.[20] Likemindedness and agreement reflect stifling conformity in this situation. Such uniformity is not usually an attribute of the cooperative pattern, since conditions encourage high involvement by all participants. It is more likely, however, to occur in the cooperative setting in which active opposition is discouraged.

In the pluralistic conflictual pattern, participants view each other with some degree of caution because their interests and goals are not fully compatible. Differences are resolved through a bargaining process in which compromise and tradeoff occurs until a common acceptable position is established. Participants push their position as far as they can, depending on their power resources and skill and commitment in using them, and adjust their position in response to successful blocking efforts by others. Everyone may win at least a little bit in the compromise distribution of payoffs. The polarized conflictual pattern, on the other hand, is characterized by such great dissension that participants do not trust each other at all. Since payoffs are zero-sum, they cannot be shared between opposing sides. Resolution comes only through victory by one side over the other.

Relationship of Patterns to Political and Service Functions

There is a superficial similarity between the conflictual and cooperative patterns and the political and service functions advanced by Banfield and Wilson. Distinguishing between the two approaches is important to clarify the nature of the interactional patterns. The political and service functions refer to purposes for which government is organized. The former is the resolution of conflicts within the political process.[21] The latter entails the provision of essential services that people in cities require of government. The political function is essential to governance, given the diversity of the urban population. Banfield and Wilson felt that advocates of city government reform believed that politics had no place in local government and tried to orient government to the service function only to the exclusion of the political function.[22] Stressing services and ignoring conflict produces the appearance of cooperation in city government.

Other scholars have accepted this theme as an organizing principle. Lineberry and Sharkansky argue that governmental institutions were chosen to enhance either the premise of "professional management" or "political accountability."[23] Jones suggests that "two broad conceptions of government exist": in one, government is an "exercise in technology"; in the other, governmental power is used to "resolve competing interests."[24] Finally, Yates discusses two conceptual models for designing governments: "administrative efficiency" and "pluralist democracy."[25] In each pair, the first-mentioned model describes a situation that appears to be conflict free, although power used by elites and administrators actually suppresses or excludes expression of divergent views. This approach has been the only one available in the urban politics literature to explain the absence of conflict.[26]

The conflictual and cooperative patterns of interaction in the governmental process, however, are not proxies for Banfield and Wilson's functions or for the opposing governmental models identified by others. Rather, they refer to alternative modes of interaction within the governmental process through which the political and service functions are provided. Although the political function involves managing conflict, that conflict may be kept largely outside the governmental process. Officials may deal with each other in a cooperative manner in handling a dispute between citizen groups or dealing with public opposition to a proposed action, that is, they handle community controversy with a sense of shared values and trust. Alternatively, conflict may also arise among officials as they become parties to the dispute. In this case official conflict takes on a life of its own and must be "managed" along with the community controversy.

Furthermore, conflict among officials may characterize the service function. Divergent goals and blocking actions produce struggle over control of services and convert them into a power resource to be used for political advantage. Conflict is present in the service function (1) when mayors hold services hostage to secure compliance from council members, (2) when council members interfere in the work of staff to obtain special benefits for constituents, or (3) when departments wage turf battles that impair service delivery or effectiveness. Thus, it is possible for the political function to be handled cooperatively and for the service function to be fraught with conflict.

In conclusion, the assessment of official roles and behavior may be guided by two divergent models of interaction in the governmental process. To use one model exclusively is to run the risk of serious omission or misinterpretation. Each model will be described in greater detail.

Characteristics of the Patterns

To many observers of city government, conflict is endemic and ever-present, whether manifest or latent. If conflict is not expressed, the opposition has been temporarily won over or suppressed, either of which requires the expenditure of political resources. Conflict may also be concealed by a stable balancing of forces, but the tension remains. The internal process of government so reflects the characteristics of the total political process in the community that cleavages in the population find expression among officials. Conflict is inevitable in cities and city governments because of the insolvable problems they face, the scarcity of resources, and the tensions produced in providing some services.[27] Conflict imposes strains on policy making and implementation and, if it is extreme and unchecked, the city is ungovernable.

This approach also implies a conflict theory of organizational behavior.[28] The superficial form of organizational structure can not be equated with its internal dynamics. An organization that appears to have an orderly hierarchy of offices controlled from the top may actually be rife with power politics in spite of (or some would argue because of) the formal bureaucratic structure. If conflict conditions, characterized by contentious struggle among self-interested parties, prevail within the administrative organization, the organization is uncontrollable. Democratic governance, which presumes implementation consistent with policy, can not be secured if staff are unmanageable or unmanaged.

Opposing interests and differing perspectives contribute to incompatible goals. For mayors and other elected officials, the "first rule" in the political game is to "enhance [their] likelihood of re-election,"[29] so they look after their own interests. To do so, they must observe the second rule: "The principal coin in the realm of politics is power." Politicians work hard to get power and to maintain it. Competition among elected officials for resources is a given in the conflictual pattern. Elected and administrative staff also have different values, priorities, and timetables, which reflect in part their differences in background and training.[30]

The administrative agencies of government can become the "new machines"—entrenched, self-centered, concentrations of power impervious to control from superiors.[31] Professional administrators resist outside control and seek to limit the scope of decision making by elected officials.[32] They strive to keep what resources they have and to expand their budgets.[33] Departments in government are "competing fiefdoms, actuated by different sentiments and views—but all dedicated to survival."[34] Parochialism shaped by office or department is difficult to overcome. Divergent line and staff orientations and needs within the organization can lead to a struggle over the freedom to operate flexibly versus pressure to conform to general procedures.[35] The staff in control "downtown" see the world differently from those providing services at the street level.[36]

The problems of internal fragmentation may be magnified by external cleavage. Although the governmental process can be distinguished from the political process, in the conflictual pattern the two are intertwined. Contention among groups in the larger political process has a direct bearing on the governmental process in three circumstances. First, insofar as "outside" forces are represented or mobilized by city officials in decision making, then dissension among the groups so represented becomes part of the governmental process. Mayoral candidates who use the "electoral arena" to generate support for use in the "governmental arena" or appoint leaders in the electoral coalition to positions in government can, in the process, transfer external conflicts into the governmental process.[37] Other examples are council members who act as advocates for neighborhood groups qua council members; a director of human relations who advances the cause of a civil rights group in the exercise of his duties; or a police chief who mobilizes citizens concerned about law and order to pressure the council to block the initiation of a police review board. Second, if the governmental process is permeable to outside groups to the extent that official decisions are shaped by external pressure, then conflicts in the political process are blended with conflicts in the governmental process. Third, when polarization in the community is so great or conflicts are so intense that officials are immobilized by cross-pressure, then outside forces have undermined government's capacity to act. Whether officials become a party to "street-fighting pluralism" or are helpless in the face of it, governments become reactive.[38] "Hyperpluralism" engulfs official actors leading to "segmented" decision making[39] and "crisis-hopping."[40]

Finally, since formal authority is divided and nongovernmental forces impinge upon the relationships within government, the formal resources of officials are inadequate as a power base. Therefore, it is presumed that an official needs allies and must accumulate informal resources in order to be effective.

The cooperative pattern, given the shared values that characterize it, presumes that officials want to work together constructively to accomplish common goals. Disagreement may be commonplace, but conflict is contained within bounds, self-limiting and episodic. Cooperation is the reflection of common purpose which induces the participants to work together. Elected officials seek to rise above conflict and do what is best for the community as a whole.[41] Among administrators as well, there may be a sincere commitment to serve the public.[42] Professional administrative values can be public serving in character rather than a mask for autonomy.[43] The governmental process is separated from the political process, more or less open to input but still insulated. Thus, the governmental process can be different in character from the encompassing political process in the community.

The tendencies within the administrative organization will be toward a "collective orientation," even though competition is not absent. This commonality is based on either shared values, a controlling structure, or both, depending on which organizational theory one finds most congenial. In either case, the organization is neither uncontrolled nor uncontrollable. The theories of organization that are consistent with the cooperative pattern include three major perspectives.

Classical bureaucratic theory provides the basis for control through hierarchy, division of labor, and formal rules. It emphasizes political supremacy and administrative insulation. To the extent that these conditions are found in an organization, one has the conditions for control and compliance with decisions of elected officials that are part of the cooperative model. In humanistic theories of organizations, the common bond becomes shared values and common purpose such as that manifested in Likert's System IV.[44] Participative management, with its emphasis on shared decision making, decentralization of authority, and responsiveness to clients, rests on the assumption that all members of the organization are tied together by common goals. Both of these theories may seem too simplistic—a common assessment.[45] If so, it is possible to conceive of a decision-making theory based on the behavior of organizations as they encounter uncertainty and change, one that stresses structural controls through rules, procedures, bureaucratic organization, and standard programs as well as unobtrusive controls. Although the organization is neither monolithic nor uniformly committed to overarching goals, the definition of goals by higher levels and shared "premises for decisions" contribute to cohesion and control.[46] The leader is neither all-powerful nor totally dependent on persuading his or her subordinates to go along, but rather has substantial capacity to guide the organization.[47]

Under any of these views, the individuals and subgroups that make up the organization "are both independent actors and involved members of a larger collectivity."[48] Although the pursuit of individual goals continues, "they adhere to unifying patterns of cultural and social order as they take on responsibilities as part of a larger social entity." Acceptance of values solidifies an organization and permits a framework within which flexibility and trust are possible. Peters and Waterman identified this seemingly paradoxical trait in their "best run" companies. Organizational leaders permit decentralization and looseness at times approaching "barely organized chaos," but, at the same time, "they are fanatic centralists around the core values they hold dear."[49] Most of the companies have "rigidly shared values." When officials share basic goals and values, trust is possible, and decision making can be shared between elected and appointed officials and across lines in the administrative organization.

Shared values reinforce authority, which becomes a distinct support to cooperation. The right and power to command and expect obedience orders relationships among officials. Power arrangements, Pfeffer has observed, can "become legitimized over time, so that those within the setting expect and value a certain pattern of influence."[50] Such power is authority. Authority represents the "institutionalization of social control." Having been established, authority is not resisted, and—unlike power—is not diminished by its use. When authority is present, compliance can be secured without expending resources. Under these circumstances, management—coordinated, goal-oriented behavior—is possible. Since effective management is a necessary though not sufficient condition for effective governance, the manageable city is potentially a governable one.

A particular form of authority is political supremacy, the control of elected officials over staff. Despite eloquent defenses of the concept such as Redford's discussion of "overhead democracy,"[51] realists have stressed the difficulty of achieving control over the bureaucracy.[52] Their rationale is based on a conflictual perspective that weighs the resources possessed by elected officials and administrators and declares the former to be outmanned and outgunned.[53] This assessment, though accurate in some situations, discounts the importance of authority and exaggerates resistance to control.[54] Elected officials and their political appointees are "supposed" to be in charge, and, in the cooperative setting, they are typically obeyed. In contrast, when authority is divided among elected officials, it is natural that there should be conflict between those who possess parts of it, and as a consequence the influence of legitimate authorities may be diminished.

Implicit in these conditions is the insulation of the governmental process from the political process, and the separation of management from interference by elected officials. The presumption that one can have shared values, respect for political and administrative authority, and rational management assumes that the governmental process can be different in character from the political process. Cleavage, divergent values, and scarcity naturally produce conflict among the nongovernmental actors in city politics. The interaction among competing groups is nonrational and devoid of generally accepted goals and values or widely recognized authority. For the governmental process to operate differently, it must by necessity be shielded to some extent. Cleavages within the population are not necessarily transported into the governmental process. Providing a hearing for groups and accepting portions of their demands does not require officials to become advocates for their point of view and take on the contentious attitudes of others in their own relationships.

Finally, the characteristics of the cooperative pattern enhance the significance of formal structure. Lines of authority do matter, and officials are able to rely more fully on the formal resources of the position to discharge their responsibilities.

Potentially, any city can manifest either pattern. It is likely, however, that there will be an association between the form of government used in a city and the characteristics of the governmental process.

Forms of Government and Patterns of Interaction

The institutional arrangements of city government provide a framework that channels behavior in important ways. In view of the sources of conflict and cooperation, the aspect of governmental structure that is crucial to interactional patterns is the degree of fragmentation of authority. Separation of powers is intentional fragmentation, in which offsetting powers or authority are given to different offices or branches in the government, such as the power of a legislature to pass a law and the power of the executive to veto it. Separation of powers produces checks and balances that prevent any one officer or branch from exercising complete power. They can also produce stalemate if no one is able to develop superior influence.

There is a basic distinction to be made. On the one hand, there are governments with no separation of powers, in which a governing body delegates authority to an appointed executive. On the other hand, governments may be based on a separation of powers in which case there is a political executive and a legislative body, each separately elected.[55] Although Banfield and Wilson suggest that the council-manager form "carries the separation of powers a step further" because all administrative authority is given to the manager,[56] this form is typically characterized as one without separation of powers. The council and manager have distinct roles to play, but there are no checks and balances. Rohr suggests that Madison's basic test be used to determine whether or not separation of powers is present. In *Federalist 47*, Publius defined nonseparation as one in which "the *whole* power of one department [i.e., branch of government] is exercised by the same hands which possess the *whole* power of another department."[57] Nonseparation is found in council-manager government since the council can choose, control, and unilaterally remove the manager.

The argument developed here is that form of government is the key factor that produces conflict or cooperation with other institutions contributing to variations on the dominant pattern. The methods of electing city council members do not have a direct bearing on distribution of authority, despite their potential impact on representativeness, access to government by parties and citizens, and relationship among officials. We may start with three plausible generalizations about authority, responsibility, and the nature of the governmental process. First, the more widely dispersed authority is, the more likely it is that conflict rather than cooperation will characterize the governmental process. Second, any division of responsibility can produce disagreement, which may turn to conflict if the parties have sufficient influence to support their side or if they view their goals to be incompatible. Third, the degree of conflict or cooperation will, therefore, depend on the attitudes and actions of officials concerning division of responsibilities as well as being influenced by formal structure. Officials may shape their relationships to reflect their own preferences, although the task is more or less difficult, depending on structural arrangements and other sources from which conflict may arise. Separation of powers predisposes officials to conflict for reasons that will be elaborated in this section, but official behavior is not structurally determined.

Slightly more than half of the municipalities in the United States over 2,500 in population use a mayor-council system in which separation of powers between the executive and legislature is the organizing principle of the governmental structure, although these cities differ among themselves in the degree to which authority is concentrated or divided.[58] Over a third of the cities use the council-manager form, and these (along with the small number of commission cities) have no separation of powers. The remainder—approximately 7 percent—use the town meeting or representative town-meeting forms of government. The commission and town-meeting forms will not be discussed since responsibilities of officials in these forms differ markedly from those of officials in the dominant forms.

Mayor-Council Forms of Government

The mayor-council governments are the most commonly used form of government in very large and small cities, as indicated in Table 2-2. All of the six cities with 1980 population in excess of one million population and thirteen of the seventeen cities over 500,000 have a mayor with executive powers. On the other end of the population scale, a majority of cities under 10,000 use the mayor-council form. Regionally, this governmental type is the most frequently used form in the Northeast and Midwest, where the reform movement has not been as successful as in other regions. The regional variation may be explained by the greater

Table 2–2. Distribution of Major Forms of Government among Cities
of over 2,500 in Population (1981)

Classification	No. of Cities Reporting (A)	Mayor-Council	% of (A)	Council-Manager	% of (A)	Commission	% of (A)
Population Group							
Total (all cities)[a]	4165	2155	51.7	1894	45.5	116	2.8
Over 1,000,000	6	6	100.0	0	0.0	0	0.0
500,000–1,000,000	17	12	70.6	5	29.4	0	0.0
250,000–499,999	26	13	50.0	11	42.3	2	7.7
100,000–249,999	95	29	30.5	62	65.3	4	4.2
50,000–99,999	230	82	35.7	140	60.9	8	3.5
25,000–49,999	471	150	31.9	302	64.1	19	4.0
10,000–24,999	1026	439	42.8	556	54.2	31	3.0
5,000–9,999	1066	569	53.4	476	44.7	21	2.0
2,500–4,999	1228	855	69.6	342	27.9	31	2.5
Geographic Division							
Total (all cities)[b]	4157	2148	51.7	1893	45.5	116	2.8
New England	191	75	39.3	115	60.2	1	0.5
Mid-Atlantic	647	429	66.3	177	27.4	41	6.3
East North Central	869	561	64.6	288	33.1	20	2.3
West North Central	471	280	59.4	167	35.5	24	5.1
South Atlantic	560	194	34.6	359	64.1	7	1.3
East South Central	252	193	76.6	45	17.9	14	5.6
West South Central	458	199	43.4	254	55.5	5	1.1
Mountain	225	113	50.2	112	49.8	0	0.0
Pacific Coast	484	104	21.5	376	77.7	4	0.8

[a]For breakdown by population size, supplementary information gathered by the author was added to include all cities with populations of 500,000 and over.

[b]Totals from original source.

Source: Sanders (1982: 180). Table 3/2 from *The Municipal Year Book 1982* used with permission of the International City Management Association.

concentration of European ethnic groups and the salience of ethnic politics in the Northeast and Midwest; Dye and MacManus concluded that the ethnicity is the best predictor of the use of mayor-council form of government.[59] Smaller cities are more likely to have a *weak* mayor, whereas larger cities are somewhat more likely to have a *strong* mayor. Generally, the weak mayor structure has been subject to piecemeal change, which leaves part of its nineteenth-century character intact, whereas the strong mayor was created by substantial change in the original form to centralize power in the hands of the executive.

The *weak mayor-council form of government* is characterized by extensive fragmentation of authority. This form divides up power into many small parcels, has many instances of shared authority, and widespread popular participation through electing many officials. The weaknesses of these mayors stem from (1) their limited powers to appoint staff, some of whom are directly elected, some appointed by the council, and some appointed (or removed) by the mayor but only with the concurrence of the council; and (2) their inability to develop the budget as an executive proposal that reflects overall policy. A committee of the council (or one composed of the council), the mayor, and other elected officials typically draft the budget. The council, therefore, has both legislative and administrative responsibilities, since it passes laws and creates programs and also appoints staff and shares in the supervision of administrative departments. Because of weakness with respect to personnel and budgeting, the mayor lacks integrated administrative control over the staff and operations of city government.

Some formally weak mayors have been able to augment their influence with informal sources, such as political party support, and by using their limited powers with creativity and energy. As Banfield concluded in his study of Chicago, "a single actor . . . can pursue a course of action only insofar as the formal decentralization is somehow overcome by informal centralization."[60] Two well-known examples are Daley of Chicago, who used the party, and Lee of New Haven, who used both party and extensive personal political skills to transform the character of their respective offices.[61] Even if the fragmentation can be papered over, however, the formal structure remains as a powerful limiting factor to mayoral leadership, since the mayor must constantly expend energy and divert attention to maintaining the fragile arrangements whereby the disparate power holders work together. Overcoming fragmentation, Banfield asserted, "always represents a cost to the political head."[62] With disruption or change such as the election of a new mayor, the system can easily revert to its former (and formal) fragmented state, as has happened in Chicago after Daley. Some large weak-mayor cities such as Atlanta have attempted to permanently change governmental operations by reorganizing their governments into strong mayor systems. New Haven did the same, after the augmented influence of the mayor's office was dissipated during the tenure of Lee's caretaker successor.

The *strong mayor-council form of government* also has separation, but it is between, on the one hand, a mayor with extensive powers and integrated administrative control over staff and, on the other, the elected legislative body. This form was patterned after the strong executive in the national government and incorporated the goal of the reform movement to consolidate influence in the hands of the executive, thus eliminating the power vacuum that had been exploited by the political machine. Typically, in strong mayor cities the mayor and council members are the only elected officials. The mayor has the authority to appoint and dismiss certain department heads often without the consent of the council. Other department heads may be covered by civil service provisions, or they may, once appointed, not be removable by the mayor except for "cause" (i.e., demonstrated failure to adequately perform officials duties). The mayor prepares the budget, controls its administration, and is responsible for directing the efforts of the departments of city government. Institutionally, the strong mayor has, therefore, the integrated administrative control that the weak mayor lacks. The lines of authority for all or most departments of city government lead to the mayor's office.

In some cities, the mayor may appoint a Chief Administrative Officer (CAO), who handles whatever tasks are assigned by the mayor. These usually include extensive delegated authority over program implementation, operational concerns, and budget formulation, as well as an advisory role in developing other policy recommendations.[63] Called the CAO, or given other titles such as vice mayor, this officer augments the capacity of the mayor to attend to the broad-ranging demands of the position for political and organizational leadership. In some cities, the chief lieutenants appointed by the mayor also include officers such as a budget director and development administrator as well as a CAO.

The council, on the other hand, is confined to a limited role. Even in policy making, the council is heavily dependent on the mayor for proposals and information, and it can be checked by the mayor's veto power and favorable position for mobilizing public opinion in support of proposals. Because the council, however, must approve policies and can override vetoes, there is the potential for deadlock between the executive and legislature. The council usually has its own leader selected by the members and entitled President, Chairman, or Vice Mayor. In addition, the council president may not only have significant potential for leadership within the council but also serve as the focal point for relations with the mayor; or the presidency of the council may be a largely ceremonial post.

The major questions surrounding division of responsibility in this form concern the respective contributions of mayor and council to mission and policy. Furthermore, the mayor and council may disagree concerning the boundary between policy and administration; or the mayor, asserting executive prerogative, may exclude the council from management decisions. Since both mayor and council are legitimate interpreters of the popular will, they may come into conflict over how to translate it into governmental goals, policies, and programs. The mayor's power over information and staff and his or her greater access to the media give the mayor a natural advantage over the council. The council, especially when it lacks its own staff, is often confined to a reactive position responding to mayoral initiatives, but may be restive in this role and strike back at the mayor in various ways. The mayor has sufficient formal and informal power that he or she may make independent decisions on "administrative" matters concerning implementation and service delivery that not only displease council members but also may be seen by them as unilateral "policy" making. For example, are the admission rates and hours of operation for a major city recreational facility issues that should be resolved by the mayor as an administrative question or referred to the council as a policy matter, since they have a bearing on who in the public shall have access to this city service? If each side seeks to expand its sphere of responsibilities and to limit the prerogatives of the other, the mayor will try to act independently of the council, whereas the council will insist that the issue be brought before it for resolution.

The mayor as chief executive officer and possessor of power resources vis-à-vis the council may undertake to exclude the council from management concerns entirely. From the mayor's perspective, such exclusion increases his or her freedom of action in face of the considerable constraints that limit the executive's control of the bureaucracy. From the council's perspective, however, there are major issues such as internal organizational structure or level of productivity which it would like to address but cannot if the mayor erects a barrier around staff and operations. Thus, conflict may arise over roles and responsibilities in this dimension as well as in others.

There are general conditions associated with both weak and strong mayor-council systems which may also produce conflict, some related to the election–succession process of choosing the executive and others to the interplay of mayor, council, and bureaucracy. Transition from one executive and his or her "administration" of supporting staff to the next is a major source of discontinuity in cities with separation of powers. Adjusting to a new executive is often accompanied by considerable disruption.[64] The tension is magnified by appointments. Staffing decisions for top positions may cause resentment when the mayor picks either close followers or inexperienced outside "experts." What is viewed as political payoffs to supporters may be crucial to the mayor's need to preserve the cadre of a campaign organization and to have trusted lieutenants serving as intermediaries with and supervisors of a permanent staff that is less than fully trusted.[65] Expertise may be the criterion for selection and modernization the goal, as in Mayor Lindsay's choice of bright, young policy analysts, but the experts' lack of familiarity with city government and limited field experience may produce friction with the permanent staff.[66]

The need to take hold of the organization quickly and to preserve the prospects of reelection points to another condition of these forms that may sustain a conflictual pattern—the lack of permanence. Since mayors and their appointees serve for a fixed term, contenders may exploit this weakness by delay and even defiance, depending in part on how lame is the duck in the mayor's office. Periodically, the mayor, if he or she seeks to remain in office, is drawn again into the contention of the electoral arena. Council members and permanent staff must take sides in the election, fueling another cycle of reward and recrimination after the election. Candidates' great need for campaign funds make them increasingly subject to particularistic interest-group domination and a "new spoils" system.[67]

These problems of succession highlight the uncertain position of the permanent staff in relationship to the mayor and the council and the potential for incompatible goals among them. The "bureaucracy" becomes a third actor in the governmental process, and it may be divided along agency or departmental lines, particularly when headed by a directly elected director or board. Three-party conflicts are difficult to resolve. One party can sabotage accommodation reached through reciprocity between the other two. As a consequence, conflict may be sustained unless coalitions emerge to link two of the parties, and coalitions may be undermined by defections.

Thus, the mayor's office in these cities carries great burdens and is surrounded by conflict. A weak mayor is likely to experience frustration at having limited resources to secure accommodation among other officers empowered to act. A strong mayor is likely to generate resentment in the exercise of his or her extensive powers (relative to other officials). Despite these powers, however, the mayor may commit such great effort to simply surviving in office that the city is "governed but poorly led."[68] The council is constrained in both variations of this form, because of the multiplicity of actors in the one and the superiority of the mayor in the other. Council members must cope with the frustrations of an ambiguous role and limited resources. The permanent staff is likely to be restive both because of the direct control of "outsiders" who are viewed as unprofessional political cronies of the mayor or imported experts with limited knowledge of city government and also because of the efforts by the council to direct and oversee its activities independently of the mayor. They may protect themselves by promoting constituency support and by playing the mayor and council off against each other. The mayor-council forms are likely, therefore, to be characterized by a rich variety of conflict manifested by divergent goals, jockeying for advantage, and efforts to block the preferences of others.

Council-Manager Form of Government

The council-manager form of government provides in effect for specialization of roles that avoids piling so many tasks on one person. The council and mayor occupy the overtly political roles in government, and the manager directs the administrative apparatus, an activity which provides ample opportunity for influencing and shaping policy without the burdens (or opportunities) attendant to elected leadership status. The council-manager form is used in a majority of the cities between 10,000 and 250,000, and in over 40 percent of the cities just above and below that population range in Table 2.2. The council members are the only elected officials in city government. The council possesses all governmental authority, except as it delegates authority to the manager, and, thus, there is no separation of powers or checks and balances in the system. The mayor is typically the presiding officer of the council and has no formal powers different from those of other council members, except for the veto power in 13 percent of council-manager cities. Mayors, directly elected in 62 percent of these cities, can be an important source of policy guidance and coordination of participants, although they rarely exercise any administrative authority.[69]

The manager is the executive officer with extensive authority for directing staff, drafting and (after approval by council) expending the budget, and controlling operations. Given the great scope of the manager's influence and authority, some feel that the form weakens public control. Jones's assessment is typical of this view.

In council-manager cities, the manager is formally responsible to the city council, but city council members are often part-time volunteers with little expertise in municipal government. The manager often acts as policy initiator, and his or her recommendations are usually followed by the council. This is a far cry from the theory of democratic accountability as normally stated.[70]

Others contend that democratic government is not jeopardized. "In this system," Newland has contended, "executive authority can safely be great, because limits on the executive are even larger, and they may be exercised swiftly and decisively."[71] Although an influential member of the community elite, the city manager, as Loveridge observes, is under "the close and jealous supervision of the city council" and must be "highly responsive to their preferences and interests."[72] Northrup and Dutton provide evidence that managers, less stable and more vulnerable than the elected executives, "tend to perceive a wider range of groups as influential than chief executives in unreformed governments."[73]

The manager is appointed by the council with no voter involvement and serves at the pleasure of the council without term, although it is becoming more common for managers to have a contract that sets forth their rights and benefits if removed from office.[74] The manager is typically the only staff member hired by the council (in some cities, the city attorney and/or clerk are selected by the council as well,) and all other employees are hired under the authority of the manager. If the council is displeased with a staff member (e.g., they would like to have the police chief removed), the council can only attempt to persuade the manager to make the change and, if unsuccessful, either accept the situation or fire the manager. In some cities, direct communication between council members and any staff members except the manager and attorney is prohibited, and even if not explicitly proscribed, the norm of the system is for elected officials to respect the insulation of staff from "political" interference.

The characteristics of the council-manager form tend not only to promote cooperation but also to arrest and reverse conflict when it arises. Since the council ultimately wins all battles with the manager, tests of will are self-limiting. The appointment process for selecting the manager puts a premium on experience and professional competence. Such an executive, even if appointed from outside, has fewer points of disparity with existing staff, especially if they too have been chosen on the basis of merit criteria. The integrated organizational authority vested in the manager gives him or her greater potential for control over staff than in weak-mayor cities in which that authority is fragmented and lines of authority lead to many officials. The manager's appointment without fixed term means that staff cannot know when a manager will leave.

The dynamics of executive change are different from mayor-council systems. The manager can be replaced at any time without a battle between the incumbent and a challenger. Even though struggle and replacement may have occurred among council members, a new manager comes into office with few political commitments, debts, or enemies. There is usually a honeymoon period after a new appointment, during which the council tends to respect managerial prerogatives, rather than exploiting the newcomer's weakness. Still, managers do not come into office without broad expectations concerning their performance. Flentje and Counihan find that in Wichita, the desire for change and reorientation was reflected in the selection of an outsider who meets the qualities desired by the council, whereas periods of consolidation are overseen by managers selected from inside.[75] Choice of the manager itself, then, contributes to the formulation of mission by the council. By the nature of the selection process, the manager must be acceptable to a majority of the council, and he or she has a reasonable chance of establishing a pattern of interaction that will promote and sustain cooperation with the council. An exception is a city that has evenly balanced political factions. In these cities the shift of a council majority from one faction to another is likely to be accompanied by replacement of the manager.[76] In this situation, the characteristics of the council-manager form do not deflect conflict because the political conflict of the community clearly extends to the governmental process. Still, conflict is exceptional, rather than typical in council-manager governments.

In conclusion, the degree of fragmentation of authority and the method of selecting executives predispose city governments to patterns of conflict or cooperation. Weak mayor systems with highly dispersed authority need some informal factor to create enough cohesion for the government to function properly. Mayor, council, and administrative staff—some responsible to other elected officials or boards—are independent claimants for decision-making responsibility. Strong mayor governments with separation between the executive and the council may experience dynamic tension, sniping and guerrilla warfare, or an impasse between the two seats of power. In both weak and strong mayor systems, the election of a new mayor and the transition from one administration to another are likely to produce discontinuity and conflict. The staff may sense a disparity between their own orientation and interests and those of nonprofessional outsiders above them in the hierarchy. The mayor and political appointees may be resisted. In council-manager cities, on the other hand, there is no question about who has ultimate authority, and thus there are few battles to protect prerogatives. The executive is selected without a public contest among competitors, and staff are likely to respect the new manager as an experienced professional, even if from outside the city.

It is likely, therefore, that in the absence of special conditions that will overcome it, conflict will be commonplace in the mayor-council forms. Conversely, unless special circumstances are present, the council-form will not experience high-level, persistent conflict. Instead, cooperation, based on concentration of authority and shared goals, is likely to be found among officials.

There are several factors other than the form of government per se that may explain the greater harmony in council-manager cities. The kind of cities that tend to use this form are likely to have less community conflict than those which typically use the mayor-council form. They are less likely to be very large (although population growth puts five council-manager cities on the verge of one million in population.)[77] The form is found in New England, the agricultural Midwest and the mountain states, and the Sunbelt (except for the east south-central states) to a greater extent than in the industrialized states of the Northeast, mid-Atlantic region, and Midwest. It is more common in suburban and rural than in central cities. As a consequence of these differences, council-manager cities have higher income, more growth, and better "quality of life."[78] The distinctness of the two sets of cities should not be over-drawn (as Wish illustrates with examples from a Sunbelt mayor-council city and a Coldbelt council-manager city), but it provides a political culture—as opposed to a political structure—explanation for the differences in the governmental process in mayor-council and council-manager cities taken as a group.

Empirical Test of Differences in Patterns

The field research I have conducted attempts to hold constant characteristics of the population and measure differences produced by the form of government. Six pairs of moderately large—population 120,000–650,000—mayor-council and council-manager cities which share many demographic and economic characteristics were studied. A comparison of features in the six pairs of cities (presented in Appendix, Table A-1) would not lead one to expect great differences in the governmental process attributable to population characteristics, fiscal health, or governmental institutions other than the form of government.[79] Although this research was not organized with the explicit purpose of measuring conflict, there is some direct and indirect evidence of differing levels of conflict in the opinion of officials from these twelve cities.

Surveys were distributed to council members and department heads.[80] Measures of council-executive relations and attitudes toward staff in Table 2-3 indicate that greater distrust and tension exist in strong mayor-council cities than in council-manager cities. Although a majority of these council members and department heads consider the council's relationship with the mayor to be positive, the proportion is far higher in council-manager cities. Less than 30 percent of the council members feel that the mayor provides them with sufficient policy alternatives, whereas over three-quarters of the council members rate the manager's policy recommendations positively. Council members are less likely to make effective use of staff, perhaps because their access to staff is blocked or because of tension in the relationship. The council in the strong mayor cities is perceived to lack time to deal with important

Table 2–3. Council-Executive Relationships in Council-Manager (C-M) and Strong Mayor-Council Cities (SM-C)

| | Percent Agreeing | | | |
| | Council Members | | Dept. Heads | |
	C-M	SM-C	C-M	SM-C
The council and manager (or) mayor have a good working relationship	100.0 **	56.5	75.7 **	52.1
The manager (or) mayor provides council with sufficient alternatives for policy decisions	76.9 **	29.1	90.9 **	56.2
The council effectively draws on the expertise of professional staff	76.9	54.2	76.1 **	47.9
Intervention by a council member is necessary to get adequate response to citizens' complaints	34.6 *	66.7	7.4	14.6
The council's appraisal of the manager's (or) mayor's administrative performance is satisfactory in depth and frequency	73.9 *	39.1	68.4 **	33.4
6 C-M and 5 SM-C cities (1 weak M-C excluded): $N =$	26	24	67	48

*$p < .05$ based on chi-square for comparable officials by form of government.

**$p < .01$.

issues. The burden of policy decisions may reflect the greater difficulty these council members have in getting information from the executive.

Council members are much more likely to feel that their intervention is necessary in order to secure adequate response from staff in the strong mayor cities. Although department heads in both types of cities overwhelmingly disagree with this assessment, there is much less difference of opinion between elected officials and staff on this matter in council-manager cities than in the strong mayor-council cities. Furthermore, council members in the council-manager cities not only work more effectively with staff and have a higher level of trust, they also feel that they provide adequate appraisal of the manager's performance. The department heads share in these assessments. Most council members and department heads in strong mayor-council cities feel that their assessment of performance is not satisfactory. Council members lack the opportunity, therefore, to check those behaviors they deem to be unsatisfactory through appraisal of the elected executive. Appraisal as a formal control mechanism appears to reinforce positive relationships.

It is interesting to contrast relationships in the strong mayor cities with the one weak mayor city in the study. (The results from the latter are not included in Table 2-3.) In this case where the council members are full-time officials with extensive staff and active committees, the council appears to be able to set the terms of the relationship with the mayor and staff. Most council respondents feel they work well with the mayor and use staff well (department heads tend to disagree on this point). A majority of council members and staff express the opinion that appraisal is adequate. They are likely to feel, however, that the mayor does not provide enough alternatives and that council intervention with staff is needed to get adequate response to citizens.

Assessments of the mayor by council members display other similarities and differences in the strong and weak mayor cities. Although most council members consider the mayor to be open and responsive to councils inquiries (63 percent and 72 percent in strong and weak mayor-council cities, respectively,) only a bare majority of the council members in strong mayor cities feel that the mayor complies with the spirit of council directives, as opposed to over 70 percent of the council members in the weak mayor city. In both types of cities, most report that the mayor does not regularly consult with the council as policy proposals or the budget are being formulated. A third of the council members expressed the opinion that the strong mayor applies excessive pressure on the council to support his proposals, and over 60 percent agree that they are on guard to keep the mayor from taking advantage of the council.

The weak mayor council members do not perceive pressure, and most are not on guard. In both kinds of cities, approximately three council members in ten feel that the council can rarely defeat the mayor if he is determined to get a program he wants adopted.

The picture that emerges, then, is one of tension and wariness (but not open warfare) in the relationship between the mayor and council and distrust of staff in the mayor-council cities in contrast to positive interactions and trust between the council and the manager. These differences would be expected if one compared the *typical* mayor-council and council-manager city, because regional, demographic, and structural characteristics of the cities that use each form diverge in ways that will commonly induce or retard conflict. Although the data analyzed here are from a small, nonrandom sample of cities, the findings suggest that differences may also be produced by the characteristics of the form itself in cities that are otherwise similar.

From the conflictual perspective, the council-manager form and other reform institutions do not eliminate conflict. Rather, they only suppress conflict by shifting power from the political arena and elected officials to administrators.[81] Reform institutions in this view contribute to bureaucratic power and weaken political control. The tranquility of council-manager cities (community characteristics aside) has been explained by the likemindedness of officials and their conservative bias,[82] the weakness of the mayor,[83] domination of business elites who impose fiscal restraint on city government,[84] and the influence of professional administrators.[85] The evidence presented to this point indicates that this argument needs to be reexamined and subsequent chapters will question each of the reported findings that support it. There are inherent features in the major forms that predispose officials to relate to each other differently. Council members and department heads in the council-manager cities studied appear to be neither docile nor domineering, respectively, but to work within a constructive partnership controlled by the council.

Implications for the Study of Official Leadership

Political scientists have tended to view city government from a conflictual perspective and to feel that the absence of conflict masks the exertion of political power to exclude or suppress those with dissenting opinions. The cooperative pattern is, however, a theoretically and empirically defensible alternative model for interpreting the governmental process in some cities.

Conflict and cooperation are alternative patterns of interaction among officials in the governmental process resting on contrasting premises and conditions. The models describe opposing tendencies that may be found in isolation or in combination. Using both approaches to interpret and analyze a particular government may reveal important features missed if either is used alone. Still, it is expected that one of the patterns described by the models will be dominant. Conflictual and cooperative behaviors tend to be self-reinforcing and thus stable. Furthermore, features of one pattern do not work in the other setting: trust is a "weakness" that is exploited in a conflict setting. Self-serving competition and conflict tactics are unsettling and even insulting in a cooperative setting. When trust is highly valued, to criticize and challenge excessively is to impugn motives of other participants. Such actions challenge the connections that tie participants into a common endeavor, and a typical reaction is to close ranks until the threat is isolated and removed. The interpretation of city government in terms of the conflictual pattern is not meant to be pejorative, nor is cooperation necessarily positive. Rather the patterns are descriptive of conditions that obtain in certain cities, each of which has negative and positive consequences.

Use of the two patterns encourages reexamination of generalizations about who receives services from government and who contributes to governmental decisions. If the governmental process is not necessarily a clash of wills to determine who shall control decisions, and if it is insulated from the political struggle of the community, then the distribution of benefits from governmental programs does not necessarily reflect the power balance among officials and groups in the city. Governmental responsiveness need not depend on a wide range of demands and bargaining among competing claimants to produce a fair distribution of governmental services. From the conflictual perspective, the absence of conflict produces inequity. The presence of cooperation based on shared values, however, can be equitable if the values include a commitment to fairness and public service. Government is better able to serve weak groups when conflict does not dominate the governmental process. In the next chapter, we shall reexamine the association between form of government and governmental outputs to determine whether this alternative interpretation has empirical support. Similarly, the two patterns present very different opportunities for contributions by officials in city government. Contributions are not necessarily proportionate to the power of competitors. These issues are explored in the next chapter.

3

The Significance of Structure

The governmental process, the interaction among officials determining and implementing policy and managing city government affairs, may be characterized by patterns of conflict or cooperation. Among the factors that influence the nature of the governmental process, the most important one inside government is the degree of formal fragmentation determined by the form of government and the assignment of power to officials within it. The tendency of cities with mayor-council forms to experience conflict and of cities with the council-manager to cooperate is important in itself but does not tell us all we need to know about governmental performance. It is also critical to assess the effects of governmental form on governmental outcomes and the contributions of elected officials and administrative staff. Who receives the benefits of government action? How democratic is the governmental process under different forms of government and, by extension, when the governmental process is conflictual and cooperative? Outcomes and contributions may be more important than interactional patterns.

Our collective wisdom on these matters may be summarized as follows: conflict in government in mayor-council cities may be unpleasant (at least to the tidy and the squeamish), but it is necessary to assure responsive government. Through checks and balances, elected officials limit the power of administrators and make government open and responsive. The pursuit of cooperation in council-manager cities, on the other hand, is a nice way of suppressing the interests of the poor and minorities, and enhancing the position of the upper stratum. Administrative staff dominate the governmental process. These conclusions, however, are not supported by the existing literature on the relationship between form and consequences nor by the results of my own research regarding the involvement level of officials. Council-manager governments are as fair and responsive as mayor-council governments. Council-manager officials manifest a mixture of sharing and separation of responsibilities to which elected officials and the manager both make substantial contributions. Mayor-council governments, on the other hand, have competing claimants for responsibility in each of the governmental dimensions. The division of power between the mayor and council works to the disadvantage of one elected official or the other depending on which mayor-council form is used.

This chapter, then, delves into the murky relationships between structure, on the one hand, and outcomes and the characteristics of the decision-making process, on the other.

Governmental Structure, Process, and Consequences

Is governmental form—and, by extension, the pattern of interaction in the governmental process—related to certain outcomes? This question must be answered to remove a cloud that would obscure the further consideration of structure and behavior in city government. If fragmented forms and the conflictual pattern are associated with outcomes deemed to be desirable, then changing either structure or process could have harmful consequences. Put differently, one may prefer cooperation to conflict, but if process characteristics that seem beneficial are likely to produce outcomes that are deleterious, then one would probably choose to leave the process alone. There is a pervasive sentiment in discussion of urban politics that council-manager governments are more harmonious and efficient but less effective and responsive.

The differences between forms of government will be explored in five areas: election institutions used and the representativeness of city councils; interest group participation; representativeness of administrative staff; the level of expenditure and "responsiveness" of city government; and patterns of service delivery. In addition, it would be useful to examine differences with respect to efficiency, but, if one excludes the studies of spending levels, there appear to be virtually no empirical studies of differences in efficiency related to form of government.[1]

Elections and Representativeness

The first consequence to examine is difference in electoral systems and the representativeness of councils. Representativeness is largely a product of electoral institutions, insofar as council composition is related to structural as opposed to demographic or mobilization factors, but it is considered here for two reasons. First, the electoral institutions, and consequently the characteristics of elected officials, may vary systematically with form of government, which could help to explain policy and service outcomes. Second, form of government is used in some research as an independent variable to measure election results (i.e., council membership is compared in cities with different form of government). A complete discussion of election systems and council characteristics will be found in Chapter 5.

The packaging of institutions in the Model City Charter has created a tendency to link council-manager government with particular methods of electing council members. Doing so may lead to the impression that this form invariably has (and even produces) a certain kind of council.[2] By implication, more politicized mayor-council forms produce a different kind of council from that found in council-manager cities. Despite the widespread acceptance of the association between the institutional package of council-manager form / at-large / nonpartisan elections and "unrepresentative" city councils, the evidence is more complex.

First, form and electoral method are combined in various ways. Most cities do not use partisan elections: only two-fifths of mayor-council cities and one-fifth of council-manager cities do so.[3] Among cities over 10,000 population in 1972, one-third of the council-manager cities did not use either at-large or nonpartisan elections, and over two-thirds of the mayor-council cities did not have both traditional election institutions.[4] Furthermore, since that time, change in the constituency type of elections has been common. Between 1970 and 1980, 6 percent of all cities and 14 percent of cities over 50,000 in population changed their election system, most of them abandoning at-large elections.[5] Heilig and Mundt report that in cities with over 15 percent black population using at-large elections in 1970, 55 percent of southern cities and 22 percent of nonsouthern cities had efforts to create districts during the seventies.[6] Districts were adopted in 33 percent and 16 percent of these cities, respectively. Between 1981 and 1986, the proportion of all cities over 2,500 population using at-large elections declined from 67 percent to 60 percent.[7] Two-thirds of the council-manager cities still use at-large elections (as opposed to 49 percent of the mayor-council cities), but that proportion represents a decline from three-fourths of the council-manager cities in 1981. Thus, the association between form of government and use of at-large elections is diminishing.

Second, when representativeness is measured in racial terms by comparing the percentage of blacks on the council with their percentage in the population (using all central cities in 1976 with at least 15 percent black population), the mean index in council-manager cities is twenty-five points lower than in mayor-council cities, approximately 50 percent versus 75 percent of the expected representation, respectively.[8] This was partially a result of the more widespread use of at-large elections as the constituency type in council-manager cities. Such elections resulted in only 42 percent of fair representation for blacks whereas mixed district / at-large produced a 73 percent rate and pure districts, 85 percent. When the effect of form is measured controlling for constituency type of election, it is still related to representation rate, but at a much lower level.[9]

Third, other studies conclude, however, that electoral institutions are less important than the black percentage in the population in determining the racial composition of the council. The relative income levels of whites and blacks is another important factor.[10] MacManus concluded, when controlling for the socioeconomic conditions of the city and measuring differences among different types of elections more carefully, that there was no independent relationship between the election plan and minority representation.[11]

Finally, when the representation of other groups is considered and controls are employed to remove the effects of community characteristics, the use of at-large and nonpartisan elections has modest effects that are not wholly exclusionary in their impact. The income of council members is higher when either reform institution is used, and education level is higher when elections are at-large.[12] The election of women is enhanced, however, by at-large elections.[13]

In conclusion, council-manager cities do not necessarily use at-large elections, and institutions including form may have limited effect on lowering black representation, in comparison with the social and economic characteristics of the minority and total population. The more common use in council-manager cities of nonpartisan and particularly of at-large elections (and small councils) have adverse effects on socioeconomic, geographic, and ethnic diversity of councils, but the form of government itself is not necessarily responsible for these characteristics. Representativeness on the council, then, should be viewed as a product of demographic and socioeconomic characteristics and electoral institutions rather than a consequence of the form of government.

Group Participation

A separate argument is that reform structures depress group participation and produce a governmental bias toward middle-class and business organizations.[14] These effects may be attributable to election systems rather than form of government, as we have observed with respect to the representativeness of the council. Some have suggested, however, that it is plausible to expect reform structures to expand the role of groups in local politics.[15]

Dutton and Northrup, having surveyed the number and kind of groups that are influential in cities over 50,000 in population, offer evidence to sort out these competing views about the impact of reformism in general and the council-manager form in particular. First, party organizations are less influential in reformed cities. Parties were either quite or very influential in 36 percent of these cities, 70 percent of the cities with a mix of reformed and unreformed institutions, and 83 percent of the unreformed cities.[16] Second, a wider range of groups were influential in council-manager cities than mayor-council cities.[17] Third, the council-manager form is associated with greater influence by certain business and middle-class groups (e.g., bankers and executives, building developers and real estate brokers, and good-government activists) and environmental groups. There is a negative association with the influence of labor unions, ethnic groups, local medical groups, and church leaders. Finally, there is virtually no relationship between the form of city government and the influence of minority groups, neighborhood groups, the Chamber of Commerce, industrial leaders, the bar association, and newspapers. The conclusion one may reach is that council-manager cities are likely to have more pluralistic local politics. Their array of influential groups, though differing in some respects from what is found in mayor-council cities, is not generally exclusionary. The political climate is less inviting to labor unions and ethnic groups and more open to groups concerned with environmental issues. Minority and neighborhood groups fare equally in either type of city. Thus, the council-manager form cannot be equated with generally restricted group participation.

Representativeness of Staff

Another form of representativeness is reflected in the makeup of the municipal work force. Ethnic and racial groups have struggled to gain positions for their members both as a symbol of recognition and as a means of acquiring a share of the economic and political resources of city government. In addition, the national government has given strong encouragement (until the Reagan administration) to the practice of affirmative action, consisting of special efforts to hire and promote minority employees. The obligation to support affirmative action has been widely proclaimed as a professional norm among public administrators. Thus, one might suspect growing black employment because of increasing support for civil rights and the expanding political clout of blacks. Council-manager cities might have changed their employment practices less, if one accepts the lower responsiveness thesis, or may have been more accepting of minority employment because of the adherence of professionals to law, regulation, and professional norms. Overall, the highest levels of black employment are found in cities with large black populations and with black mayors.[18] When one examines the percentage of black employees compared to the black percentage of the population—a measure of affirmative action effort—different patterns emerge. "Relatively speaking," Eisinger concludes, "black employment is highest in those cities with healthy economies, cities, moreover, headed by white officials."[19] Although Eisinger does not discuss differences based on form of government, when the forty-nine cities for which data are provided in his study are divided into mayor-council and council-manager categories, the latter have a higher average "effort score" than the former. Among council-manager cities, black employment was 130 percent of the black population, whereas in mayor-council cities, it was 116 percent. Greater commitment to affirmative action among professional managers supported by more favorable economic conditions would seem to account for the relatively higher response to black demands for employment in council-manager cities.

Spending Levels and Responsiveness

Measuring expenditure patterns among city governments and differential responsiveness to groups in the population has been a concern of political scientists. Lineberry and Fowler concluded that reformism produces lower levels of taxing and spending and reduces responsiveness.[20] Both spending levels and responsiveness have been the subject of additional research.

Much of the difference in the amount of taxing and spending can be accounted for by variation in the functional scope of city government rather than in its form,[21] although the number of governmental functions provided is itself related to form of government with reform governments tending to provide fewer services.[22] In a study of fifty-one cities, Clark found that with controls for community population characteristics and economic conditions there was a strong positive correlation between reformism and overall spending and no relationship to spending for urban renewal.[23] Lower spending was not found in a comparison of cities over 25,000 in population which had changed their governmental institutions between 1948 and 1973 and similar cities which had not. No consistent, substantial differences appear between the cities shifting in different directions—adopting or abandoning reform—and the control cities. Morgan and Pelissero conclude that "government structure may matter very little—at least when it comes to city taxing and spending policies."[24] Another study by Morgan and Brudney examining all cities over 50,000 concludes that reform institutions reduce per capita expenditures modestly, but far greater variation is produced by the scope of functions provided by city government, intergovernmental aid, and environmental factors such as the percentage of citizens who are nonwhite, who are 65 years and over, or who are high school graduates.[25] Lyons concluded that unreformed cities are likely to increase their spending to take advantage of external funding sources and to respond to pressures for increased spending, whereas reformed cities are more responsive to demands for slower growth in expenditures and less spending.[26] Johnson and Hein also report that manager cities have lower levels of revenues and expenditures than nonmanager cities.[27] The results are somewhat mixed, but overall council-manager governments appear to spend somewhat less than mayor-council cities.

With respect to responsiveness, Dye and Garcia reach the same conclusion as Lineberry and Fowler: "It is true that reformed cities are generally less responsive to the social and ethnic character of their populations than unreformed cities."[28] This assertion, however, is not clearly supported by the reported findings. Their results highlight a problem in defining responsiveness. There are two distinct forms: responsiveness to demands and responsiveness to needs, whether or not clearly articulated by individuals and groups. If one takes the latter approach and assumes that responsiveness means that spending "should" increase when the nonwhite population increases and when socioeconomic conditions decline, one finds that generally reformed governments are more responsive.[29] Unreformed cities are more responsive to *ethnic* groups, whose presence may be manifested in greater demands for governmental action. With respect to the other groups, cities with reform institutions not only are more responsive to minority groups and blue-collar families (i.e., spending is more strongly related to the size of these groups in the population in reformed than in unreformed cities) but also tend to ignore income differences. Both reformed and unreformed cities tend to spend more as the education level declines and as homeowners become fewer. On balance, the reformed cities appear to act in a more socially responsible way to minorities and the less well-off.

Morgan and Brudney provide stronger support for the hypothesis that there is less responsiveness to population characteristics in reformed cities, although reformism has "much less impact than the functional responsibilities of city governments, their receipt of intergovernmental aid, and the environmental variables."[30] Reform institutions, therefore, mute the translation of environmental factors into policy and may diminish responsiveness to ethnic groups in the city, but do not necessarily diminish response to need based on race or socioeconomic status.

Karnig reports that civil rights groups had greater success in unreformed than reformed cities.[31] Lineberry and Sharkansky take this as evidence that reform institutions "tend to insulate decision makers from potential conflicts of urban life and give professional managers and bureaucracies more power."[32] This reasoning suggests that public administrators in reformed cities are less concerned with civil rights than are elected officials in unreformed cities. This conclusion does not seem warranted in view of the minority hiring evidence noted above, although it may suggest that officials in council-manager cities are less sympathetic to organized *group* demands for civil rights action, even though their civil rights performance is generally good.

A similar result appears in response to demands for assistance to businesses and developers to promote economic development. In cities over 50,000 in population, council-manager governments are less likely to create business assistance centers, provide tax rebates, or seek Urban Development Action Grants from the federal government than are mayor-council cities.[33] Executive mayors—as well as council members elected from districts and in partisan elections—are strongly inclined to engage in "credit-claiming" activities. They have an "incentive to provide some form of visible—if only symbolic—benefits to a great array of potential supporters."[34] Despite the common association between reform institutions and business interests, executive mayors and partisan and district council members may be more prone to accede to certain business demands than officials in reformed governments.[35]

Thus, there may be less difference in substantive commitment than in decision-making style in response to particularistic demands in the two types of cities. As noted above, responsiveness to demands may be different from responsiveness to needs in the two forms of government, resulting in part from greater insulation of officials in council-manager cities. Insulation may reduce the impact of demands on governmental officials without reducing the attention to needs of the population.

Ironically, some studies from the 1960s of decision making in the face of controversy surrounding both school desegregation and fluoridation concluded that the presence of a strong political party produces an "'insulation' effect" that "reduces the pressures playing directly on the decision-making machinery."[36] As parties have progressively declined in American cities, one may speculate that officials in mayor-council systems have less of a buffer to resist pressure from groups, whereas council-manager systems retain some measure of insulation from specific demands. The competitive atmosphere in the former causes council members and the executive to seek allies through positive responses to groups, relying on compromise and trade-offs to reconcile offsetting demands. Such demands come from business and development interests as well as the grass roots. Council members and managers, on the other hand, are more likely to treat these demands as one of many factors to consider when deciding an issue. Presumably, the increased use of district elections in council-manager cities will decrease the insulation effect by establishing a closer linkage between constituencies and council members.

Distinct values that can be traced to conflictual and cooperative patterns of interaction may contribute to differing modes of responsiveness as well. Russell and Crain found that more school desegregation plans were adopted in council-manager than mayor-council cities in the North during the period 1964–1972. This decision represented response to the need for change and an effort to address the problems of the black community. Although the decisions were not made by city government officials themselves, the authors speculate that the communities with different forms have distinctive ideologies. The reformed government is more likely to be found in a community that is committed to the "unitary ideal of the public interest and loyal to a commitment to doing things that are 'right' rather than expedient."[37] In the cooperative pattern, overarching goals provide the basis for agreement on controversial issues. The likelihood of resolution increases if decision makers are somewhat insulated and do not feel pressured to arrive at a compromise that accommodates each contending group. In the conflictual pattern, agreement is likely only if the issue can be converted into a positive-sum bargaining situation—a difficult task in desegregation decisions— or by mobilizing sufficient power to overcome opposition. Thus, insulation from direct demands and commitment to the public interest in council-manager governments need not work to the disadvantage of the poor, working class, or minorities.

Service Delivery

The supposed lack of responsiveness of council-manager governments has rested in part on a presumption: whenever greater attention is given to professional considerations in decision making, less attention is paid to the concerns of all groups in the public. The argument would be that professional administrators are more concerned with advancing their own and their agency's interests than in addressing the needs of citizens.[38] This supposed incompatibility of interests, however, should be reexamined in light of evidence on service delivery. When decisions for delivering services are based on professional norms, the consequences for responsiveness may be observed in the way that services are allocated in different parts of the city, since the professional staff play a large role in this administrative process.

The research on service delivery, in which bureaucratic considerations are found to be the major determinant of distribution patterns, shows that professional criteria are public serving in concept and in their impact. The norms of the professional (or quasi-professional) groups that staff city government stress responding to need, equity, and standards for "adequate" service level and accessibility. One might argue that the opinions of expert staff concerning the maximum distance to a park facility or the number of library books per capita are generous to the interests of their professional groups, but they are at the same time providing services directly responsive to population characteristics and needs. A budget fashioned by each professional group might be too costly to provide, but it would probably not be unfair nor unbalanced to the advantage of the politically powerful or to the detriment of politically weaker segments of the community. "Political" grounds for decisions about service delivery may be more likely to take into account electoral support, favored status, or prejudice.[39]

The conclusion that "distributional decision making is routinized and largely devoid of explicit political content" has been reached in studies in reformed cities as well as unreformed.[40] Two studies find some indication that political and economic factors influence service distribution, although neither provides the basis for concluding that powerful groups are accorded pervasive preference or that minorities and the poor are subjected to discrimination. Bolotin and Cingranelli found in Boston evidence that support for the winning mayoral candidate slightly increased the level of police services in Boston neighborhoods.[41] Boyle and Jacobs determined that for "property" services, such as fire and sanitation, the contribution of the area to the city's tax coffers was the strongest predictor of expenditures in New York, whereas police services and "human" services were distributed in a compensatory fashion.[42] Jones's study of housing services in Chicago does show that electorally strong wards served by a disproportionately large number of patronage appointees have higher demands and do receive more services. Party workers also help to "coproduce" services by intervening with landlords and testifying in housing court.[43] He also makes clear that the normal agency response stresses need—the severity of the violation—whereas party workers offer favoritism and special treatment not normally permitted under standard rules.

The coincidence that the first two studies were conducted in mayor-council cities does not permit any conclusions about difference in performance for cities with different forms of government. The normal administrative response in Chicago would have been like other cities without the intervention of party workers, as Mladenka has shown in studying delivery of other services in Chicago. The thrust of service delivery research calls into question the inference that bureaucratic influence necessarily produces unresponsive allocational patterns. If responsiveness implies linking services to need, then city governments generally have been responsive.[44] The decision rules often followed in service delivery have typically emphasized equality or compensation in distribution. If reform governments are more professional, they may be more responsive in this sense. If responsiveness implies responding to articulated group demands, reform governments may be less responsive.

Thus, the relationship of form of government to characteristics of elected officials and city employees or to responsiveness and service provision is mixed at best. In most respects, council-manager governments perform as well as or better than mayor-council governments, and shortfalls such as the socioeconomic and racial disparities in council membership are not inherently a product of the council-manager form but rather of at-large elections, the use of which is declining in all cities. This does not mean that particular governments of either form will not deviate in a positive or negative direction from these generalizations. The major thesis of this discussion is that individual officials make a substantial difference in the performance of their government for good or ill, depending on the observer's perspective.

Division of Responsibility and Form of Government

The form of government used in a city is likely to produce differing patterns of interaction among officials and affects the contributions of elected officials and administrators. A commonly held view is that the council-manager form weakens elected officials and strengthens the position of professional administrators. Lineberry and Sharkansky are typical: "Municipal bureaucracies have more power and autonomy in reformed systems, and elected decision makers have corresponding smaller bases of power."[45] Consequently, decisions are more likely to be based on professional criteria rather than on narrowly defined political factors, and the "key arena of decision making" in reformed cities is the bureaucratic rather than the electoral sphere.

There is, however, little empirical evidence for this generalization as it applies to council-manager governments, and on logical grounds it is not obvious why this generalization is generally accepted. One might argue that the "new machines" observed in mayor-council systems are more powerful because they are able to use separation of powers to their advantage.[46] Council-manager administrative agencies are not only more circumscribed by weak formal position vis-à-vis the council, but also they are presumably more subject to the formal administrative authority of the manager. Furthermore, this approach ignores the possibility that decisions by professional managers may be made within a framework of political control. The division of responsibilities among officials in cities with different forms of government should be reexamined. The dichotomy-duality model, based on observation of council-manager cities in North Carolina, contradicts the bureaucratic power assumptions about how decisions are made in council-manager cities.[47] Elected officials are primarily responsible for the formulation of mission, administrators are largely responsible for management, and there is extensive sharing of responsibility for policy and administration.

The model has been tested further by measuring with more precision how mayors, council members, and administrators divide responsibility for decisions in the four dimensions of the governmental process—mission, policy, administration, and management. The research was also conducted in mayor-council governments in order to compare the involvement of officials in different forms of government. Questionnaires were distributed to members of the city council and to department heads in the matched pairs of similar mayor-council and council-manager cities described in Chapter 2.[48] Officials were asked to rate the actual and preferred level of involvement by the council and by the executive and staff in twenty-nine different decisions. These ranged from broad choices that determine the city's future to operational details. The items and explanations of the involvement rating from the questionnaire are provided in Appendix, Table A-2. These decisions were then grouped in the four dimensions, and an average rating of involvement was calculated for council members and administrators in each dimension. The ratings of actual involvement in decision making in the three types of cities are presented in Table 3–1.

In the council-manager and strong mayor-council cities, the council's involvement is highest in the mission decisions and recedes markedly across the other dimensions. Still, the council in the cities with managers has a substantially higher level of involvement than its counterpart in the strong mayor cities in all dimensions. The executive mayor and manager have high to very high involvement in all dimensions.[49] The manager's rating is lower than the mayor's only in the mission dimension. These responses are similar to findings of Abney and Lauth. They report both that the manager's recommendations are given greater weight by the council than are the mayor's in mayor-council cities and also that the "councils have more influence in reform cities than they do in nonreform cities."[50] The council-manager form combines a strong

Table 3–1. Levels of Involvement in Four Dimensions of Governmental Process among Officials[a]

Involvement by:	Council-Manager Cities				Strong-Mayor Cities				Weak-Mayor Cities			
	Council		Executive		Council		Executive		Council		Executive	
	C[b]	D[b]	C	D	C	D	C	D	C	D	C	D
Dimension												
Mission	3.7	3.6	3.4	3.5	3.1	3.2	3.6	3.9	3.8	3.8	3.7	3.4
(average)	(3.7)*		(3.5)*		(3.2)		(3.8)		(3.8)*		(3.5)	
Policy	3.4	3.1	4.0	3.8	2.7	2.7	3.8	3.9	3.6	3.4	3.7	3.2
(average)	(3.2)*		(3.9)		(2.7)		(3.9)		(3.5)*		(3.3)*	
Administration	2.7	2.7	4.3	3.9	2.4	2.4	3.9	4.0	3.4	3.4	3.6	3.2
(average)	(2.7)*		(4.0)		(2.4)		(4.0)		(3.4)*		(3.3)*	
Management	2.2	2.4	4.5	4.0	2.0	2.0	4.0	4.0	3.3	3.3	3.3	2.9
(average)	(2.4)*		(4.2)		(2.0)		(4.0)		(3.3)*		(3.0)*	
N =	26	67	26	67	24	48	24	48	7	14	7	14

[a]T-test of difference in means of involvement ratings for each group of officials comparing (1) council-manager and strong mayor-council respondents and (2) weak mayor-council and strong mayor-council respondents. For example, an asterisk for the rating of council-manager council members means that it is significantly different from the rating for council members in the strong mayor-council cities.

[b]Respondents are council members (C) and department heads (D). Entries are the composite rating of involvement by the council and the executive (i.e., the mayor or manager and staff) in decisions made by city government. Each dimension is based on ratings for 6–8 specific decisions. Involvement is measured on a five-point scale. See Appendix, Table A-2 for interpretation of scale and a list of items that go into each dimension.

*$p < .01$.

council and a strong executive. The strong mayor takes a large share of responsibilities, leaving the council weak and confined to a reviewing and reacting role. Although the mayor's opinion may not be valued as highly (in part, as noted in Chapter 2, because the mayor is not trusted to provide a full range of policy options), the mayor has power resources to prevail despite council suspicion.

In the weak mayor-council city, the council has a higher level of involvement than the mayor in all four dimensions. The council also has higher ratings than those for elected officials in the council-manager cities, particularly in administration and management. In the weak mayor-council city, the mayor's involvement recedes whereas the other executives maintain or increase their activity across the dimensions. There is not in Table 3-1 a direct measure of the activity of permanent administrative staff as distinct from the mayor's staff. As we shall see, however, that staff influence expands as the mayor's contracts.

The results reveal graphically the different position of the mayors in the two mayor-council forms. The strong mayor is a true executive—highly involved in administration and management as well as the policy dimensions—whereas the weak mayor is most active in broad policy making. The department heads give the mayor a markedly lower rating than the council does suggesting that the mayor is not perceived to be a central player from the perspective of staff. It appears that the council identifies actions in the "administration" with the mayor, whereas department heads may view the mayor as somewhat less directly involved. By implication, either no one is responsible for these areas or department heads themselves—but not the mayor—are.

Follow-up questions in the mayor-council cities asked respondents to divide influence between the mayor (and his appointees) and the permanent staff in selected decisions. For those that involve policy and organizational initiatives, there was little difference between respondents in the strong- and weak-mayor cities. With regard to allocating services, approximately half the respondents in the former felt that the permanent staff had influence equal to, or greater than, the mayor and "political" appointees, whereas two-thirds of those interviewed in the weak-mayor city expressed this opinion. Both in evaluating programs and in assessing the performance of the organization, 57 percent considered the permanent staff to be at least as influential as the strong mayor while 90 percent considered the permanent staff to be at least on a par with the weak mayor. Thus, in the weak-mayor form, the council overshadows the mayor, and the mayor's influence over staff recedes in the allocation of services and the assessment of performance.

The council-manager form combines an active council that limits its involvement in administration and management with an appointed executive who is active across the board. Although the manager's involvement level virtually matches the strong mayor, the manager's lack of formal powers over the council decreases the likelihood that he or she will constrict the council's contributions. Unlike the strong mayor-council cities in which the council members and department head have virtually identical ratings of their own and each other's involvement, there are several cases in which the ratings differ. One would suppose that one consequence of conflict in the strong-mayor cities would be a testing of limits and a general awareness of relative involvement. In the council-manager cities, on the other hand, the council puts its own involvement in policy at a higher level than the department heads do, a result that suggests the council's rating may be inflated. In administration and management, they rate the manager's involvement quite a bit higher than do the department heads. Council members appear to see these areas as being more fully the manager's responsibility than department heads do. This is not, however, an expression of a sharp disjuncture in defining the manager's roles nor tension in the relationship between the council and the manager as some have noted.[51] The council members recognize substantial involvement by the manager in the mission and policy dimensions.

Not only are there differences in the actual level of involvement across the cities that have different forms of government but there are also great divergences in the relationships associated with the division of responsibilities. The council and manager are satisfied with existing involvement levels in sharp contrast with the officials in mayor-council cities. This judgment is based on a comparison of the actual and preferred ratings of involvement. (See Figure 3–1.) Council members and staff in council-manager cities have preferences that differ little from the actual division of effort. They share a mild preference for more council involvement in mission, and the staff would like to see less council activity in management, although it is already moderately low. In the weak-mayor city, there is a desire by council members to be quite a bit more involved in mission formulation, despite their high actual rating. Department heads, on the other hand, wish that the council would decrease its activities in administration and management. They do not, however, want the mayor to assume a larger role in these areas above his actual moderate level of involvement. In the strong mayor-council cities, the department heads are generally satisfied with involvement levels as they are. They support more council contributions to mission, although they consider the actual involvement to be only moderate.

The council members in the strong mayor-council cities, however, express great dissatisfaction with the division of responsibilities. They would like to be substantially more involved in all dimensions. The differences in their ratings of actual and preferred involvement approach a full step on the scale—from a position of reviewing and advising to initiating and actively revising the formulation of mission, and from reacting and rubber stamping to systematically reviewing management decisions. In policy and administration, they would like to shift from moderately low to moderately high involvement. Their preferences are for an involvement profile very close to that of the council in the weak-mayor form. They would also prefer that the mayor and staff be somewhat less involved across the board than is currently the case.

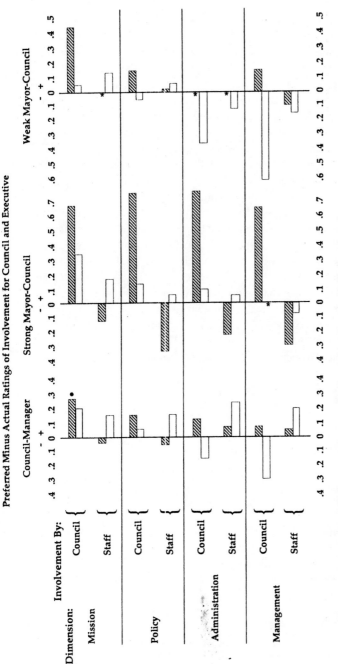

Figure 3-1. Comparison of Ratings of Actual and Preferred Involvement for Council and Executive

Graph measures difference between preferred and actual rating, e.g. + .29 reflects a preferred rating of 3.99 and an actual rating of 3.70. For rating of actual involvement, see Table 3-1.

* = +/- .01, i.e., preferred and actual are virtually identical.

• Type of respondent: ▨ = Council members ☐ = Department heads

These differences in preference indicate the substantial potential for conflict in the mayor-council form. The council cannot feel that its official interests are compatible with those of the strong mayor. Department heads are generally pleased with the council's limited role and would presumably resist greater activity, as would the mayor. This tension is found to a lessor extent in the reported differences in the weak-mayor city, and the mayor is likely to feel disadvantaged by the opinions of both the council and the department heads who prefer that his involvement be relatively low.

These results are consistent with the original formulation of the dichotomy-duality model in the council-manager cities. The behavior preferred by both elected officials and staff would reflect it even more clearly since the council would be more active in mission formulation and less involved in management than is currently the case. The manager's contributions are extensive in all dimensions, but the division of responsibility is determined by the involvement level chosen by the council. Given its formal authority, when the council chooses to be highly involved it necessarily also has the controlling influence. As is true of the council in the weak mayor-council city, the department heads may prefer that the council do less in an area but they are limited in their ability to change the council's behavior. The council limits itself in administration and management—in contrast to the council in the weak-mayor city.

The same cannot be said for the strong mayor-council cities. Even if the mayor and council were equally involved, the mayor's resources would give him greater influence. In fact, there is relatively little involvement by the council. The mayor is able not only to win contests but to fight fewer battles because the council's participation is restricted. If the council had its way, this would not be the case, but the mayor and department heads have walled the council into a small sphere of activity. If one combines the involvement of the mayor and staff, one has a modified dichotomy model of division of responsibilities rather than the dichotomy-duality division. The council's involvement is limited except in mission formulation. In administrative decisions, the mayor may be seen as a block to council involvement. One hears the claim from executive staff in these cities that the council should "stay out of administration," even though their involvement is less than in council-manager systems. The perception of interference may be attributable to the council's having to forcefully assert itself in competition with the mayor to guide implementation, obtain information, or secure response to citizen complaints. The council-manager council can be involved in these ways without necessarily clashing with the manager. The strong mayor can take active measures to exclude the council from administration, whereas the manager cannot block the council's involvement.

In the weak mayor-council city, there is an even division between the mayor and council in all the dimensions. By implication, since the mayor is not as highly involved as the executives in the other types of cities, the permanent administrative staff and other elected officials make a greater contribution in all dimensions as well. The permanent staff has greater influence vis-à-vis the mayor in decisions about allocating services and assessing programs than is the case in the strong-mayor cities. The council also maintains relatively higher involvement in administration and management. Thus, the division of responsibilities is closer to the duality model with a tripartite division of all dimensions. Tensions are evidenced by the squeeze on the mayor, the council's preference for more involvement, and the department heads' desire that the council back out of administration and management.

The original premise that council-manager governments restrict the activity of elected officials and expand the power of the bureaucracy must be revised on the basis of the evidence presented. Only the council-manager form has an active body of elected officials with a strong executive. Because of the acceptance of the division of responsibilities, the issue is not who is stronger but how are their respective activities combined. The former question is more appropriate to the mayor-council cities. One mayor-council form constricts the council and the other hems in the executive. Although it has extensive and wide-ranging participation by elected officials, the weak-mayor plan curtails executive leadership. It simultaneously permits more staff influence but offers less protection to staff from incursions by the council in administration and management.

Comparing the council-manager and strong-mayor systems, one must distinguish between representative democracy and executive democracy. The latter provides stronger democratic leadership in the sense of having greater concentration and range of potential actions under the direct control of an elected official. The former has stronger democratic leadership because it is more broadly based and more clearly provides citizen control of government. The council in the council-manager form is active and works with and through an executive who shares its goals and who is as capable a manager as the council chooses to hire. To dismiss this council as impotent is to fall prey to the assumptions about politics in the conflictual pattern. Thus, forms of government differ in the kind and extent of involvement by elected officials, but none has the corner on democratic leadership.

Summary of Conceptual Framework

The discussion in the first three chapters provides the framework within which the characteristics and behavior of mayors, council members, and administrators will be addressed. The major concepts are the following:

governmental process: the interaction of officials within the institutional structure to make decisions in the four dimensions of government.

patterns of interaction: the characteristic ways that officials relate to each other.

conflictual pattern: interactions based on incompatible goals and competing interests with no central authority.

cooperative pattern: interactions based on compatible goals and complementary interests usually with a central authority.

dimensions of governmental process: mission—goals and purpose; policy—programs and plans to accomplish goals; administration—the implementation of policies and delivery of services; and management—the coordination and control of resources to accomplish the purposes of the organization.

dichotomy-duality model: a division of responsibility among officials for the dimensions of the governmental process in which elected officials are primarily responsible for the formulation of mission; administrative staff are primarily responsible for management; and responsibility for policy and administration is shared.

In mayor-council governments there are structural factors that reinforce the conflictual pattern and in council-manager governments factors that sustain the cooperative pattern. The fragmentation of authority created by separation of powers produces incompatible official interests and promotes conflict. It is difficult to keep the conflicts of the larger political process from entering the governmental process, because mayors, council members, and staff are advantaged by securing support from groups in the community. Accommodation based on compromise is achieved through bargaining among competitors. Positive reciprocity may emerge within the conflictual pattern and keep conflict in check, but it does not eliminate the conflict.

The interactions among officials in council-manager cities are likely to be characterized by cooperation because of the presence of central authority in the council and the integrated organizational authority of the manager, as well as a tendency for officials to share values. The insulation of the council from direct pressures reduces the transfer of community conflicts into the governmental process. Still, conflict can arise in council-manager government if participants perceive that they have incompatible goals.

With respect to outcomes of the governmental process, there is no dramatic difference between the cooperative pattern and council-manager government, on the one hand, and the conflictual pattern and mayor-council government, on the other. In all city governments, delivery of services reflects the desire of administrators to observe agency or professional norms and the commitment to fairness in accomplishing agency goals. Still, in council-manager cities, there is greater insulation of governmental officials from political forces in the community and a greater tendency to respond to needs, whereas in mayor-council cities the governmental process is more permeable to the larger political process and responsiveness to articulated demands is likely to be greater.

Thus, the impact of the patterns of interaction and the forms of government depart from the common wisdom expressed at the beginning of the chapter. Conflict in government is not necessary to assure representative or responsive government. The cooperative pattern, as associated with the council-manager form, is not dependent on unrepresentative official leadership, nor does it produce less responsiveness to racial minority and lower socioeconomic groups than the conflictual pattern. With the cooperative pattern, one is likely to find greater insulation from popular pressures in governance and management. The evidence for this insulation is less variation in spending when ethnic population increases and lower responsiveness to the articulated demands of civil rights and business groups. This condition, however, does not negate universalism and fairness in the actions of government. Indeed, it may enhance it. Identification of the interests of the community as a whole does not necessarily mean exclusion of the concerns of lower income groups or racial minorities from civic priorities.

It is not appropriate to assert that administrators have more autonomy in council-manager government, although they often have considerable influence over decisions in partnership with elected officials. Indeed, council members have a larger role in all dimensions of the governmental process than their counterparts in strong mayor-council cities, although the council in weak-mayor cities takes an active part in administration and management as well as mission and policy making. In council-manager governments, the council is freer to define the terms of their involvement in administration and management, for example, the level of oversight review and organization appraisal they will conduct. Executive mayors, on the other hand, constrict the amount of activity by council members in their cities. The absence of conflict often observed in council-manager cities cannot be interpreted as the suppression of elected officials by bureaucrats. Rather, the norm is active cooperation resulting from high levels of involvement by both council and staff.

Regardless of form, officials need to understand their roles and establish effective working relationships if government is to function well. By understanding the significance of governmental form and likely tendencies associated with it, they are better able to take advantage of the opportunities and work around the constraints of their governmental structure. Despite the effects of form of government, the behavior of officials is crucial to fashioning the governmental process for better or worse in each locality.

In the following chapters, roles for each set of officials are examined with recognition that there are certain similarities across all cities and other characteristics of the position that are unique to one structural arrangement. The conceptual framework of these introductory chapters will be applied to determine what contributions officials make to the governmental process in cities with various forms of government. Three questions will be examined. First, what roles do officials play in the generation or resolution of conflict and/or the enhancement or diminution of cooperation? Second, how are each set of officials involved in the four dimensions of decisions made by city government? Third, how do officials relate to each other?

4

Mayors: Driving Force Versus Guiding Force

The mayor occupies a position of great visibility, and constituents have high expectations about the leadership that the mayor will give to the city. The mayor is viewed as the "problem-solver-in-chief" in city government. Unfortunately, for incumbent and citizen alike, the power available to "his or her honor" to get things done autonomously is either (1) more or less insufficient or (2) nonexistent depending on the form of government. If we define executive leadership to include the initiation of proposals to deal with problems in the community and the implementation of policy through control of the bureaucracy, then such leadership is a challenge for the strong mayor, difficult for the weak mayor, and impossible for the council-manager mayor.

The mayors in cities with and without separation of powers differ to such an extent that only those in mayor-council cities can be considered executives. They have administrative authority, whereas the mayor in council-manager cities does not. "Executive" mayors must be treated separately from the mayors who occupy a position closer to that of chairman of the board. For the time being, we shall label this kind of mayor as "nonexecutive" although it is not particularly satisfying to be defined by what one is not. The same analysis of roles cannot be applied to both, even though there are commonalities that apply to the mayoralty generally.

This difference does not imply, however, that one variety of mayors is better or more complete than the other. Each can make substantial contributions and has distinct roles to play. These roles are determined by the "requirements" of the form of government and by the pattern of interaction that characterizes the governmental process. Separation of powers, fragmentation of authority, and the conflictual pattern that are commonly found in mayor-council cities make the mayor the focal point of action. The system "depends" on certain kinds of leadership to function beyond the level of maintaining current operations. By establishing direction, forging coalitions, galvanizing the bureaucracy—in general by managing and resolving conflict in all dimensions of the governmental process—the executive mayor becomes the *driving force* in this form of government.

The nonexecutive mayor need not take on these roles, but makes a different kind of contribution. This office is important (if not crucial) to the city government's operation, but what the mayor can do beyond filling ceremonial roles has been largely unrecognized. To be sure, the government may operate adequately with minimal leadership from the mayor, given the formal features of council-manager government and assuming a cooperative pattern of interaction among officials. Policy initiation is shared by the entire council, the manager draws upon professional expertise and staff support to generate proposals, and executive powers are vested in the manager. An active and effective mayor, however, can elevate the level of performance of other officials and the governmental system as a whole. The mayor's roles are to foster communication and facilitate effective interaction among other officials and to provide a greater sense of purpose to city government. In this sense, the mayor is a *guiding force* in city government who helps insure that all other officials are performing as well as possible and that all are moving in the right direction.

Thus, all mayors have a special responsibility to the public at-large to lead their cities to higher levels of performance. In this sense, all mayors provide political leadership, a possibility sometimes overlooked in reformed cities. "The council-manager plan," according to Sanders, "represents the importance of professional competence and efficiency values with little emphasis on political leadership."[1] There is increasing recognition, however, that these cities, as well as those with the mayor-council form, need (or at least benefit from) a dynamic mayor.[2] As mayors seek to discharge this responsibility with varying degrees of success, they will fill distinct roles and manifest different types of leadership, depending on their form of government and the characteristics of the governmental process.

In this chapter, we shall reexamine how the office differs conceptually in the two forms of government, the resources for leadership—some common and some peculiar to the governmental form—and the distinct leadership roles and types of both kinds of mayors. To conclude, the possibility for convergence of the distinct types and exchange between the forms will be examined.

Perspectives on the Mayoralty

The mayor's office was examined extensively during the sixties and early seventies as a source of leadership in dealing with the problems of urban decay, poverty, and unrest. Most of those studies focused on the executive mayor. A shortcoming in much of the limited literature on council-manager mayors is a tendency to measure the office and performance in terms of the executive mayor. Although an occasional council-manager mayor might be considered to be an effective leader by this standard, it is unfair and inappropriate to compare all mayors to the executive mayor. This and other preconceptions stand in the way of identifying what constitutes the office and the leadership roles that the council-manager mayor may fill.

It is not simply the executive version of the office but a particular way of filling the office that has dominated thinking about the mayoralty. The innovator or entrepreneur type emerged from studies in mayor-council cities as the norm for mayoral leadership.[3] The effective mayor, as innovator, sets goals, builds coalitions, and influences the council, bureaucracy, and public to act according to the mayor's preferences. Although formal resources are of some help in establishing this type of leadership, mayors must also pyramid resources from informal sources in order to gain leverage over other actors. Because of the conflict common in city government, mayors face obstacles in establishing their position and must contend with challengers, including the council and entrenched department heads inside government. The central thrust of this approach was that mayoral leadership is necessary to overcome the "considerable fragmentation of authority and dispersal of power characteristic of the formal governmental structure" of American cities.[4] To do so, Ferman argues, "formal tools and informal resources must be manipulated in such a way that the mayor establishes the conditions for increasing executive power."[5]

Some discussions of the nonexecutive mayor are based on the same premises despite the fact that authority is formally concentrated and centralized in council-manager governments. Two case studies of individual mayors examine the office from the strong executive perspective. They share the assumption that the "normal" council-manager form does not provide the opportunity for mayoral leadership.[6] Pressman's study of a reluctant mayor in one city—Mayor Reading of Oakland—has strongly colored perceptions of the office. For example, in their urban politics text, Lineberry and Sharkansky assert that the "ribbon cutter" type of leadership is "the common role in council-manager cities."[7] When leadership is displayed, it will be largely "hortatory in nature," given the characteristics of the form.[8] Sparrow, who charts the creation of a "new municipal chief executive model" by Mayor Pete Wilson of San Diego, demonstrates that broader leadership is possible, but argues that basic precepts of the form of government must be altered to achieve it.[9]

Beyond providing interesting details of the trials and triumphs of two mayors, however, both studies suffer from preconceptions about the nature of the office and the form of government that may not be warranted. There are four shortcomings: assessing mayors as if they were executives, overstating the centrality of the mayor, distrusting the role of manager, and presuming a climate of conflict. Each of these points needs to be elaborated.

First, the studies by Pressman and Sparrow illustrate the inappropriateness of the executive mayor perspective in council-manager cities. To be sure, in most cities, mayors have to augment their limited formal assets. These studies argue further that all mayors must increase their resources in order to acquire leverage over other participants or to induce support. "Without governmental jurisdiction, staff, and financial resources," Pressman writes, "it is hard for any mayor to direct, or even influence, the actions of others."[10] The obstacles to achieving this kind of leadership are particularly great in council-manager government. Influence must be based on personal resources to overcome the limitations of structure. Sparrow as well stresses the need for informally pyramiding power. Mayor Wilson's leadership in San Diego was based on "adroit accumulation of political, policy-making, and administrative power" culminating in de facto control over the selection of the manager.[11] Only by tapping resources outside the formal structure or altering the form, it appears, is leadership possible. The authors assume that the mayor must have his or her own power in order to be effective. The studies give no attention, however, to the possibility that the formal authority normally available to elected officials in council-manager government will provide the basis for influence. Furthermore, they fail to recognize the inherent resources that are available to the council-manager mayor.

Two other studies demonstrate that the council-manager form of government does not preclude leadership. Boynton and Wright, who examined mayor-manager relations in forty-five large cities, found that the mayor provides significant leadership in the councilmanic and public arenas.[12] Wikstrom, in a study of forty-one cities in Virginia, found that almost all mayors in Virginia at least provide council leadership, and 38 percent also provide political leadership.[13]

The second and third preconceptions in the Pressman and Sparrow studies are closely related: the centrality of the mayor to the governmental process and the distrust of professional administrators. It is assumed that the mayor must activate the lethargic city government and give it direction, if any elected official is to do so. The manager, they suggest, will manipulate the council, pursue a personal/professional agenda, and take cues from outside influentials, but will not provide leadership responsive to elected officials nor supportive of their exercise of democratic control. The manager, Pressman observed, "may be responsive to citizen's preferences because he deems it to be a wise policy to act in such a manner," but superior resources permit the manager to dominate the governmental process.[14]

Sparrow suggests that managers generally seek to promote the growth of the city because in the process their "personal worth" increases through "larger and more professional staffs, an increasing tax base, and greater influence."[15] The manager was responsive to the council in San Diego only so long as it supported growth, and the staff resisted a change in policy. Only when Mayor Wilson secured the appointment of a manager who was willing to settle for a limited scope of responsibilities and accept the mayor's broad-ranging activities was political control achieved. Thus, mayoral leadership is essential to providing direction and to curtailing the power of staff.

There are two implications of this approach. One is that leadership cannot be collective, either exercised by the mayor and manager or by the council as a whole. The other is that it is assumed that the manager will not be responsive to the mayor and council. Boynton and Wright, however, characterized the mayor-manager relationship in large cities as "collaborative or team relationships."[16] This finding indicates that cooperative relationships between elected and appointed officials are common, and clearly contradicts an assumption of inherent conflict in relations among officials. Wikstrom as well concludes that council-manager government has evolved into "teamwork governance; mayors and managers need and depend upon each other."[17]

Finally, and underlying the other preconceptions in the executive-oriented studies, is the presumption of conflict within the governmental process. Sparrow viewed power in San Diego as a hydraulic system "whereby decrease in the manager's power would result in increased mayoral power,"[18] and Pressman's analysis of Oakland also rests on a zero-sum conception of power. As discussed in Chapter 2, when participants in the governmental process view the payoffs of interaction in this way, conflict is likely. When the mayor's winning depends on the manager's losing, distrust is also likely to be present. Thus, even without separation of powers, the characteristics of the conflictual pattern would be present. Sparrow and Pressman advise the mayor to play the game accordingly.

The defect in this approach is that the behavior appropriate for the executive mayor may be not only unnecessary in council-manager government, but may also produce conditions that would otherwise not be present. Conflict may be introduced when the mayor takes actions to advance his or her own interests and block those of others. If a mayor uses power tactics on the assumption that a manager will resist the mayor's control (as opposed to control by the entire council,) these actions are likely to provoke the very resistance the mayor anticipated. Anticipation of resistance, thus, becomes a self-fulfilling prophecy. One should not presume that the governmental process is characterized by the conflictual pattern unless conditions support that conclusion.

As we have discussed extensively in Chapter 2, the conditions associated with conflict are not invariant in the urban governmental process. When Mayor Henry Cisneros of San Antonio called upon council-manager cities to create "models of consensus" for decision making, he was not being naive according to this reasoning.[19] He was seeking to promote the potential for cooperative relationships in this form of government, and his experience as mayor demonstrates that high caliber leadership can be provided by a council-manager mayor.[20]

When the cooperative pattern obtains, the mayor does not need to be an autonomous power wielder who activates and checks other officials. Rather, the mayor may be seen as the single most important agent of cooperation in relations among officials. The challenge to the mayor is to achieve and maintain a situation in which each set of officials fulfills their responsibilities with the least possible interference in the activities of others.

This argument counters the presumption that "stronger" leadership by the mayor in council-manager cities transforms the structure. In this way of thinking, the mayor-council model continues to be the norm. Wikstrom, who avoids most of the preconceptions of the executive mayor approach, still suggests that when the mayor's policy role expands and the mayor becomes more broadly involved in administrative matters, the council-manager form resembles a "skew version of the mayor-council with a CAO [chief administrative officer] form".[21] Sparrow concludes that "the city manager is losing power" as the mayor expands his own.[22] He approves of the mayor having effective control of the selection of the manager which, in effect, converts the manager into a CAO. George identifies a trend toward the emergence of a "strong-mayor, council-manager" form of government.[23] All three assessments appear to be reverting to the familiar in describing a largely unrecognized phenomenon—the active, visible mayor who makes substantial contributions to the council-manager form without altering its basic features.

To counter this tendency, the mayor's office should be defined in terms of the form of government in which it is located. The roles and types of leadership provided by the mayors in the two forms of government are distinct. The council-manager mayor is not *limited* in his or her leadership but rather is *different* in the kinds of leadership provided. All mayors potentially offer political leadership regardless of the form of government. As we shall see in the next section, such leadership depends more on personal characteristics than on formal or informal power resources.

What then is different about the council-manager mayor? If this mayor does not execute—or directly promote task accomplishment—what does he or she do? The answer is that this mayor *facilitates,* that is, accomplishes objectives through enhancing the efforts of others. This distinction makes a great difference in the orientation of the mayor. Rather than seeking power as the way to accomplish tasks, the facilitative mayor seeks to empower others. Thus, our perspective on the mayoralty needs to be broadened to include both executive and facilitative mayors who will typically be associated with the mayor-council and council-manager forms of government, respectively.[24]

This approach does not ignore the possibility that characteristics of the governmental process may require borrowing approaches from the other form. For example, a mayor with a truly entrenched and unresponsive manager who has cowed the city council will need to adopt power tactics. On the other hand, a mayor in a mayor-council city in which the council has active leadership and permanent staff is attentive to the wishes of the mayor and council may be more effective by providing facilitative leadership like that of council-manager mayors. In conclusion, there are two kinds of mayoral leadership that are equally appropriate to different forms or circumstances. To understand what is common and different about them, it is useful to review the resources for leadership available to the executive and the facilitative mayor.

Resources for Leadership

The office of mayor is not firmly defined by legal structure nor tradition. Rather, individual incumbents, operating within broad limits set by the form of government and the political context, shape the office by the way they utilize various resources. Because the individual puts his or her stamp on the office, it is helpful to distinguish which resources are tied to the legal arrangements or the political characteristics of particular cities and which are generally available to all mayors.

The resources may be categorized by source (legal or formal versus informal) and by their impact on the office. Some contribute directly to defining the character of the office—whether it is executive or nonexecutive. Others affect the way the job is performed, but usually do not by themselves determine the nature of the office.

Resources that determine whether the mayor functions as an executive are the formal and informal power resources that determine whether or not the mayor will (at least potentially) play an important role, independent of the council, in policy formation, policy implementation, or management. The formal powers include control over budget formulation and hiring of staff, appointment of members of boards and commissions, *ex officio* membership on boards, the veto, and the right to issue executive orders and fill vacancies in elected offices. There is, in addition, organizational authority over departments of city government proper and, on occasion, over semi-autonomous units of government (e.g., a housing authority or redevelopment commission).

Yates suggests that the characteristics of an organization are important as well as the formal control over it. Richard Lee of New Haven secured strong support from redevelopment and antipoverty agencies because he created them from scratch paralleling the traditional city hall departments. John Lindsay in New York, on the other hand, was hampered by the need to work with the "recalcitrant, outmoded bureaucracy," which resisted his "guerrilla raids from city hall."[25] Kevin White in Boston used his powers over administrative organization to shift functions he considered important from semi-autonomous agencies to ones under the mayor's office. For example, the responsibility for community development programs in neighborhoods was shifted from the Boston Redevelopment Agency to the Neighborhood Development Administration in his office. Between 1967 and 1976, the staff in mayoral agencies more than doubled from 284 to 584 and the funds expended mushroomed from $378,752 to approximately $6.5 million.[26]

Other formal provisions that may be either power resources or simply enhance performance are staff support for the mayor and salary to make the job full-time. For example, Wilson used his financial analysts to develop leverage over the manager.[27] Other mayors use these resources to augment the number of and range of tasks they perform without taking on executive functions and exerting power over other participants.

The formal power "profile" of the mayor varies widely across cities. Depending on their number, they provide the basis for a lot, some, or no assertive goal setting, leverage over council decisions, and control over the actions of administrative staff. The variation in formal powers is illustrated by the mayor's veto authority and appointment powers. Virtually all mayor-council mayors have the veto power (91 percent), and half of these can veto all actions. The mayor has appointment authority for none or one of four key positions—police chief, fire chief, city attorney, and chief personnel officer—in 23 percent of the cities, for two or three of these positions in 32 percent, and for all four in 46 percent.[28] Thus, the chief executive in the mayor-council city may or may not have direct authority for those who occupy key administrative positions. In council-manager cities, mayors usually do not appoint any staff. Only 13 percent have any veto and less than 30 percent of these can veto all actions, that is, a broad-ranging veto power is available in only 3 percent of all council-manager cities.[29]

The variations in charter provisions defining the mayor's position in mayor-council cities are illustrated in Table 4-1. The nine cities included are representative of the variety of institutional settings in which the mayor operates. In Minneapolis and San Francisco, there is extensive fragmentation of authority. Different parts of city governments are

Table 4-1. Illustrations of Formal Power Resources of the Mayor

City	Appointment	Limitation of Budget Authority	Other
Minneapolis	Major department heads (except Parks and Library) appointed by Executive committee consisting of Mayor, President of Council, and three other council members, with approval of City Council. Staff department heads appointed by City Coordinator. Park and Library directors selected by their own boards.	Prepared by Mayor and approved by Council. Its proposal goes to Board of Estimate along with Library and Park budgets. Council cannot exceed levy set by Board.	
San Bernardino	Mayor appoints Chief Administrative Officer (CAO) and department heads with approval of council; may be removed by mayor with approval of two-thirds of council.	None	
San Francisco	Mayor appoints CAO (10-year term), Controller (serves for life) with confirmation of Board of Supervisors (council). Mayor appoints executive staff (deputy for development, social programs, etc.) and a number of commissions (e.g., City Planning, Fire, Housing, Police), which appoint their own department heads. CAO appoints certain department heads, including Public Health and Public Works. Mayor and Council both appoint members to major regional agency boards. A number of officials, including the Sheriff, Assessor, and Treasurer are directly elected.	Controller prepares budget. Mayor (and Council) can only decrease budget requests. Only indirect control over budget requests from departments under CAO and separate boards.	Limited to two terms. Shares executive authority with CAO.
New Haven	Mayor appoints and may remove at pleasure up to four "coordinators," usually in areas of community development, human services, public administration, and finance; appoints for two-year term Corporation Counsel, Director of Public Works, Director of Welfare, Board of Finance; appoints, if vacancy, but may not remove (except for cause), Controller, City Assessor, City Engineer, Police Chief, Fire Chief, Director of Parks and Recreation, Planning Director, Personnel Director, and Director of Traffic and Parking.	Board of Finance, chaired by Mayor, prepares budget for Board of Aldermen. It may change line items, but can not raise the total figure.	

City	Appointment and removal powers	Budget/Veto	Council relations
Akron	Mayor appoints members of most boards and commissions, although there are some restrictions regarding staggered terms and party representation. Mayor with consent of the Council appoints and removes members of boards and commissions; appoints and removes all department directors, except Director of Health, who is appointed by Health Commission, and the Personnel Director, who is appointed by the Civil Service Commission. Appointment and removal is unrestricted for positions in unclassified service—including Directors of Public Service, Finance, Law, and deputies to the mayor; all other officials are covered by restrictions of classified service (i.e., nomination by Personnel Director and removal only for cause). Department of Public Safety is under the direct supervision of the mayor.	None	Council may not attempt to dictate to Mayor any appointment nor give orders to any subordinates of the Mayor.
Memphis	Mayor appoints CAO with approval of Council but may remove for cause; appoints department heads with approval of Council, who serve for a term concurrent to that of appointing Mayor and may be removed with approval of Council.	None	Veto may be overridden by majority vote of Council.
Atlanta	Mayor appoints CAO; nominates with confirmation by Council department heads for term of four years; may remove department heads with written notice subject to override by two-thirds vote of Council.	None. Mayor has line-item veto.	
Boston	Mayor appoints most department heads, very few require council approval. Mayor has no formal authority over parks and roads, welfare, transportation, or schools.	None. Council may only decrease appropriations.	
Knoxville	Mayor with consent of Council appoints members of boards and commissions; appoints and may remove department heads; appoints members to standing committees in the Council.	None	Mayor presides over Council meetings but may not vote, except to break ties.

Source: Information is from city charters, except for Boston and San Francisco, which comes from Ferman (1985: 24–29).

run by different officials. San Bernardino provides integrated executive control in the hands of the mayor, but limits the mayor's appointment of department heads. They must be approved by the council and cannot be removed without two-thirds approval from the council. In Atlanta, on the other hand, although the council approves appointments, it must have a two-thirds vote to block the removal of a department head. Memphis offers another variation; council approval is needed for appointment and removal, but the mayor can appoint a new complement of department heads at the beginning of a term. New Haven and Akron, on the other hand, combine unrestricted mayoral appointment power over certain officials with protected tenure for others. The mayors in Boston and Knoxville have extensive autonomy in choosing department heads.

Most mayors do not directly control large numbers of city government jobs. Civil service protection of most positions limit the jobs a mayor can dispense. Kevin White in Boston and Richard Daley in Chicago were notable exceptions. By a combination of formal authority and skillful manipulation of the personnel process and a passive civil service system, White had over 4,000 patronage jobs at his disposal out of a workforce of 24,000. He was able to create "provisional" slots during election campaigns, approximately 1,200 in 1975 and 1,600 in 1979.[30] The patronage pool available to the mayor as head of the Democratic machine in Chicago in the mid-seventies was estimated to exceed 9,000 out of 45,000 employees.[31] Most mayors, however, cannot count on the firm control secured by providing supporters with a job; nor are they able to dispense patronage as a way of controlling other elected officials.

With respect to formulating the budget, mayors share that function with others in Minneapolis and San Francisco but can develop executive budgets in the other cities. Mayors can use this control to induce and reward support or to punish opposition.

Despite the number of formal powers, they must be supplemented with informal power resources. In mayor-council cities, the weaker the formal, the more important the informal resources. It is probably a truism that no mayor feels the office is powerful enough. Support of a political party or community elites, strong popular backing, and a host of private backers indebted for jobs, favors, contracts, and recognition can give mayors the added political clout they need in the council and their own administration to get ideas accepted and acted upon. Such support permitted Daley of Chicago to convert a weak mayoralty into the power center of city government. Greer describes how the mayor of Waukegan built widespread constituency support by tapping slack resources in the private sector and service agencies to augment the services available from city government.[32]

The difficulty in acquiring resources is affected by the characteristics of the governmental form and the "organization" of community politics. When the mayor uses extensive formal resources to control the council and bureaucracy, he or she is also favorably situated to expand control over nongovernmental actors as well. This "centralized control" model, Ferman has observed, provides far more opportunities for the mayor than a "consolidated influence model" in which the mayor "attempts to pull power from the sides"—outside government—"to the center."[33] When groups in the community are organized in broad coalitions, the mayor is better able to tap these external resources without expending his or her limited supply than when the groups are small, fragmented, and at odds with each other. Mayor Alioto in San Francisco was more successful in consolidating influence from a coalition of labor and business backers than were Mayors Moscone and Feinstein, who sought to fashion a coalition from a variety of groups.[34] Thus, limited formal resources and fragmented political systems limit the likelihood of strong mayoral leadership.

The weak mayor, although limited in executive powers, is an executive nonetheless. This mayor has some direct control over policy making and implementation, which may be augmented by informal resources. On the other hand, the council-manager mayor typically has no such independent control to build on. Therefore, *executive* control exercised directly or through the manager must be derived from outside support or from backing by a majority of the council. It appears that Mayor Wilson in San Diego became the de facto executive by determining who would be manager and by limiting the scope of the manager's authority over policy and budget formation while expanding his own capacity to shape the content of policy. Without building formal powers into the charter (which Wilson unsuccessfully attempted to do), the executive council-manager mayor will be inherently unstable, however. If formal powers are added, one may question whether the form has also been converted into a government with separation of powers.

In sum, the power resources—formal or informal—are particularly important in the mayor-council form or conflict conditions. Accumulating and retaining them in the council-manager form will be difficult and will normally not be necessary unless the mayor wishes to take on executive functions.

The mayor's performance is also affected by individual characteristics, such as experience, personal or occupational financial and staff support, personal attributes (charisma, reputation, wisdom,) commitment to the job (time, resources, and energy expended), and relationship with the media. These factors determine how well and how fully the mayor fills the position, whatever the scope of the office. The personal resources in themselves cannot make up for nonexistent formal powers or weak informal sources of influence, despite the relationship between individual talents and the accumulation of power resources. The charismatic or adroit weak mayor may be able to win substantial support from the community and wring more advantage from limited powers than others have done. Political entrepreneurship entails identifying and creatively utilizing slack resources. Ferman has argued that "effective political skills" are the critical factor for strong mayoral leadership.[35] But there are limits. A council-manager mayor, relying entirely on energy and resourcefulness, cannot acquire the power to appoint staff. These individual traits may explain, however, why one nonexecutive mayor is generally perceived to make a significant difference in the way the city operates whereas another is merely a figurehead. Thus, the personal resources are important for all mayors, whereas the power resources are primarily relevant to mayor-council mayors.

Kotter and Lawrence provide a framework that assesses the impact of mayors based on the range of their interactions and the quality of their ideas and places less emphasis on their power over other officials. They use a single typology for all kinds of mayors. In twenty cities, including seven with council-manager form, they analyzed mayoral behavior in three processes: agenda setting, network building, and task accomplishing. They argue that the "scope of the mayor's domain"—those areas in which the mayor "behaves *as if* he has some responsibility"—is determined more by the nature of the mayor's agenda-setting activities than by the assignment of formal responsibility.[36] Also, mayors can establish a broad network of relationships regardless of formal powers. Task accomplishment will, however, largely be limited to an "individualistic" approach, in which mayors work on tasks by themselves, unless they have the formal control over the bureaucracy or supportive staff—typically absent from council-manager government—or they have unusually great entrepreneurial capacity. As a consequence, four of the seven council-manager mayors were placed in the minimum leadership category (only council-manager mayors were placed in this category), and two were characterized as "individualist" type mayors. Thus, their framework leads to conclusions similar to those of Pressman and Sparrow who explicitly stress power resources: leadership by the mayor in council-manager cities is likely to be limited unless the mayor has rare personal characteristics.

One may challenge, however, the contention that their treatment of resources is equally appropriate for both kinds of cities. A conceptual approach that does not include task accomplishment would be more relevant to council-manager mayors. Furthermore, their emphasis on the need to build networks and the inclusion of control over staff and authority to reorganize in networking fails to recognize the inherent potential for mayors in this form to handle communication and promote cooperation, starting with the close relationship to the manager.

Thus, most of the existing literature has been tilted toward how to be (or become) an effective executive mayor. Only scant attention has been given to the additional resources that support facilitative leadership in council-manager cities. In fact, the council-manager mayor has resources to draw upon that extend beyond individual characteristics. Although these are derived from the position, they are not power resources available only to the mayor.[37]

Wikstrom identifies leadership roles that draw on essential features of the council-manager form and the tasks assigned to the mayor. These are (1) presiding over the council, (2) representing the city, and (3) facilitating constructive interaction between the council and manager. Out of these activities, the mayor may be able to provide leadership to the council, offer political leadership, and help realize goals.[38] Boynton and Wright identified three significant spheres of activity in city government—legislative, public, and bureaucratic. The mayor's significance derives from the dominant role typically played in the first two spheres by virtue of the nature of the position and from the unusually close relationship to the bureaucratic sphere as a result of extensive interaction with the manager.

The mayor has ample opportunities for facilitative leadership by virtue of the attributes and duties of the position. As ceremonial head and spokesman for the council, the mayor has much more extensive public and media contact than other council members. As presiding officer, the mayor can guide the conduct of meetings and have some impact of the flow of debate and the timing of resolution. As liaison with the manager, the mayor links the two major components of the system—the legislative body and the administrative apparatus—and can foster communication and understanding between elected and appointed officials. As official representative, the mayor has extensive dealings with officials in other governments and may serve as a key participant in formulating agreements with state or federal officials, developers, and others who seek joint ventures with city government.

By performing these activities, the mayor occupies a strategic location shaped by his or her special and close relationship with the council, manager, and public. Unlike Kotter and Lawrence's approach, which stresses creating a set of relationships and controlling staff, the mayor's distinctive interaction with the participants provides a network that is readily available if the mayor chooses to use it. This network is illustrated in Figure 4–1. All the major interactional channels pass through the mayor. By virtue of this favored position, the mayor is able to tap

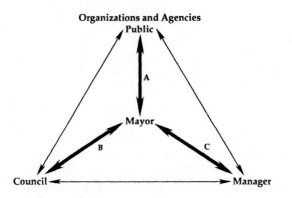

COMMON ACTIVITIES THAT PRODUCE EXTENSIVE INTERACTIONS

A. Ceremonial activities, spokesman, official representative and delegate.

B. Presiding officer, work sessions, informal contacts.

C. Frequent meetings, agenda setting—formal or informal--, scheduling, briefings, and other preparations for mayor's "official head" tasks.

* Arrows indicate communications among actors. The double arrows for the mayor suggest the extensive interactions the mayor is likely to have with these actors, which are greater than they have directly with each other.

Source: Svara (1986b) reprinted with permission from *National Civic Review*.

Figure 4-1. The Strategic Location of the Mayor in Council-Manager Cities

into various communication networks among elected officials, governmental staff, and community leaders. Although they can and do interact with each other independently, the mayor can transmit messages better than any one else in the government because of the breadth of knowledge and range of contacts he or she is likely to have. In so doing, the mayor has a unique potential to expand the level of understanding and improve the coordination among participants in the governmental process.

To be sure, the mayor must recognize the strategic potential of his or her position and seek to maintain and expand the network. Eberts and Kelly have found that mayors differ in the importance they assign to facilitating citizen participation as well as their desire to establish links at the state and national level. When mayors are active locally and extralocally, however, they "perform a central coordinative role" not found in "any other community position."[40]

The mayor's opportunity for policy leadership is based on the goodwill that is generated from providing coordination, from superior knowledge about all the participants, and from the ability to insert her or his own ideas as well as transmitting the "messages" of others. In contrast, the mayor-council mayor will typically find it harder to be a facilitative leader because of the prevalence of conflict. Behaviors that depend on trust and openness will be ineffective at best and may be self-defeating for the executive mayor.

In conclusion, executive mayors whose impact is evidenced by altering the behavior of other officials depend ultimately on power resources, whereas facilitative mayors in council-manager government utilize the characteristics of the form to foster communication and improve interaction among officials. Just as it is difficult for the council-manager mayor to be an executive due to limited power resources, it is also difficult for the mayor-council counterpart to be a facilitator because of the prevalence of conflict conditions and the absence of trust. For both kinds of mayors, performance varies depending on the personal characteristics and style of the incumbent.

Mayor-Council Mayors: Roles and Types of Executive Leadership

An array of typologies have been developed for understanding the variations in mayoral leadership. The dimensions used in the literature to construct typologies are listed in Table 4–2. They fall into four distinct

Table 4–2. Scholarly Perspectives on Dimensions of Mayoral Leadership

Source	Variable Used to Construct Typology
Resources	
LS	Formal authority
LS	Political resources
L	Resources
Y	Political and financial resources
KL	Resources for networking: resources available to build network; capacity to reorganize; extent of staff support
Assessment of Performance	
C	Initiation of policy
KL	Agenda setting: muddling through to rational-deductive
G	Implementation
C	Organizational ability
KL	Accomplishing tasks: through individual efforts, bureaucracy, or "organization," augmented by pyramiding resources (i.e., entrepreneurial)
L	Performance: centralizes community politics; mobilizes community involvement; integrates diverse interests; activates innovative programs
Style	
Y	Degree of activism and innovation they display in their daily work
S	Stance regarding problem-solving: passive versus active
B, SC	Active-passive/positive-negative
C	Style: originality, risk-taking, energy, openness, and promotional ingenuity
KL	Agenda setting: how broadly mayor defines scope of domain
S	Visibility: low versus high
CF	Populism: relying on the electorate versus established parties and interest groups
S	Political methods: personal versus mass appeals
F	Skill: manipulation of resources in order to increase executive power; also bargaining, persuasion, manipulation of conflict, incentives, media, and image
KL	Relationships in networks: nature of appeals to build network; degree to which network is altered
EK	Localism and cosmopolitanism: network building at local level and at state and national level
S	Administrative methods: traditional versus modern
SWM	Expressive leadership: stressing social or emotional content of an issue rather than its substance
Policy or Ideology	
L	Goals: collective goods versus private goods
S	Type of policy orientation: Nonredistributive versus redistributive
CF	Fiscal issues and social issues: conservative versus liberal
Context	
L	Community characteristics: pluralized versus polarized

Sources:

B	Barber (1972)	L	Levine (1974)
CF	Clark and Ferguson (1983)	LS	Lineberry and Sharkansky (1978)
C	Cunningham (1970)	M	Maier (1966)
EK	Eberts and Kelly (1985)	SC	Shank and Conant (1975)
F	Ferman (1985)	S	Stone (1982)
G	George (1968)	SWM	Stone, Whelan, and Murin (1986)
KL	Kotter and Lawrence (1974)	Y	Yates (1977)

categories: power resources, assessment of performance, style, and policy preference or ideology. The dimensions reflect four broad questions that we ask about executives:

Power resources: With what do they work and how do they gain control?
Assessment of performance: How well do they perform and how much do they accomplish?
Style: How do they operate?
Policy Preference or Ideology: Toward what policy ends do they strive?

The factors are used separately and in combination to produce models or typologies of leadership. For example, some examine the interaction of formal and informal power resources. Others combine them with style.

The typologies have been presented as universal models applying to all mayors. When one examines the dimensions on which these typologies are based, however, it is evident that most are more properly viewed as typologies for the executive mayor. Those that utilize power resources as a criterion for classifying the mayor are inappropriate for facilitative mayors, who do not rely on power resources. The typologies based on assessment of performance measure certain behaviors—policy initiation and implementation or task accomplishment—that are widely shared in council-manager government and are not the exclusive preserve of the facilitative mayor. Thus, a new typology using different factors and indicators is needed for mayors in council-manager cities. Such a typology will be developed in the next section.

Keeping in mind this limitation, the executive mayor typologies illuminate various aspects of the office and the behavior of incumbents. The resource factors include formal authority, informal or political resources, financial support, and staff support. The performance factors emphasize initiation and implementation of policy. The resource and performance factors may be blended with considerations of style. How a mayor forms a supportive network of persons and groups depends in part on formal resources such as the power to reorganize staff or the extent of staff support. The nature of appeal to supporters and the inclination to reshape or expand the network are matters of personal style. Similarly, agenda setting combines performance in the ability to generate ideas and link specific actions to general goals as well the scope of issues a mayor chooses to be concerned with, in part a matter of personal choice. Typologies by Cunningham (1970), Kotter and Lawrence (1974), Levine (1974), Lineberry and Sharkansky (1974), and Yates (1977) all use resource and/or performance in fashioning a classification of leadership types (as indicated in Table 4–2).

There is another set of typologies that emphasize personal qualities and attitudes separate from what a mayor has to work with and how well he or she uses power resources. Because these style and policy factors avoid the resource and performance factors that are specifically relevant to executive mayors, they have the apparent advantage of being broadly applicable to all mayors. They are not, however, very useful for differentiating among types of leadership. Knowing that a mayor is, for example, active or passive, visible or invisible, or utilizes expressive leadership does not tell us much about the quality of leadership he or she provides. Symbolic actions may be a substitute for attacking problems or may accompany substantial action.[41] If one is active and visible but ineffective in a key performance dimension, the style characteristics are of little interest. Using goal orientation or ideology as the basis for classifying leadership injects an unneeded normative bias. The quality of leadership provided by the incumbent may be assessed independently of the mayor's policies, that is, one may have effective or ineffective mayors who are liberal or conservative.

The community context has been stressed by Levine. In the polarized city with a persistent cleavage between two major segments of the population, the mayor's actions have a different focus than in the pluralistic city with many competing groups. A different typology is needed, one that emphasizes how the mayor contributes to overcoming the warfare or stalemate in this situation.

These dimensions have been used to generate a plethora of mayoral leadership types. These labels have been assembled in Table 4–3. There is a basic agreement about minimal, low, medium, and high levels of leadership, but no consistency in usage. The same or similar terms are used in more than one level by different authors, and the same kind of leadership has been given various labels. This comprehensive reference list is useful because some factors may be more or less obvious at different times in a mayor's career, or in a campaign among candidates for the office. There is presumably a fundamental connection among some of the indicators.[42] The rating one can give a mayor or prospective mayor on a readily observed factor (e.g., network building) may be a clue about how less obvious aspects of the position are being or will be handled.

My own preference is to use the performance factors as the basis for differentiating among executive mayors.[43] Other factors are best used to explain the variations in this key criterion. Power resources, as dis-

Table 4-3. Scholarly Perspectives on Types of Executive Mayoral Leadership

Source	Type and Characteristics

Minimal Leadership

KL	Ceremonial pattern: "minimum mayor"
SC	Figurehead (or evader): passive-negative
L	Bystander: passive observer of conflict in polarized city
EK	Ceremonial (manager) low local/national network building
LS	Ribbon cutter: weak formal and political resources
M	Caretaker: weak in initiation and implementation; reactive, fails to mobilize machinery of government

Low Leadership

Y	Broker: weak in political/financial resources and passive
	Caretaker:
KL	—muddling through, limited networking, bureaucratic and individualistic task accomplishing
EK	—high local/low national networking
SC	—passive-positive
C	Trustee-manager: characterized by caution, inflexibility, bureaucratic authoritarianism, physical inertness, heavy-handedness, and organizational confusion

Moderate—Active or Strong in One Dimension, Inactive or Ineffective in Other

S	*1. Traditional Methods/Individual or Organization Appeals*
C	Broker: weak initiation and strong implementation
Y	Boss: strong political/financial resources but passive
SC	Modern boss-politician: active-negative
LS	Conservative: weak in either formal or political resources
	2. Loner
KL	Personality/individualist: short-term perspective, largely reactive, personal and purposive appeals with limited network and staff, individualistic task accomplishment (usually weak formal resources)
SC	Maverick-independent: active-positive
SC	Renegade: active-negative
SC	Polarizing leadership: active-negative
L	Partisan: promotes one side in polarized city
S	*3. Modern Methods and/or Mass Appeals*
M	Reformer: strong in initiation, weak in implementation
LS	Frustrated activist: weak in either formal or political resources
Y	Crusader: weak political/financial resources and high activism
SC	Cosmopolitan: active-positive; disparity between constituency and audience (see Wilson [1969])
EK	Entrepreneurial (innovator): high on national/low on local networking
KL	Executive: moderate-range agenda, varied appeals (more reliance on staff), more bureaucratic
S	Manager: low visibility, passive, nonredistributive, impersonal and modern

High Leadership

LS	Power broker: strong formal authority and strong political resources
S	Social reformer: high visibility, active, redistributive, impersonal and modern

(*continued*)

Table 4–3. (*Continued*)

Source	Type and Characteristics
CF	New fiscal populists: populist, conservative on fiscal and liberal on social issues.
C	Innovator: high in initiation and implementation
	Entrepreneur:
Y	—high political/financial resources and high activism
S	—high visibility, active, nonredistributive, impersonal and modern
SC	Program-politician: active-positive
EK	Activist (executive): high local and national networking
KL	Program entrepreneur: broad agenda setting, all types of network building, and all task accomplishing with emphasis on entrepreneurial
L	Hegemonic leader: centralizes community politics; mobilizes community involvement; integrates diverse interests; activates innovative programs in polarized city.

Sources:

CF	Clark and Ferguson (1983)	LS	Lineberry and Sharkansky (1978)
C	Cunningham (1970)	M	Maier (1966)
EK	Eberts and Kelly (1985)	SC	Shank and Conant (1975)
G	George (1968)	S	Stone (1982)
KL	Kotter and Lawrence (1974)	SWM	Stone, Whelan, and Murin (1986)
L	Levine (1974)	Y	Yates (1977)

cussed in the previous section, help explain the potential for executive leadership. Individual style, such as creative drive and originality, and policy orientation are personal factors that shape how the mayor will use resources and approach performance within the job. The following discussion, which assumes that the city is not polarized, will be organized in terms of a typology based on an assessment of mayoral performance.

This approach answers the basic question asked by incumbents or observers of the mayor, "How well is the mayor doing?" The question can be answered in terms of success in providing two elements of leadership—policy initiation and direction of program implementation. This approach assumes that the mayor (at least potentially) has power resources beyond the threshold which permit executive roles. For such mayors, it is not especially useful to examine resources per se, because mayors differ so much in how fully they exploit and augment a given resource base. Thus, resources serve only as a screening factor or prior condition for inclusion in this typology. Only executive mayors with formal and informal power resources are included.

Initiation includes the formulation of policy and the generation of sufficient agreement and support to secure its approval. Initiation presumes that the mayors have imaginative ideas (or supporters who will generate them) and the desire to undertake change. Energy, imagination, and risk taking will be required if the mayor wishes to promote innovation. The resolution of conflict to reach agreement on action is often difficult to achieve without resourceful leadership. The mayor who successfully initiates policy is able to win the support of the council and other elected officials and overcome resistance of opponents or detractors. The ability to build a coalition of supporters among individuals, groups, and institutions within and outside the community is needed. Finally, the mayor must be able to get requisite help from his or her own appointees and the permanent staff to formulate creditable and supportable proposals. Depending on the emphasis on rationality among participants and the level of conflict in the governmental process, the mayor will engage in more or less bargaining, compromising, and trading to launch new policies. The mayor needs considerably less effort and resources to successfully block initiatives he or she opposes.

Policy implementation refers to getting things done and making government work, that is, the manipulation of administrative staff, organization, and resources to execute policies and direct programs to accomplish policy objectives. This task is important because the bureaucracy of local government may be resistant to change, hostile to cooperation across departmental lines, and subversive of policy intent by various forms of "bureaucratic vetoes." The council may wish to take an active part in implementation before or after decisions are made. Citizens may also oppose or seek to influence the direction of implementation. Opposition to adverse impacts, aversion to unwanted facilities or programs, or competition to secure an attractive activity are likely from one or more groups. All these inputs serve to clutter the implementation process with controversy and additional decision points.[44] Successful effectuation of policies requires persistent attention and reinforcement from the executive.

Variation in these two components of policy making provide the primary bases for elaborating role types. There are four major types of leadership. The innovator combines both elements whereas the antithesis of this type, the caretaker, provides neither. Two intermediate types that stress one element over the other are the broker and the reformer. A summary of the types is given in Figure 4–2. Several other types contained in the previous figure have been included in this figure to accommodate some common hybrids that deviate from the four major ones.

Three of the four major types are "incomplete" leaders because they are weak in one or both elements of leadership. *Caretakers* are executives who fill the office in such a limited way that they fail to realize the

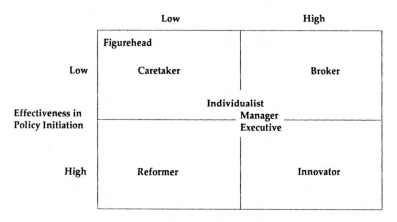

Figure 4-2. Summary of Leadership Types for Executive Mayors Based on Performance in Policy Initiation and Implementation

policy-making potential of the position. The mayor's perspective is limited to dealing with problems as they occur, and the mayor fails to organize the machinery of government for action. Although not the minimum mayor represented by the *figurehead,* the caretaker "accepts the limitations of his power and seeks to keep peace in the city by carefully balancing and adjusting conflict, demands, and interests."[45] The caretaker muddles through rather than having a clear plan for the future, has a limited network of supporters and few contacts outside the city. This mayor is cautious, inflexible, inert, and authoritarian. He or she relies on the bureaucracy for implementation and handles many tasks personally.

The *broker* also lacks a broad set of policy goals, but accumulates and manipulates power in the system to maintain control. This mayor relies on traditional political-organizing strategies, emphasizing exchange of favors for support. The broker acts as a gatekeeper to determine which proposals will be considered and succeed, but the broker picks battles carefully preferring to invest resources in ways that will generate future payoffs rather than consuming them.[46] This cautious use of resources in weak-mayor systems reflects the difficulty in overcoming the formal fragmentation in that form of government. All mayors choose to avoid certain difficult issues that appear to carry greater costs than benefits, but this is the typical reaction of the broker.[47]

The *reformer* concentrates on policy initiation to the detriment of effective implementation. Henry Maier, former mayor of Milwaukee, describes the reformer's approach as that of "dramatically enunciating the 'oughts' of city life without consideration of the day-by-day effort necessary to execute the steps that must be taken toward concrete achievement."[48] Thus, the good ideas may never be accepted and may be undermined through poor implementation. The reformer may be more interested in outside audiences than ones inside the city.[49] This mayor cannot match his or her activism and visibility with local support and accomplishment.

Several hybrids of these two intermediate types can be identified. The individualist or maverick may be somewhat more balanced in the emphasis on initiation and implementation than the broker or reformer but is characterized by a tendency to go it alone. This behavior will limit coalition building for new ideas and the generation of support for implementation. The executive and the manager are more complete than the broker, reformer, or maverick. These mayors have programmatic and process goals and use organizational resources to advance them.[50] These types are limited in comparison with the innovator, however, by their moderate-range agendas, emphasis on the bureaucracy for task accomplishment, low profiles, and greater concern for the process of government than its impact.

The *innovator* is the complete executive who is strong at both initiation and implementation. Also called the entrepreneur, this executive charts the long-term course for local government and works on a broad front to get his or her program accomplished. Local and national networking are highly developed. As a democratic leader, the executive more than any other local official is expected to reflect popular concerns and respond to popular needs in shaping policies, and to mobilize popular support and build coalitions among groups in the population. As policy leader, the executive guides the deliberations of elected representatives drawing upon extensive contact with voters, close ties with the media, and staff expertise to set the agenda and shape the proposals for governmental action. As administrative head of government, the innovator manages the complex and often fragmented machinery of government to get things done, although this may require generating influence not provided through the formal governmental structure.

In short, the innovator is the central moving force in local government, a role that requires extensive investment of time and energy along with the creative use of the legal powers available. Maintaining this role is extremely demanding and draining. Several observers have noted that mayors shift the type of leadership over time. In New York City,

Lindsay retreated from being a change-oriented innovator to a manager.[51] In Boston, White shifted from social reformer to entrepreneur to broker over his sixteen years in office.[52] In San Francisco, Alioto used his formal power in an individualistic way in the last two years of a mandatory final term rather than stressing the coalition building that had characterized his first six years in office.[53] Yates argues that mayors generally will become caretakers as the other options are closed off: Unable to sustain the innovator role, they will lack the power resources to be brokers and find that the symbolic politics of the reformer generate more conflict than the mayor is capable of resolving.[54]

Still, one could argue that forms of government headed by an elected executive require a leader with the qualities of the innovator to function most effectively. Without this high level of leadership, innovation is lacking or conflict is not managed. Either reactive policy making prevails or contending actors dominate the governmental process. It is difficult for leadership to arise from another source within the government to offset mayoral weakness. Council members cannot replace a mayor whose leadership is deemed inadequate. Thus, the mayor-council form has high-level leadership requirements that are difficult to achieve and sustain.

Council-Manager Mayors: Roles and Types
of Facilitative Leadership

The media and scholarly literature alike suggest that only by achieving de facto chief executive status does the elected leader in a council-manager government become a "real" mayor. Rarely, however, will the preconditions be favorable for acquiring executive status. More importantly, the case not been made that the innovative executive model is necessary or appropriate to the council-manager form. Rather, the council-manager mayor may be seen as a facilitative leader. There is a type of leadership that is parallel to the innovator type in that it is comprehensive and consistent with the basic features of council-manager government and the cooperative pattern of interaction among officials. The preconditions for this kind of leadership are readily attainable within the council-manager form, although they are not necessarily used to their fullest.

Central to effective performance in the job is understanding the possibilities and limitations of political leadership for the facilitative mayor. Mayors have been handicapped by the limited appreciation of what the office entails. It is possible, however, to construct a job description and identify leadership types that fill the position more or less fully.

Long-term research in Greensboro indicates that mayors have opportunities for two kinds of leadership beyond traditional ceremonial functions. One is a coordinative component in which the mayor pulls together the parts of council-manager government to improve their interaction. The second opportunity is guidance (as opposed to control) in the initiation and execution of policy. The mayor has great potential to guide other officials toward the accomplishment of goals favored by the mayor. From 1965 to 1987—despite relative constancy in conditions and governmental structure—five different mayors have varied in performance, some realizing neither of the opportunities, some one of them, and some both, although all filled the basic ceremonial component of the position.[55]

Drawing from interviews with and about the mayors of the five largest cities in North Carolina, another major component and specific roles that make up the mayor's job have been identified.[56] Mayors also devote considerable attention to the development needs of the city. Eleven roles that a mayor may or may not perform have been isolated from content analysis of the interviews. These roles grouped into the four components of leadership are presented in Table 4–4, along with the proportion of respondents who referred to that role. Whether and how effectively the mayor fills the roles are separate questions which provide the basis for distinguishing among the types of mayoral leadership.

Typically perceived by observers of council-manager government is the mayor's responsibility for a variety of *ceremonial tasks,* representing the city, and appearing at many and various meetings, dinners, and other special occasions. The mayor also serves as *spokesperson for council* enunciating positions taken, informing the public about upcoming business, and reacting to questions about the city's policies and intentions. This activity, though commonplace, may be merged with other ceremonial and representational activities in the minds of many observers; it was identified as a separate role by less than one fifth of the respondents. In these two activities, the mayor builds the extensive contact with the public and the media which can be a valuable resource in performing other roles. As Boynton and Wright observed, the mayor's "unique relationship to the public provides him with leadership resources not available to any other . . . actors."[57] As representative

Table 4–4. Dimensions and Roles of Mayoral Leadership
in Council-Manager Cities

%[a]	Dimension/Role
Ceremony and Presiding	
82.8	1. Performer of ceremonial tasks
17.2	2. Spokesperson for council
51.7	3. Presiding officer
Communication and Facilitation	
10.3	4. Educator: informational and educational tasks vis-à-vis council, manager, and/or public
29.3	5. Liaison with manager: promotes informal exchange both ways between the council and the manager and staff
29.3	6. Team leader: coalescing the council, building consensus, and enhancing group performance
Organization and Guidance	
29.3	7. Goal setter: setting goals and objectives for council and manager; identifying problems; establishing tone for the council
13.8	8. Organizer: stabilizing relationships; guiding council to recognition of its roles and responsibilities; defining and adjusting the relationship with the manager
32.8	9. Policy advocate: developing programs; lining up support or opposition to proposals
10.6	10. Directing staff: giving orders to staff; directing the manager; expediting action by staff
Promotion	
35.5	11. Promoter: promoting and defending the city; seeking investment; handling external relationships; securing agreement among parties to a project.

N = 58

[a]Figures in the percentage column refer to the proportion of respondents mentioning activities associated with each role. Respondents were council members, administrators, and community leaders from Charlotte, Durham, Greensboro, Raleigh, and Winston-Salem.

Source: Svara (1987a), used with permission of *The Journal of Politics*.

and spokesperson, the mayor also becomes an important channel for citizen input. Wikstrom found that 66 percent of the mayors in Virginia spent more than three, and 16 percent more than ten, hours per week dealing with citizen inquiries and complaints. In addition, the mayor serves as *presiding officer* at meetings, a role mentioned by half of the respondents. In so doing, he or she sets the tone for meetings and may exert mild influence over the timing and outcome of deliberations.

These traditional roles, sometimes perceived to be the full extent of the job, are important for establishing the relationships with the council and the public. Mayors also send signals to staff about their attitudes toward them in their public conduct. This public demeanor can influence the nature of that key relationship. Some mayors never move beyond ceremony and presiding. For other mayors, additional activities that build on these foundation roles were also identified by respondents.

The mayor contributes to higher levels of communication and facilitates action by officials. Beyond the straightforward transmission of council views to the public, the mayor may also serve as an *educator.* Although only mentioned by 10 percent of the respondents, this role is conceptually distinct from spokesperson or advocate (defined below). In relations with the council, the public and media, and the manager, the mayor, without promoting a favored position, identifies issues or problems for consideration, promotes awareness of important concerns, and seeks to promote understanding across the city by exchange of information.

As the chief *liaison channel* with the manager, the mayor links the two major components of the system—the legislative body and the administrative apparatus—and can facilitate communication and understanding between elected and appointed officials. The mayor increases the manager's awareness of council preferences and can predict how the council will react to administrative proposals. Although the manager must maintain positive relations with each member of the council, the mayor-manager interaction is an efficient way to exchange information. Despite the benefits that can be derived by filling this role, however, and its accessibility to the mayor, the role of liaison is not necessarily filled. Over 70 percent of the respondents perceived the mayor to have a closer relationship to the manager than other council members, but only 29 percent cited the liaison role as a part of the mayor's performance.

Finally, 29 percent identified the mayor as a *team builder,* one who works to coalesce the council and build consensus. Wikstrom found that "practically all mayors take the lead in promoting consensus when the council is divided over policy matters."[59] Promoting cohesion is conceptually distinct from taking the group in a particular direction. The mayor as team leader seeks to promote full expression, help the council work through differences expeditiously, and encourage the council to face issues and resolve them decisively. Several managers noted that it is much easier to work with a council that operates in this fashion.

The roles considered so far have been concerned with communication and coordination, whereas the next group of roles involves influencing the direction of city government affairs and the content of policy. As *goal setter*—a role identified by 29 percent of the respondents—the mayor establishes goals and objectives for council and manager, identifies problems, and sets the tone for the council. Some mayors keep track of a set of key objectives so that the council and manager undertake to accomplish these priority items. Thus, this role may encompass the accomplishment as well as the setting of goals. Similarly, Wikstrom reports that 56 percent of the mayors in his study considered themselves to be primarily responsible for ensuring that the manager implements the council's policies.[60]

In addition, the mayor may be active as an *organizer* and stabilizer of the key relations within city government. The mayor guides the council to recognition of its roles and responsibilities. If the council has standing committees, the mayor can use appointments and assignments to advance his or her view of how the council should be operating. The mayor in this role helps to define the pattern of interaction between council and manager, monitors it, and makes adjustments in order to maintain the complex sharing and separation of responsibilities between the council and manager.

The mayor is uniquely situated to control that relationship and better able than any other official to correct it, if change is needed. By the same token, the mayor who handles this role inappropriately can do more to interfere with the council and manager's performance than any one else. The mayor's actions must be guided, therefore, by the goal of enhancing the performance of other participants and strengthening their interaction. For example, the mayor may advise the manager to bring more matters to the council, intervene with a council member who is intruding into operational matters, or seek to alleviate tension between the council and staff before a serious rift develops. The mayor may also undertake to augment the council's capacity for information and decision making vis-à-vis the manager. Some of Wilson's changes in San Diego were intended to enhance the role of both mayor and council.[61] In the North Carolina cities, the mayor often handles these organizing and stabilizing activities informally and in private. Indeed, a number of respondents noted that the mayor's ability to make such adjustments out of the glare of publicity is one of the greatest resources of the office with sunshine laws that limit private deliberations among elected officials.

Finally, the mayor was perceived to be a *policy advocate* by 33 percent of the respondents. As an active guide in policy making, the mayor develops programs and lines up support or organizes opposition to proposals. In these activities, the mayor most closely resembles the executive mayor's public persona as the city's problem solver. In addition, the mayor may influence others' policy choices. Wikstrom reports that two-thirds of the managers informally discuss major issues with the mayor before submitting a proposal to the council. The same proportion of managers "sensed that council members usually followed the policy posture of the mayor."[62] The mayor's role in advocating and shaping policies may be based on all the other roles, or pursued to the exclusion of others when the mayor launches a public drive to win acceptance of a proposal.

Finally, 10 percent of the respondents mentioned activities that involved *directing staff:* issuing orders, requesting reports, and monitoring the performance of certain department heads. These actions, unlike those discussed in the previous dimensions, may constitute interference with the prerogatives of the manager and contradict the norms of the form of government. The mayor's activities in administration may "conflict with," "displace," or "complement the manager's activities."[63] When complementary, these actions can be thought of as part of guiding and organizing officials. Displacing the manager—or controlling the position independently of the council—is a different matter.

Care must be taken to distinguish between administrative actions that are part of the extensive traffic between elected officials and staff and those that constitute executive control. The mayor is a party to the council's involvement in administrative matters. When mayors seek information from the manager "on behalf of solicitous councils" regarding the "implementation and success of a policy,"[64] they may be filling the liaison, goal-setter, or organizer role, or acting as a quasi-executive, depending on how the inquiry is handled.

Conceptually distinct from the preceding are the mayor's activities in promoting and defending the city. This was the most commonly mentioned role—by 36 percent—beyond the foundation roles. The mayor may be involved in external relations and help secure agreement among parties to a project. For some mayors, the *promoter* role is a simple extension of ceremonial tasks. Others are active initiators of contacts and help develop possibilities for the city. As official representative, the mayor has extensive dealings with officials in other governments and may serve as a key participant in formulating agreements with state or federal officials, developers, and others who seek joint ventures with city government. The mayor may also take the lead in projecting a favorable image of the city and seek to "sell" others on investment in it. This role has contributed to the emergence of the mayor as a central figure in council-manager government.[65]

A pronounced form of administrative direction not found in any of the North Carolina cities studied is that of the mayor assuming control over the manager. If the mayor chooses the manager and defines the scope of the office, as Sparrow claims happened in San Diego under Wilson, then the mayor becomes the de facto executive officer with the manager acting as an administrative officer to the mayor. The role of *selecting and overseeing the manager* can be added to the eleven identified by the respondents in North Carolina to form a comprehensive list of potential roles.

What kind of mayoral leadership is provided by an incumbent depends on which roles the mayor performs and how well he or she handles them. There is infinite variety in the combinations of activities pursued by individual mayors, but certain general types have emerged from this and previous research. Mayors develop a leadership type for themselves by the way they combine the five dimensions of leadership. In Table 4-5, the twelve roles are used as an ex post facto inventory of the scope of leadership provided by the mayors in the five North Carolina cities. The proportion of respondents mentioning activities associated with each role provides a profile of the salient aspects of leadership in each city. For comparison, a column is added to reflect the roles filled by Mayor Wilson of San Diego, as inferred from Sparrow's description.

It is apparent that the performance of more demanding roles is not evenly distributed among the cities. The mayor may invest so little in the office and define its scope so narrowly that he or she simply is a *caretaker*—a uniformly underdeveloped type of leader, who shirks virtually all aspects of the job. For most mayors, the presiding and ceremonial tasks are inescapable because legally required or an integral part of the job. A mayor who fills these roles actively but performs no others can be called the *symbolic head* of government. This was the kind of leadership provided by Mayor Reading of Oakland as described by Pressman.[66] The mayor in city C demonstrates this type of leadership: he was perceived to be filling virtually no other roles. Although such mayors preside and attend to the interactions with the public, their narrowly defined leadership docs not address division within the council, and the manager's influence is likely to expand. Mayor Reading's

Table 4-5. Activities and Leadership Types of Council-Manager Mayors

Roles	Proportion of Respondents Noting that Mayor Performed Role in Five Study Cities					San Diego
	A	B	C	D	E	
Selects manager (12)	XXX[a]					*[b]
Directs staff (11)	XXX	XX				*
Promotes city (10)	XXXX	XXX		XXXXXXXXX		*
Advocates policy (9)	XXXX	XXXXXXXX		XXX		*
Organizes relationships (8)	XX	XXXX				*
Sets goals (7)	XXXXX	XXXXXXXX		X		*
Forms team (6)	XXXXX	XXXX				*
Acts as liaison with manager (5)	XXXX	XXXX	X	X	XX	*
Educates (4)	XX	X	X	X		*
Presides (3)	XXXX	XXXXX	XXXXXXXX	XXXXX	XXXXXXXXXX	
Is spokesman (2)	X	XX	XXX	XX	XXXXXX	
Performs ceremonial tasks (1)	XXXXXXXXX	XXXXXXXXX	XXXXXXXXX	XXXXXXXXX	XXXXXXXXXXX	
	N = 14	N = 13	N = 12	N = 13	N = 6[c]	

Roles Filled by Different Leadership Types

Caretaker: None fully
Symbolic Head: Roles (1)–(3)
Coordinator: Roles (1)–(6)
Promoter: Roles (1)–(3), (10)

Activist/Reformer: Roles (1)–(3), (7)–(10)
Director: Roles (1)–(10)
Chief Executive: Roles (1)–(12)

[a] For study cities in North Carolina, each X means that 10 percent of the respondents mentioned that activity in response to an open-ended question, "What are the responsibilities and roles of the mayor in [name of city]?"

[b] An asterisk indicates that this activity was attributed to the mayor of San Diego by Sparrow (1984).

[c] In this city, seven interviews were conducted before the inclusion of the question concerning the mayor.

Source: Svara (1987a), used with permission of The Journal of Politics.

limited leadership and the manager's extensive influence in Oakland presumably were mutually reinforcing, although it is also possible that individual council members will intrude excessively in the manager's sphere in this situation since the mayor will not seek to alter the behavior of other elected officials.

If the next set of roles is performed as well, the mayor becomes a *coordinator*. Pursuing these activities effectively contributes to a smoothly functioning council-manager government with strong collective elected leadership. The council does not necessarily work together well, nor do the council, manager, and public necessarily interact smoothly without coordinative leadership from the mayor. The coordinator is a team leader, keeps the manager and council in touch, and interacts with the public and outside agencies—all contributing to improved communication. This mayor helps to achieve high levels of shared information but contributes little to policy formulation (at least, no more than any other member of the council.) The coordinator is not a "complete" type of leadership since the organizing and guidance roles are not part of the mayor's repertoire. The mayor in city E represents this type in part. He is perceived as providing liaison with the manager, although the perception of his team leadership is less common.

A third incomplete type of leadership was found in the study cities, and a fourth (with two variants) can be defined even though it was not observed in pure form in these cities. The mayor in city D is a *specialized promoter*. This mayor provides effective guidance in that single role. Observers give him high marks for bringing together support from state and federal sources, drawing upon extensive political activities and governmental service prior to becoming mayor, and commitments from the private sector, with which he has strong occupational ties. The extraordinary contributions to promoting the city are not matched by effectiveness at activities in other roles. The specialized promoter leaves a vacuum of responsibility for tasks involving coordination, organization, and policy guidance. In city D, the manager must pay more attention to these activities. As indicated in Table 4–5, the mayors in Cities A and B are also commonly perceived to be promoters, so this type of leadership does have to be a specialty. Indeed, hard times and increasing competition among cities virtually forces this role on the mayor.

The fourth and fifth types are similar to the maverick or personality-individualist and the reformer. The activist and reformer types emphasize policy guidance and advocacy but neglect coordinative activities, especially team building, essentially going it alone. The *activist* wants to get things accomplished quickly, and succeeds by force of personality and the presence of a working majority. Although influential, the activist is viewed by some members of the council (perhaps even the mayor's own supporters) as abrasive and exclusionary. The tenure of this type of mayor is marked by successful policy initiatives along with friction and disgruntlement among the council members.[67] Too much emphasis on the policy roles can induce mayors to overreach their position and alienate the council. Such mayors would then fall into the *reformer* type of leadership, which is possible for any mayor who ignores or maladroitly handles the tasks of coordination. These mayors stress the policy enunciation activity, but are not very successful at securing acceptance of their ideas.

The *director* is a complete type of mayor who not only contributes to smooth functioning of government but also provides a general sense of direction. A primary responsibility of the council is to determine the mission of city government and its broad goals. The director contributes significantly to a consideration of broad questions of purpose. One former mayor observed that "my toughest job was keeping the council's attention on the horizon rather than on the potholes." The mayors in Cities A and B demonstrate this comprehensive type of leadership.

This mayor stands out as a leader in the eyes of the council, the press, and the public, and uses that recognition as the basis for guidance rather than control. He or she enhances the influence of elected officials by unifying the council, filling the policy vacuum that can exist on the council, and guiding policy toward goals that meet the needs of the community. Furthermore, this mayor is actively involved in monitoring and adjusting relationships within city government to maintain balance, cooperation, and high standards. No one else can attack the causes of friction between the council and manager (which may be produced by failing of either party) nor promote the constructive interaction that is needed for effective performance. This mayor does not supplant the manager's prerogatives nor diminish the manager's leadership, although this mayor is occasionally perceived to be directing staff. The organizer role is oriented toward enhancing the ability of the manager to function as the executive officer. Wikstrom has observed that "managers prefer a mayor who provides policy leadership and direction."[68] In sum, although this mayor does not become the driving force as the executive mayor can be, the director is the guiding force in city government.

The contrast is clearly seen in Sparrow's portrait of Wilson as a *chief executive*. When a mayor achieves this type of leadership, however, he or she belongs in the executive typology and should be analyzed accordingly. In addition to the changes that augmented the role of the entire council, he added a fiscal analyst in his office, handled certain federal programs (CETA, Model Cities, and General Revenue Sharing), and used his appointment power over council committees and members of boards and commissions to expand his control over policy formation and administration. The most striking change in power was acquiring the de facto ability to hire the city manager, presumably by driving out those who did not adjust to his leadership style and influencing appointments until he found one who did. Sparrow concludes that Wilson achieved through informal means the concentration of power in the mayor's office which the voters had refused to approve in a charter change in 1973. Wilson displayed comprehensive leadership across all roles to be sure, but he appropriated power to himself that weakened the other participants in city government.

In sum, the analysis suggests that a mayor is able to fashion a unique type of leadership by the roles that he or she chooses (or happens) to develop. Certain types are cumulative, building on the successful exercise of more easily accomplished roles. To be a successful director, it is necessary to maintain strong support from the council and from the public. And this support can flow only from the mayor's performance of traditional and coordinative roles. The existence of incomplete types indicate that some mayors do not adopt more difficult roles—the ceremonial heads and coordinators—or experience the consequences of emphasizing higher ranking roles over lower ones—the activist, reformer, and specialized promoter.

Mayoral leadership of the director type does not depend on a superior power position if relationships are cooperative but rather on utilizing the resources for coordination and communication inherent in the mayor's office. Mayors who possess both a clear conception of the job—its possibilities, interdependencies, and limitations—and an appreciation of the governmental process within which they operate are the ones likely to make better use of resources.

In council-manager governments, the foundation roles—ceremonial and presiding activities, education, liaison, and team building—support goal setting, organizing, policy advocacy, and promotion. The highly committed, assertive, and impatient mayor may jump into the higher level roles without developing the others, but runs the risk of having only the short-term success of the activist or of being an isolated reformer.

If the mayor is inclined to fill the roles that make up the director type of leadership, other preconditions for leadership follow. The mayor must have ideas and a sense of purpose. The mayor must be effective at working with others and willing to give certain responsibilities to them. Inclusiveness, sharing of information, facilitation of the expression of divergent views, and ability to resolve differences are important traits for the mayor to have in dealings with the council. The relationship with the manager requires tact, respect, ability to share authority, and trust in the manager's commitment to advance the goals of the city and to achieve the highest performance from government as a whole. The mayor does not necessarily need to expend resources in order to hold an autonomous professional administrator in check.

Finally, mayors need to be flexible and capable of shifting the emphasis they place on different roles. More than any other official in this form of government, the mayor is the stabilizer who acts in those areas in which contributions are needed at a given time. He or she will be more or less central, more or less public, more or less assertive as conditions warrant. Through all the fluid shifting of responsibilities, the mayor's firm sense of purpose can provide the bearings for all participants.

Conclusion

Mayors are expected to provide political leadership in their cities. How they approach this task will vary greatly with the form of government in which they operate. Mayor-council systems depend on their mayors to be executives and they provide at least some formal tools to support this position. Council-manager systems, on the other hand, look to their mayors to be facilitators who will help the council and manager achieve a high level of performance. Stable, effective leadership of a kind that does not match the form of government is not likely to occur. The executive mayor distorts relationships in the council-manager form; the facilitative mayor is likely to be pushed around in a mayor-council city unless cooperative conditions are present.

Within the confines of each form of government, mayors display certain major types of leadership. Figure 4–3 presents a summary of these types based on performance indicators that are appropriate to the

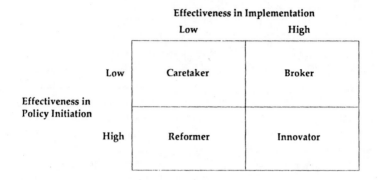

I. Mayor-Council Form: "Executive Mayor"
Resources Support Executive Functions

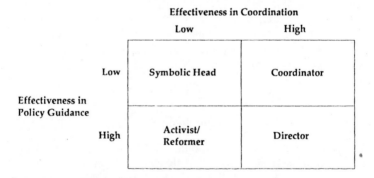

II. Council-Manager Form: "Facilitative Mayor"
Resources Do Not Support Executive Functions

Figure 4-3. Types of Mayoral Leadership

form of government and to the resource level of the mayor. In mayor-council cities, the mayor who is weak in both policy initiation and implementation becomes a caretaker, while the mayor who emphasizes the former is a reformer and the mayor who emphasizes the latter, a broker. The mayor who initiates policy proposals and who controls implementation is an innovator. In council-manager governments where the mayor can make a special contribution to coordination of actors and to policy guidance, the incumbent who proves to be weak in both these areas ends up as a symbolic head, one who handles only the ceremonial and presiding dimension of the position. The mayor who plays the role of coordinator helps to improve the interaction within the council and with the manager, whereas the mayor as activist or reformer stresses policy guidance to the exclusion of enhancing relationships. The mayor who is able to act as a director is strong in both areas.

The mayor in the mayor-council form faces choices that are at once simpler and more complex. The executive mayor must take charge of the governmental structure to the extent that the definition of the office will permit. Less flexibility and shifting of roles is needed because the mayor is generally expected to be the central leader. The greater complexity comes from working with and through others with whom the mayor is likely to be at odds. By virtue of the mayor's need to carve out and preserve a sphere of operation between the council and the permanent staff, the mayor is necessarily engaged in conflict. The coordination and communication techniques available to the council-manager mayor as primary tools are less effective in a conflict setting. The executive is weakened when sharing of information is exploited by others and is not reciprocated. Still, this mayor cannot have sufficient power to dominate other officials and can usefully borrow from the council-manager mayor by strengthening partnerships with the council and permanent staff.

Council-manager mayors can contribute substantially to the performance of their governments and the betterment of their communities. The position is not a pale imitation of the executive mayor's office in mayor-council city, but rather a unique leadership position that requires distinctive qualities. This mayor, to make the most of the office, must utilize opportunities for coordination and policy guidance present in the form. In turn, these opportunities are shaped in large degree by the mayor's personal resourcefulness and drive, self-restraint, commitment to enhance the position of other participants in the governmental process, and flexibility. For council-manager mayors, effective leadership is built upon strengthening the other participants in the governing process rather than controlling or supplanting them.

The San Diego case demonstrates that it is possible for the mayor to move beyond coordinative and guidance roles to acquire control over other actors in the system. Sparrow asserts that such leadership "has become the preferred form."[69] Two questions arise. Is this is an efficacious strategy for other council-manager mayors? And, if so, is it preferable? It is not likely that such a leadership type will be sustained permanently without formal changes in the legal position of the office.

For every mayor who successfully sustains sufficient council support to chart an independent course and significantly supplant the manager, it seems likely that many will wind up "reformers"—isolated and ineffective. The director type of leadership is comprehensive as well, and because it is also more compatible with the form of government, it is likely to be more easily achieved and more stable.

Even if possible, the evolution of executive mayors in this form may not be desirable. The emergence of mayor-centered systems of governance in council-manager cities is likely to produce greater conflict between the council and the mayor and to create ambiguities about the lines of authority between each set of elected officials and the manager. Although the executive model of leadership has been widely accepted by political scientists, the evidence about differences in performance is scant.

The experience of mayor-council cities suggests that dependency on a single leader chosen through the electoral process to provide broad-ranging leadership can lead to poor performance as well as to spectacular success. Without strong executive leadership, Ferman warns, the power of bureaucracy rises and special interests can block efforts to alter the status quo.[70] The antipower bias in the American political culture should be set aside, and the executive given clearer, less diluted authority over city government. The mayor should be supported by a strong (but not dominant) political party which will both broaden the base of the mayor's power and also help to insure that the substantive ends of politics are not ignored. The reemergence of a strong, responsible political party system—long a hope of politically oriented reformers—seems at present to be an unlikely prospect. Executive mayors are likely to depend on individual organizations rather than on stable party support. Consequently, they may be so concerned with obtaining and preserving power to support their survival in office that politically costly change is unlikely. If the mayoral leadership in policy initiation or implementation is inadequate, it is difficult for other city officials to take up the slack or to secure change. Thus, the elected executive leadership model is no panacea for resolving urban problems.

The council-manager government may be less capable of resolving community conflicts or of coalescing divergent interests, because it lacks a single leader who can forge compromises. It is less likely, however, that the governmental process would be dominated by conflict so there will be little internal conflict to manage. Further, if this form has a mayor who provides comprehensive leadership without assuming executive control, a council-manager city has the advantages that accrue from blending the distinct talents of elected officials and professional administrators and may evidence greater consistency in governmental performance. The consequences of weak or ineffective mayoral leadership are less serious in the council-manager form. The operation of the administrative organization is not hampered—if the manager is capable—so long as the mayor's faults stem from omissions rather than commissions. With support from the manager, some degree of collective leadership can emerge from the council in spite of the mayor. In sum, the benefits of one form or the other with regard to the "quality" of leadership are mixed.

Because there are advantages and disadvantages to each kind of mayor, they must be understood in light of the characteristics of the form of government. The mayor's office in different forms cannot be compared in isolation from the structure and the governmental process in which that office is located. To some extent, the executive and facilitative mayors may learn and borrow from one another. Typically, however, they will provide leadership in divergent ways. The mayor-council mayor will be the driving force—determining direction, establishing support for goals, and mobilizing the governmental apparatus to accomplish goals. The executive mayor must acquire power for himself or herself to be effective. The council-manager mayor will be the guiding force—coordinating the contributions of council and manager and providing a sense of direction and purpose to city government. The facilitative mayor increases the involvement of all officials and adds to the leadership capacity of the system as a whole.

5

Councils: Counterweight Versus Senior Partner

The city council links the people with government in a variety of ways. Members of the city council fill the representational function in city government. They speak for and make decisions on behalf of the citizens of the community, committing the body politic to certain courses of action. Derived from representation is the legislative function. "Lawmaking" defined broadly consists of policy leadership, enactment of ordinances and resolutions, debate, criticism, and investigation. By implication, there is a third function common to legislative bodies— controlling the executive.[1] Council members respond to problems that their constituents have with administrative agencies—a representational task—by seeking to bring about corrective action—a control task. They also attempt to exert control by overseeing the execution of policy in order to insure that the purpose of their lawmaking is accomplished. Less commonly, the council members fill a judicial function either in the informal sense that they serve as the "court of resort" for certain kinds of appeals from citizens who feel they have been harmed by city government, or in the more formal sense, in a few cases, of following strict procedures to adjudicate regulations or settle legal disputes.

Political scientists have used a number of approaches to categorize the roles filled by council members starting with the representational and including a wide range of other roles determined by how council members define their purpose, policy orientation, and relationship with other actors in the political system, for example, interest groups, the executive, administrative staff, and other council members.[2] The approach taken here is to examine roles as they pertain to areas of responsibility assumed by council members.

To encompass the complex and multifaceted nature of the council member's job, it is necessary to think of it in terms of four related but distinct roles. The council member is a representative, governor, supervisor, and judge. As representative, the council member speaks for and acts on behalf of constituents. As governor, the council member not only legislates but more generally gives "direction to the collective affairs of the whole."[3] The council's primary role, in the view of some, is "formulating policy and overseeing its execution."[4] As supervisor, the council takes on tasks associated with the executive (e.g., appointment and appraisal of staff). As judge, the council member resolves specific disputes. Our discussion will emphasize the first three roles, although the significance of the judicial role is briefly noted in the introductory section. The roles will not be equally developed in all governments, owing both to structural and idiosyncratic differences among cities.

Despite the scope and complexity of the job and its potential significance in the governmental process, the council's actual performance may pale upon close inspection. In practice, it may be more a ratifying and reacting body than a policy initiator. It is more or less limited in its capacity to control the executive and administrative staff. In many cities, there are structural constraints that limit how council members fill their roles or what roles are available to them. They lack independent resources in most cities. Whether this condition is a deficiency that limits the council's ability to get information and other forms of assistance depends on the council's relationship with the executive and staff. More than the other officials in city government, council members experience a gap between potential and realized contributions. One suspects that they also suffer from a disparity between the effort they expend, on the one hand, and the recognition they receive, on the other. These community leaders offer extensive but often unheralded service as the representatives of the citizenry, policy makers and overseers, and supervisors.

The capacity of the council to fill the governance and supervisory roles differs markedly in mayor-council and council-manager governments. The council in the weak mayor-council system is involved in more activities than in the other kinds of cities. For example, in Minneapolis, the council approves the appointment and removal of most department heads upon recommendation of an executive committee that includes the mayor and four council members. Council committees oversee the departments and their implementation of policies established by the city council. Although the weak-mayor council has more legal authority than the councils in the other major forms, its impact is potentially offset by an informally powerful mayor. The capacity of all officials to act is limited by the wide dispersion of authority throughout city government. Neither the council nor the mayor exercise comprehensive authority over city government.

The council in strong mayor-council cities, on the other hand, is likely to be restricted to representational role and the legislative function (i.e., a portion of the governance role). It may encounter a narrow definition by the mayor of what is "policy" requiring its approval. The city charter of Knoxville—a strong-mayor city—gives the council legislative power and permits it to "prescribe the manner in which any powers of the city shall be exercised." Still, it lacks both executive power and explicit oversight authority except as the mayor interprets his obligation to be "responsible to the council for the proper administration of all city affairs." In the strong mayor-council form, the council is most likely to ratify rather than initiate. Emphasis is on its debate activity to bring public attention to mayoral proposals. Its investigative activities will occur from a greater or lesser distance, depending on the ability of the mayor to erect a barrier between the staff and the council.

The council-manager form gives members the opportunity to define the governance role broadly and to fill it actively. The Model City Charter, the norm for council-manager cities, provides that "all powers of the city shall be vested in the council."[5] There is no competitor in the use of formal authority. It has supervisory authority in its power to appoint the manager and to conduct "investigations into the affairs of the city and the conduct of any city department, office, or agency." The council acts as employer, assigning work to and appraising the performance of the manager and the organization.[6] Although the manager exercises executive authority and the council is prohibited by the Model Charter from appointing or removing city staff, the council may intervene in any aspect of city government. Despite the fact that the council can set the terms of the relationship with the city manager, it too may become dependent on full-time administrators who monopolize information and expertise.

This chapter will examine the representational role of the council, how council members are selected, their characteristics, contributions to the governmental process through the governance and supervisory roles, and variation in council performance associated with form of government. A major question is whether council members are more alike than different across forms of government. Two additional topics are important to note at the beginning of the discussion of councils—the judicial role and sunshine legislation.

In addition to the representational, governance, and supervisory roles, the council also serves as the adjudicator of certain disputes. This function affects the workload, image, and process of interaction of councils. Some councils hear appeals from citizens for all manner of problems, for example, relief from an enormous water bill that resulted from an unknown leak or overruling a housing condemnation order. They may also take a quasi-judicial approach to matters such as regulating rates under a franchising agreement for cable or bus service. In nine states, the courts have ordered that small-tract rezonings cannot be considered a legislative act because their direct impact is limited to particular individuals. Rather, they must be treated as adjudicative and handled following some aspects of judicial procedure. One characteristic of the judicial process is the elimination of ex parte contact outside the hearing between interested parties and those who must hear and decide such cases. "Legislative acts, on the other hand," Lyons observes, "generally do not require such procedural safeguards."[7] Council members who operate under such procedural restrictions generally endorse the procedures, including the limitations of the ex parte rule for judicial questions, even though it "strikes at the very heart of the relationship between elected legislators and their constituents."[8] Thus, acting in a nonrepresentative way appears to be acceptable in this situation. We may surmise that council members are able and willing to distinguish other roles from the representational if their values lead them to feel it is appropriate behavior. The council member acting as governor or supervisor may behave differently than he or she does as a representative.

Open-meeting laws have had a substantial impact on council operation. To a greater extent than the mayor, on the one hand, or administrative staff, on the other, the council must operate in the "sunshine." Since they ultimately exercise the policy-making authority for the jurisdiction, they have been constrained from assembling a majority of the members to deliberate matters that may become law. In most states, members may meet in closed session to discuss certain sensitive topics such as personnel, legal matters, and collective bargaining.[9] In other states, even portions of the council cannot meet in private regardless of the nature the discussion. The significance of this development for the current discussion is that councils have limited ability to meet informally without outside observers to strengthen their cohesion as a deliberative body. Thus, in addition to the other disadvantages that the council has in its dealings with other officials, constraints on interactions among members limit their ability to develop effective working relationships.

This chapter moves from the known to the unknown in research about the city council. Of all the officials included in this book, the city council members are the least studied. The research is not sufficient to encompass the variation in council characteristics, attitudes, and behavior that is produced by differences in methods of selecting council members and form of government. There has been much more emphasis on the representational role than the others. That topic shall be our starting point.

Perspectives on Council Roles I: Representation

The orientation of local legislators is heavily influenced by how they define their official role in relationship to their constituents. A basic distinction can be made between the legislative role of *delegate*, on the one hand, and *trustee*, on the other. As delegates, elected representatives try to express as clearly as possible the opinions of their constituents and seek to be guided by them in making decisions. As trustees, elected representatives act in the interests of the community as a whole and use their own judgment to do what they think is best for their constituents, whether the constituents are in agreement or not. The *politico* is an intermediate type who combines the two perspectives.

The trustee orientation has been commonly found in surveys of council members. In surveys in the Bay Area of California and a sample of twenty Ohio cities, three-fifths of the respondents identified themselves with the trustee approach and one-quarter were politicos. (See Table 5–1.) The delegate was particularly rare in Ohio even though the councils included in the survey were split between partisan and nonpartisan elections and only one-third of the councils were selected entirely through at-large elections. Although nonpartisanship and at-large elections would seem likely to reinforce the trustee orientation, 18 percent

Table 5-1. Distribution of Representational
Types in California and Ohio City Councils

Type	California (%)	Ohio (%)
Trustee	60	64
Politico	22	29
Delegate	18	7
Total	100	100
	N = 434	205

Sources: California—Zisk (1973: 100); Ohio—Latcham and Hamilton (1974: 26).

of the California council members were delegates as opposed to 7 percent of the council members in Ohio.[10]

The impact of the trustee orientation has been examined by Eulau and Prewitt in their exhaustive study of city councils in the Bay area of California, the same survey from which Zisk described individual council member characteristics.[11] For analytical purposes, they divided the councils by the strength of trusteeship (none had a "nontrustee" orientation): 41 percent had a low level, 29 percent had a medium, and 29 percent a high level. The councils varied, as one would expect, in how likely they were to take stands that counter the majority opinion in the community. Most of the councils with a high sense of trusteeship often deviated from majority opinion, acting on their own judgment of what was best for the community. Over 60 percent of low trusteeship councils, on the other hand, seldom did so.[12]

There are reasons for the slant toward trusteeship besides "Burkean aloofness."[13] The member and constituents may have the same opinion. For most matters that come before the council to decide, constituents will have (or express) no opinion, and, on a few issues, constituents will be evenly divided. In all these cases, one could argue that even though a council member may wish to be responsive, he or she exercises independent judgment. Even if strongly oriented to the constituency, the council member is not necessarily an "instructed" delegate with no capacity to make up his or her own mind. The representational role will vary, then, with the strength of the council member's commitments and the level, clarity, and consistency of constituency opinion.

A strong interest group orientation increases the likelihood that a council member will be a politico or delegate.[14] When the representational role definition is related to the council members purpose for serving ("purposive role"), there is a positive correlation but at the same time evidence that different roles are handled in distinct ways.[15] Those who define their purpose for being a council member as a "tribune"—one who finds out what people want and expresses it—are especially likely to be delegates or politicos (23 and 27 percent, respectively). Brokers—those who try to balance and harmonize conflicting demands that are made on the council—are likely to be politicos (40 percent). Both passive "ritualists" who do the chores of the job, and active "inventors" who take a proactive approach to problem solving are very likely to be trustees (63 and 70 percent, respectively.) Still, even among tribunes and brokers half were trustees (50 and 55 percent, respectively.)

The trustee versus delegate approach relates to the council member's policy choices for the large number of people on whose behalf the legislator acts. Research on Congress has identified other kinds of responsiveness.[16] Besides policy responsiveness, representatives also accede to constituent demands for services and benefits and seek to offer assistance in resolving problems. Allocation responsiveness entails efforts to secure a fair share of services, facilities, and contracts or "pork barrel" benefits for the district. Service responsiveness involves providing intervention as an "ombudsman" to assist individuals and groups in dealing with the governmental bureaucracy, as well as obtaining "particularized benefits" for individuals or groups in the legislator's constituency. Allocation and service responsiveness—largely devoid of policy or programmatic content—make up a constituency service strategy to maintain support and enhance reelection, regardless of swings in public opinion or shifts associated with presidential voting. "The contemporary representative," Cain, Ferejohn, and Fiorina observe, "serves constituents individually and collectively, keeps in close touch with them, and generally tries to cultivate a personal relationship with them, based on accessibility and trust."[17] This constituency service helps to account for the increased likelihood that incumbents will be reelected to Congress.[18]

These concepts are being employed in the study of city councils. Heilig and Mundt use three roles. They label service responsiveness the ombudsman role. It consists of providing services to "individual members of a constituency in largely personal, noncontroversial ways."[19] They equate allocation responsiveness with the delegate role, which in their view, "include[s] a concern that geographic constituencies receive a sufficient share of public goods and services." It would seem preferable to reserve the delegate concept for voting or espousing positions that closely correspond to the preferences of the council member's electorate (i.e., to describe one approach to policy responsiveness). Allocation responsiveness can be used to assess the degree to which a council member seeks to deliver the goods to his or her constituents separate from his or her policy choices. They define the trustee type in the traditional way. They found that 65 percent of the council members they interviewed in eleven cities could be classified as trustees, 21 percent as "delegates" (concerned with allocations to constituents,) and 13 percent as ombudsmen.[20]

The three types of responsiveness—with no distinction, however, between trustee and delegate attitudes—are used by Peterson and Dutton in their study of council members in the Buffalo metropolitan area.[21] Rather than assigning council members to one role, they examined the relative effort devoted to all three. As indicated in Table 5–2, almost all council members provide service assistance through securing information for constituents and over half also help people with problems in governmental agencies. It was quite common for council members to seek to get grants for constituents on a regular basis—three quarters did so—although this activity was least likely to receive their greatest effort. Policy responsiveness, measured by considering the opinion of the constituency and soliciting views of those affected, was almost universal. Based on other research, we can assume that most of

Table 5–2. Frequency of Council Members' Responsiveness

	Service		Allocation	Policy	
	Secure Information for Constituents	Help with Courts and Other Agencies (%)	Work to Get Grants (%)	Consider Constituency Opinion (%)	Solicit Views of Those Affected (%)
Almost Never/ Seldom	4.6	46.9	25.0	3.1	6.3
Often/Regularly	42.2	35.9	65.6	78.1	64.1
Greatest Effort	53.1	17.2	7.8	18.8	28.1
Missing Data	0.0	0.0	1.6	0.0	1.6
Total	99.9	100.0	100.0	100.0	100.1

N = 64

Source: Recomputed from Peterson and Dutton (1982: 21, Table 1).

the council members were trustees. Perhaps trustees consider their constituents' opinions to a greater extent than we have given them credit for.

It is evident that the roles filled by council members can vary considerably in both direction and emphasis. As we have noted, policy responsiveness employs the categories of trustee, delegate, and politico. The two other aspects of the representational role may also be differentiated, although previous research has not attempted to do so. There are hypothetically distinct ways of handling the requests that come from the council member's various constituencies. With regard to allocation decisions, the council member may act as an elitist, universalist, separatist, or patron. In response to service requests, the council member may be detached, or act as an ombudsman or a fixer.

Handling allocation decisions involves the council member's attitudes about advancing (or ignoring) the needs and desires of constituents for a share of facilities and services. We can assume that constituents want positive programs and wish to avoid negative ones, but how does the council member respond to these demands? The *elitist* generally ignores demands from most constituents but is willing to direct resources to the benefit of upper income groups and the business community. The elitist might offer two arguments to support this approach. Since cities are in competition for groups with the most resources who can choose where to reside, amenities must be provided. Since a growing local economy benefits everyone, it can be argued that providing benefits to and lowering costs for the business sector is in the interests of the whole community.[22]

The *universalist* takes the position that the concerns of all citizens should be addressed directly, but uniform decision rules should determine the choice of capital investments or the delivery of services. This need not be a self-sacrificing stance. Rather the council member prefers that all be treated fairly in terms of "reasonable" criteria. Thus, if need is a basis for service allocation, his or her constituents should receive those services to which they are entitled based on relative need. In contrast, the *separatist* tries to get as much for his or her constituents as possible and seeks special treatment for the district. He or she prefers "separable" goods to "public" goods.[23] The latter are broadly available to residents throughout all parts of a city, (e.g., an air pollution control agency) whereas the former may be divided and distributed differentially to specific neighborhoods or even individuals, such as housing units or job training services. The separatist works to slant criteria to favor his or her constituents. A formula for service allocation is acceptable if it includes the right factors and weights to produce a tilt toward the favored group. The separatist is interested in the breakdown of projects and services along district lines.

The *patron* is even more particular and personal in his or her efforts to direct benefits to constituents and supporters. He or she wants to be seen as responsible for delivering the prize to an identifiable recipient. Whereas the separatist seeks an exchange of services to a class of beneficiaries for general support, the patron helps specific individuals and groups with a more explicit quid pro quo. Loyalty and a sense of obligation to reciprocate is sought.

In the third aspect of representation, only the *ombudsman* has been identified in previous research on city councils. This council member intervenes as necessary to resolve a problem between a constituent and an agency. Presumably, if the staff are accessible and responsive, the ombudsman does not need to do more than direct the citizen to the right office and insure that a satisfactory resolution has been reached. The detached council member, who deviates in one direction from the ombudsman, does not care to get involved in citizens' problems. Such members would seem, judging from the Buffalo data, rare indeed, but Heilig and Mundt found relatively few ombudsmen. Zisk reports a greater mix: 33 percent spent a lot of time "doing services for people" and another 31 percent spent some time. Only 35 percent spent little or no time performing the "errand-boy function." The aloof council member is not necessarily uncaring but rather assumes that others will adequately take care of the citizen. "Go see the city manager" would be a stock response. The *fixer* deviates in the activist direction from the ombudsman. This council member wants to take a direct hand in the problem solving by taking care of it directly (or seeming to), intervening with staff, or closely overseeing the resolution. The fixer is analogous to the patron in allocation issues in wishing to be the channel for particularized action. The fixer might be highly critical of the corrupting influence of the patron, but not view his or her own behavior as violating "good government" norms. Still, it seems likely that the two role orientations will be manifested jointly, as a council member cultivates the reputation as the person who can get things done in city hall.

These types are elaborated, despite limited empirical foundation, to expand the repertoire of labels available to scholars and practitioners. For example, the ideal council member to traditional reformers is presumably the detached trustee universalist elected at-large. Reformers in the past had a tendency of seeing the council member selected to represent a part of the city in the most negative light, that is, as patrons and fixers who are incapable of making a decision that deviates from the interests of the district constituents. It seems likely that district representatives will actually behave more "moderately" within each dimension of the representational role. As delegates, separatists, and ombudsmen, they are committed to expressing the opinion of constituents on issues when possible; in addition, they take an active interest in providing constituency service. On the other hand, critics of reform tend to view at-large council members as elitists. The universalist stance on allocation issues is probably more common. The emergence of the ombudsman is a positive development for increasing the accessibility—real or perceived—of low income and minority residents to city government, as Heilig and Mundt point out.[25] If the ombudsman becomes a fixer, however, negative consequences may outweigh positive ones. The suggested types, then, permit finer distinctions within the representational role.

A fourth type of responsiveness identified by Eulau and Karps—symbolic responsiveness—should be noted to complete the assessment of the representational role. It appears to be increasingly commonplace. In this behavior, the legislator is not so much exchanging a concrete action for support but rather seeking to promote a generalized sense of trust and support by manipulating political symbols. Just as mayors engage in "expressive leadership," so, too, council members sometimes take positions to respond to the strong feelings of constituents or to get on the right side of an issue. Just like their counterparts in the Congress and state legislatures, council members "introduce thousands of bills [i.e., ordinances and resolutions] which have not the slightest chance of ever being passed and, more often than not, are not intended to be passed."[26] When council members "play to the gallery" and the media on a policy question, seek a grant to recognize an organization in their district, or issue solemn instructions in public session to administrators in response to a citizen complaint, they may be responding on the symbolic level rather than displaying policy, allocation, or service responsiveness. Open meeting requirements and expanded television news coverage of local government increase the opportunities and the need for symbolic responsiveness.

In conclusion, the representational role is complex and the patterns of responsiveness are diverse. Council members would appear to be closer to their constituents in their response to allocation and service requests than one would surmise from the tendency of council members to act as trustees in making policy choices. The trustee or delegate distinction itself may be misleading. The trustee is likely to take constituents' opinions into account in making an independent decision and constituents' preferences may shape or reflect the council member's own. The delegate often has no constituency opinion on which to base a decision. Both will at times take their constituents' side in a symbolic stand against the unpopular or indefensible and for what is perceived to be the good.

Selection and Characteristics of Council Members

Elections of city council members are defined by two major institutional features: the nature of the ballot, and the character of the constituency. "Ballot" type refers to whether or not the candidate's party affiliation is printed on the ballot; if so, it is a *partisan election* and, if not, it is a *nonpartisan election*. This institution has nothing to do with the nature of campaigning, since parties may openly support and work for candidates who are free to declare their party preference. More commonly, however, parties have been weak or totally absent from the campaign, and candidates have approached local issues as if they were devoid of partisan content.[27] How great a factor parties are in partisan elections will depend on the level of organizational strength in each community, but at least candidates run under a party label and are identified by party on the ballot. In 1986, 73 percent of American city governments used nonpartisan elections. The mid-Atlantic states are the exception, with 87 percent of the cities using partisan elections. A sizable minority of cities employ partisan ballots in New England (44 percent), the industrial Midwest (32 percent), and the states of the interior South (21 percent). In the rest of the country, over 85 percent the cities use nonpartisan elections.[28]

The type of constituency refers to the size of the unit from which council members are elected and the number of council members elected from the unit. In *at-large* elections, the electoral unit is the entire jurisdiction, and all members are elected by the same constituency. In *district* or *ward* elections, on the other hand, the jurisdiction is divided up into smaller areas from which one council member is elected; thus, each council member represents a part of the whole. Although the terms are often used interchangeably, the term ward is sometimes used to refer to very small and, therefore more numerous, electoral units whereas district refers to a lower number of larger, more heterogeneous units. Until the 1980s, two-thirds of the cities over 2,500 in population used at-large elections, but a shift to districts is occurring. In 1987, the proportion using at-large elections had dropped to 60 percent, and 13 percent use pure districts. Over a quarter of the cities—27 percent as opposed to 19 percent in 1981—use both types of constituency together and elect some seats to the council at-large and others from districts.[29] Change has been particularly pronounced in cities over 50,000. There is now a strong association between city size and use of districts. Only 15 percent of the largest cities and less than 40 percent of the cities above 100,000 population use at-large elections. This method is found in over half of the cities between 10,000 and 100,000 population and over 60 percent of the smallest cities included in Table 5–3. It should be noted that some large, diverse cities, including El Paso and San Francisco, have gone against this trend by shifting back from district to at-large elections.

The traditional combination of institutions used in cities was partisan election of council members from wards. In contrast, the reform movement in cities advocated the use of at-large, nonpartisan elections. In

Table 5–3. Distribution of At-large (A-L) and District Elections, 1986

Category	Number	At-Large (%)	District (%)	Mixed A-L/Dist. (%)
Total (all cities)	3895	60.4	12.8	26.8
Population Group				
Over 500,000	13	15.4	23.1	61.5
250,000–500,000	23	34.8	17.4	47.8
100,000–249,999	93	37.6	17.2	45.2
50,000–99,999	227	53.3	10.6	36.1
25,000–49,999	472	55.9	11.4	32.6
10,000–24,999	986	58.3	11.6	30.1
5,000–9,999	955	62.5	12.4	25.1
2,500–4,999	1126	66.8	14.6	18.7
Form of Government				
Mayor-council	1686	49.1	21.3	29.7
Council-manager	2095	68.1	6.5	25.6

Source: Renner (1988: 14). Table 2/2 from *The Municipal Year Book 1988*, used with permission of the International City Management Association.

fact, there is great variation in the actual combination of election institutions, and it is increasing as more cities adopt districts or use both constituency types together. The impact of various election systems on the characteristics of council members can be summarized, although more is known about certain combinations than others.

At-large elections, especially if nonpartisan, usually provide an advantage to businessmen and professionals from affluent neighborhoods who have been active in civic affairs through voluntary citywide service organizations,[30] although the differences should not be exaggerated. Particularly disadvantaged in this system are those with lower incomes and less access to contributions, persons involved with neighborhood or other organizations limited in geographic scope, and minorities. Welch and Bledsoe surveyed council members nationally and have filled many of the gaps in our knowledge of the impact of election institutions. When controlling for city characteristics (median income, region, etc.), the income of council members is higher with at-large and nonpartisan elections, and education level is higher with at-large elections.[31] There is no relationship between nonpartisan elections and education. The authors estimate that with district/partisan elections the proportions of members in the lowest income and education group would be 6 percent and 13 percent, respectively. With at-large, nonpartisan elections, 2 percent would be from the lowest income group and 7 percent from the lowest education group. The proportion of council members elected from districts who are owners, professionals, or managers is 62 percent and the proportion with blue-collar jobs is 7 percent. Among those elected at-large, 70 percent have high-status occupations, and 2 percent are working class, respectively. There are no occupational differences associated with ballot type of elections.

The impact of district elections depends heavily on the number and size of districts in the city.[32] If the number of districts is large and each is relatively homogeneous, then council members may feel bound by the specific interests of constituents and use bargaining and logrolling as a means of securing council agreement, trading benefits to their district for support of citywide projects. With fewer districts, the population is more heterogeneous in each. Council members find that it is not always simple to identify or express "the opinion" of the district and need to balance competing interests among constituents. The use of districts increases the geographical representativeness and diversity of membership. All parts of the city have seats on the council and minority groups, if large enough and concentrated in certain neighborhoods, are more likely to be represented.[33] Groups widely dispersed throughout the city, however, are not necessarily represented more fairly, nor are women as likely to be elected in district elections.[34]

Business interests have less direct representation, and neighborhood groups and nonbusiness interest groups have gained influence after the introduction of district elections, according to a study by the LBJ School of Public Affairs.[35] Other conclusions of this assessment of six large council-manager cities with mixed (Houston, Dallas, and Charlotte) and pure district systems (San Antonio, Fort Worth, and Richmond) include the following:

attention to citywide issues continues, along with a greater concern with neighborhood and other geographic issues

the decision-making process is more open and, in two cities, characterized by more vote trading, and council meetings are longer and more divisive

council members' workloads increase, in part because of more constituent contacts

representation on appointed boards and commissions improves

council members become more involved in administrative affairs

there is greater interaction among the mayor, council, and city staff

There is the perception among some residents that services are more equitably distributed, but city officials and business representatives claim that there has been no change and that service distribution was equitable before the change in election.

Districts in themselves do not generate controversy in a city, but the system allows for clearer expression of cleavages that are already present.[36] Although there are no consistent policy differences associated with method of election, there is more conflict in district-based councils, and it is likely to be based on geography.[37] District elections increase the number of candidates, although their impact on voter turnout depends on the level of competition within districts, with turnout reduced if there are a number of districts in which incumbents are not challenged.[38] There is a greater tendency for officials to create mechanisms for citizen participation after the introduction of districts.[39]

Welch and Bledsoe find that the method of election affects the orientation of council members to constituents, although the impact is modest.[40] Virtually all at-large council members define their constituency as the city as a whole, and 11 percent include business interests as their *primary* constituency, whereas those elected from districts view the district as their constituency. Still, over 70 percent of district members also see the city as their focus; 15 percent consider it to be the primary focus as opposed to 13 percent whose primary focus is the neighborhood. Similarly, at-large members are concerned about neighborhoods, but almost none primarily focus on the neighborhood as their constituency. The district members were also somewhat more constituency oriented and spent a larger proportion of the time they devote to council duties doing services. In cities with mixed systems, the roles are blurred. In contrast to the differences with regard to geographical focus and service orientation, there is no difference between at-large and district members in the importance assigned to representing racial or ethnic interests, partisan and ideological interests, and the interests of labor.

Heilig and Mundt stress that the income of the district is also important to constituency orientation.[41] Whereas 95 percent of the council members elected from low-income districts stressed constituency service, 43 percent of those from middle-income districts and 13 percent from high-income districts did so. Among those elected at-large (on combination district/at-large councils), 17 percent emphasized constituency service.[42]

The use of partisan elections may produce some effects that are similar to those of districts if the parties are well organized, and nonpartisan elections tend to reinforce the effects of at-large elections. Partisan elections have higher voter turnout than nonpartisan elections and are likely to overrepresent the majority party.[43] Hawley documented a Republican and conservative bias in nonpartisan cities as upper class candidates—more often Republican—are more likely to be elected, although there was also a mild Democratic bias in cities with a Republican majority.[44] In partisan elections, there is greater turnout of persons with less education and lower income, who are more likely to be Democrats. The presence of the party label on the ballot may permit them to vote more rationally, that is, to better link their political action to their political interests, than would be the case in a nonpartisan election in which information about candidates is scant. Furthermore, council members with a stronger partisan orientation will address a wider range of issues and diverge more ideologically, reflecting the national party differences, than would be the case on a nonpartisan council.

Despite the arguments that nonpartisan elections favor Republicans, Welch and Bledsoe conclude that partisan bias does not result from nonpartisan elections except in isolated situations, particularly when at-large elections are used and also in smaller cities, ones with moderate income, and a Democratic majority. The increased mobilization of neighborhood and minority groups have strengthened the Democratic vote as has the use of district elections. "District systems," they conclude, "eliminate the Republican bias of nonpartisanship that exists in at-large systems."[45] Furthermore, nonpartisan council members are only slightly more conservative than partisan ones, and more liberal on some issues. Although there is no greater internal conflict on partisan than nonpartisan councils, the authors suggest, like Hawley, that "partisan labels subsume others kinds of conflict in these cities, thus making a more accountable system."[46]

Their data indicate, however, that the contribution of partisanship to accountability is limited. On the partisan council, conflict between the parties is rated the most important cleavage by 22 percent. The cleavages that drop in importance between nonpartisan and partisan councils are pro- versus antidevelopment forces and liberals versus conservatives; 37 percent of the nonpartisan council members consider these to be the most important conflicts as opposed to 19 percent of the partisan members. Other cleavages that would seem to have a partisan dimension—tax cutters vs. opponents, business vs. neighborhoods, anglos vs. others, business vs. labor—are equally important in the two types of councils.[47] One can hardly rely on visible party differences as a cue for many important battles on the city council.

There is evidence that the same forces that are eliminating a Republican bias are also strengthening liberal forces on city councils. In the ten California cities (whose average minority population was 18% black and 14% Hispanic) that Browning, Marshall, and Tabb investigated, they found that the activities of minority and neighborhood groups, plus labor unions and liberal Democrats, increased liberal and minority representation.[48] In Table 5–4, one can see that the Democratic advantage in voter registration, which increased only slightly between 1962 and 1977, was translated into overwhelming majorities on all ten city councils. Furthermore, a conservative majority had been replaced in seven of the cities between 1962 and 1977. Only one of the seven councils was elected from districts at the time of the ideological changeover (as was one of the "conservative" councils.) Increased activism is offsetting the Republican advantage in political resources and changing the characteristics of councils that are selected using nonpartisan, at-large elections.

Table 5-4. Changes in Partisan Composition of Council and Mayoral Offices

Cities	Percent Democratic Officeholders[a] 1962	Percent Democratic Officeholders[a] 1977	Percentage Points Difference, 1962-1977	Percent Democratic Voter Registration[b] 1962	Percent Democratic Voter Registration[b] 1977	Percentage Points Difference, 1962-1977
All Cities (mean)	40	80	+40	63	70	+ 7
Berkeley	56	100	+44	53	73	+20
Daly City	60	80	+20	66	70	+ 4
Hayward	14	86	+72	67	67	0
Oakland	11	67	+56	60	71	+11
Richmond	56	56	0	71	79	+ 8
*Sacramento	56	89	+33	63	68	+ 5
San Francisco	58	83	+25	62	77	+15
San Jose	29	86	+57	55	58	+ 3
*Stockton	22	100	+78	61	64	+ 3
Vallejo	38	57	+19	73	74	+ 1

[a]Council members and mayors; party registration was determined from voter lists at the offices of county registrars of voters.

[b]California Secretary of State, *Repor, of Registration, 1962-1977* (Sacramento, 1978).

*Used district elections in 1977.

Source: Browning, Marshall, and Tabb (1984: Table 4, p. 35), used with permission of University of California Press.

In sum, the nonpartisan at-large council has the greatest proportion of well educated, higher income, and business and professional members. Since elections are at-large, it has an overrepresentation of Republicans. It tends to be concerned with citywide issues and approaches. The relationship among members in such councils is usually collegial or impersonal, with only 26 percent characterized by antagonism.[49] These characteristics, though probably still common in at-large, nonpartisan cities, are not an accurate portrayal of all such cities. Increased activism is bringing new kinds of members and a new orientation even to city councils that use the standard reform combination.

When elections are at-large and partisan, parties may promote the candidacy of a wider range of people and offset the influence of business and citywide civic organizations and thus produce a more diverse council than would nonpartisan elections. For example, a council member in Hartford reported that the Democratic slate of at-large candidates is balanced by race and area. Connecticut's parties, however, retain greater control over the nomination process than is the case in other states. Slates of candidates chosen in citywide party primaries would not necessarily be balanced. The partisan at-large council is, in theory, the most oriented to the concerns of the national parties and drawn from the coalition that supports the majority party. This combination presumably expands the control of the central party organization over nominations with relatively less influence exerted by district party leaders.[50] Little is known, however, about this combination.

Conversely, nonpartisan district elections would presumably be dominated by whatever groups are important in the neighborhoods that make up a district. The party precinct or ward organization is not necessarily advantaged. The geographic focus of district council members is pronounced, but they display no greater party or ideological focus.[51] Council members are likely to emphasize local concerns. The separatist and the ombudsmen would likely predominate among these council members, although those from higher socioeconomic districts are more likely to be trustees and universalists who receive fewer requests for assistance with constituent problems. These council members do not ignore citywide concerns despite their interest in the district.

Finally, the partisan district election especially favors candidates from neighborhood party organizations, whose interests may be both neighborhood oriented and concerned with promoting the position of the ward party organization. Districts can protect minority party representation on the council since the second party may be dominant in certain parts of the city.[52] One would expect that these council members are the ones most likely to display the patron and fixer orientations— similar to the orientation of the "ward heeler" in the party organization—but there is minimal relationship between partisanship and constituency orientation independent of election by districts.[53] Although loyal to the party, the council member is likely to be a delegate for whom neighborhood interests weigh heavily unless they are overwhelmed by a strong central party organization.[54]

In conclusion, the method of electing members of the city council affects the composition of the council and the member's orientation to the representational role. There are general tendencies that have either been observed or are hypothetically plausible (and need to be examined further in new research). There is also a great deal of variation within these patterns. To understand council members better, we need to examine their attitudes about seeking and retaining the office and how they handle other roles besides the representational one.

Council Members' Background
and Motivation to Serve

The election institutions in use enhance the electability of certain kinds of candidates and reduce the prospects of others. Still, running for office is a highly demanding form of political participation, which is typically engaged in by persons with high educational attainment; substantial income; a professional, managerial, or business occupation; and/or unusually strong motivation. In this respect, governing board members are more or less the "cream" of the community regardless of the method of election.[55]

In addition to having resources and potential support, a candidate must *want* to seek the office and be willing to serve. The attitudes about the job and the motivations to seek it can be divided into three categories—the *ambitious* who seek office to advance their own interests, *volunteers* who seek to serve their community, and *activists* who seek to advance constituency interests or policy concerns. The ambitious council member may match the popular stereotype of local officials being full-time politicians who use council membership as the first step to higher office or to promote personal professional or business interests. Actually, the interest in running and the nature of "ambition" can vary widely among candidates for local office.

Prewitt has found that many council members manifest a spirit of volunteerism in nonpartisan cities: "the elected position is an extension of a community role formed by and spelled out in the numerous voluntary organizations" in which they have served.[56] These council members were much more likely initially to have got involved in politics through some civic activity, an occupational tie, a sense of personal investment in the community, or some specific political event, rather than through participation in partisan activities.

In his research on councils in small cities, Sokolow provides additional explanation of why council members seek office.[57] Like Prewitt, he finds that 38 percent were volunteers who wanted to serve the community. Most were "participants" (36 percent), who had an interest in government and a desire to participate or who saw public office as a personal challenge, or "advocates" (26 percent), who were critical of incumbents, interested in specific issues, or concerned about the policy direction of the community. Most of the volunteers and participants were natives of the community or had resided there for over twenty years. The advocates were disproportionately drawn from the relative "newcomers."

The desire to seek office is not highly "political" in the sense of being a partisan act. Less than 10 percent of the Bay Area council members viewed the position as political. Although many felt that it required political skills though it was not a political job, 52 percent were of the opinion that the "job is not in any way a matter of politics."[58] Although this assessment would presumably be different in cities with partisan elections or a more contentious political climate, the job is likely to be viewed as a service or an expression of personal interest in government or the community. Not only is this attitude attributable to the council members' background, it is also advanced by the nonelectoral route that many council members take to office and the relative security of council membership. Prewitt found that 23 percent of Bay Area council members were initially appointed to office.[59] The appointed members were likely to serve out of a sense of obligation or general interest and less likely to have either a sense of indignation or desire to solve problems than those initially elected to office.

Once in office, the council member is not likely to be defeated; the security of incumbency increased between the early sixties and the mid-seventies.[60] More incumbents sought reelection—72 percent versus 61 percent—and the proportion of incumbents reelected inched still higher to 78 percent. There is little variation by city size, form of government, or ballot type used. Prewitt reports virtually identical reelection rates for council members initially elected who had served more than one term (79 percent), those elected and concluding the first term (80 percent), and those appointed to office (79 percent).[61]

The volunteer council member relatively assured of reelection may be less likely to feel sensitive to public opinion. These council members are not strongly open to or supportive of citizen group activity.[62] A detached attitude may diminish the concern about public reactions to the council member's performance in office because he or she is not interested in higher office or even, necessarily, in reelection, as Prewitt has argued. To such an official, the threat from groups to withhold support in the next election will have little impact. The ambition to retain a position or seek higher office restrains elected officials, who feel a stronger need to be accountable. Although ambition is sometimes denigrated as unseemly, it may be the factor needed to close the gap between voters and officeholders.[63] Koehler included this attribute in a profile of the rare "councilman politician." "His political ambitions are generally set higher than city hall, but he definitely is an asset to his city."[64] This council member seeks information from a wide range of sources both inside and outside the city and scrutinizes the manager's proposals with great care.

The absence of ambition, at least static ambition to remain in the same office, however, may be overstated. Among Prewitt's respondents, only 18 percent intended to retire from office after their current term, 53 percent planned to seek another term, and 29 percent wanted to seek a higher office.[65] Peterson and Dutton found that 91 percent of the Buffalo area council members are willing to serve at least one more term and 86 percent desired reelection.[66] Council members, thus, are not totally insensitive to the electorate's assessment of their performance.

Furthermore, service to the constituency is provided regardless of electoral intentions. Peterson and Dutton did not find a relationship between static ambition and policy responsiveness, helping people with problems they have with agencies, or working to get grants for constituents. This is not to say that some council members do not act for self-serving reasons, but simply that responsiveness in all its aspects is as common (or uncommon) among those who do not care about reelection. Providing constituency services provides a means of helping people, which offers in return a sense of satisfaction and accomplishment that may not be found in other aspects of the job. In addition, reelection may be important for symbolic reasons. Even for those council members who are not intent on remaining in office for a long period nor obsessed with victory, electoral support may be perceived as a validation of doing a good job and making the right decisions. Reelection is the confirmation that a service is being provided to the community. The voters in effect license the activist council member to pursue his or her issues and renews or removes that license in subsequent elections. Thus, ambition is not the only reason for council members to be responsive, nor does its absence necessarily signify a weak linkage between representatives and voters.

Out of the mix of the positive and negative aspects of ambition, volunteerism, and activism, the council probably has greater diversity than it is given credit for. One would suspect that changes in the method of electing city councils are leading to more ambitious and activist members. Along with the changes in background, these shifts in attitudes make the council more lively and less deliberative, more contentious and less consensual. The council is becoming more responsive in its representation of citizens. One must also ask, however, how well council members fill their governance and supervisory roles and how do changes in characteristics and attitudes affect the council's contributions to the governmental process.

Perspectives on Council Roles II: Governance and Supervision

Council members are not only representatives. They are also governors and, at least potentially, supervisors of staff. Governance involves the determination of purpose for city government, the formulation of policies to accomplish purposes, and the translation of policies into programs and services that accomplish their intended objectives. The contribution of the council to policy making and execution is less than expected if one starts with the simplistic notion that all policy is formulated by elected officials, but the contribution is greater than suggested by some "realistic" studies of the influence of administrative staff. The more appropriate middle ground is that the typical council shapes the mission of the organization by defining the overall purpose and major goals to be pursued. More specific policies may be initiated by the council or simply ratified by them as they accept staff recommendations. The policy making by staff enmeshed in decisions about implementation and service delivery may not be explicitly approved by elected officials, and it is questionable whether the council reviews such activities carefully. Still, council members are well situated to oversee administration, and they contribute in other ways to implementation and service delivery.

Council members act in a supervisory capacity when they appoint staff and appraise their performance and when they address issues concerning organizational structure and process. Although the management dimension is largely the sphere of the mayor or manager, councils are legitimately interested in operational matters. Change in management practices may originate in the council. For example, the Greensboro City Council pushed the idea of expanded commitment to merit pay in the 1970s and instructed the manager to develop the details of such an approach. Councils are also interested in questions concerning organizational design and performance (e.g., productivity improvement). If councils also direct staff and make operational decisions about the use of organizational resources, such as who gets jobs, raises, or contracts, then they become managers themselves. The manager role is not considered to be a legitimate one by most observers of local government, but the supervisor role can be.

The representational role can be blended with the council member's other activities. For example, when a council member questions the progress of street widening in response to a constituent's complaint, he is manifesting service responsiveness and also informally overseeing the administrative process. If he goes further to alter the scheduling of projects to benefit the complainant, he is allocating a service and directing staff.

It seems likely, however, that for most members the bulk of the governance and supervisory activities has little direct connection to the relationship with constituents. In the course of making thousands of decisions and reviewing countless actions that constitute the work of the city, they must draw upon their own sense of what is right and proper for the city far more often than they respond to or reflect constituents' sentiments. The impact of many policy choices on constituents is not clear, and many decisions do not produce discernible division of opinion among them.[67] Council members oversee a far wider array of administrative activities (at least potentially) than those about which citizens complain or make inquiries. Similarly, if council members act as supervisors of staff, some—perhaps most—do not seek to advance constituency concerns in the process.

Council members fill the governance and supervisory roles well or poorly depending on their individual talents, commitment, and orientation to the office, and on the formal structure in which they operate. Council members will be more or less parochial and open to "outside" ideas, differ in their preference for things to remain as they are in their own community, and pragmatic or irrational in their approach to problem solving.[68] Some are familiar with delegating tasks to another person in an organizational setting and evaluating how well those tasks have been performed. Most are not.

The point is not that council members should seek to separate the performance of each role from the others, although we noted that insulation may be mandated when council members fill the judicial role. Rather, the council position must be seen as encompassing a number of distinct roles which will vary in their degree of integration.

Thus, council members potentially fill three roles—representational, governance, and supervisory. The roles and major activities associated with each are the following:

Representational	Governance	Supervisory
Policy responsiveness	Policy maker	Appointer
Allocation responsiveness	Implementor	Manager
Service responsiveness	Overseer	Appraiser

Each role may be approached with a distinct orientation or they may be fused. Decisions in the governance and supervisory role may be devoid of representational responsiveness except (or even when) explicit constituency issues are involved. The delegate on policy questions when constituents have strong preferences may exercise independent judgment in other policy decisions. The separatist at the program design stage does not necessarily intervene in program implementation to make additional efforts to steer benefits toward his or her district. The ombudsman may be a distant overseer except when responding to complaints. Heilig and Mundt found unexpected variations in how complaints are handled: "there are trustees who deal directly with city staff, and ombudsmen who work only through the manager."[69] Council members may have distinct ways of handling the representational role and the governance role of overseer.

In supervisory activities, a delegate and separatist may favor appointing a manager who is highly qualified and reflects the policy orientation of the entire council rather than one who reflects the policy preferences of the district or is willing to hire the council member's constituents to fill city staff positions. This council member may act as a detached appraiser and not try to manage staff and organizational resources to the advantage of supporters. The variety of combinations warrants further investigation.

There is no existing discussion of council behavior which examines all roles and the interactions among them. The governing style of councils was examined by Eulau and Prewitt. Among the at-large, nonpartisan councils who appointed managers, the governing style categorized as "benevolent" was found in 57 percent of the cities. Members are concerned with the good of the city, serve for the public interest rather than self-interest, and are open to suggestions and responsive.[70] A pragmatic style with an emphasis on planning, competence, and efficiency was displayed by 18 percent of the cities. Finally, in 23 percent of the cities a "political" style dominated. Council members mobilized and used power to achieve desired policy outcomes. The approach to the governance role might be seen as an extension of the representational orientation, for example, a trustee, universalist would seem more likely to manifest the benevolent or pragmatic approach whereas the delegate, separatist would display the political style. This correlation cannot be assumed, however, and it is just as plausible that council members will bring contrasting values to different roles.

Although there is little research that examines council roles other than the representational, there are guidebooks designed to assist elected officials in understanding and filling their governance and, to a lesser extent, supervisory roles. *Tools for Leadership* from the National League of Cities and *Elected Officials Handbooks* from the International City Management Association highlight these roles and the positive contributions council members can make to the governmental process.[71]

Positive View of Council Contributions

The guidebooks advocate a rational, team-oriented approach for council members to follow in organizing their activities and fulfilling their responsibilities. There is reliance on the standard problem-solving model of policy making which moves through the stages of problems, goals, objectives, priorities, action programs, and evaluation in goal setting generally and in the budgetary process. Although Sweetwood in *Tools for Leadership* notes that the assessment of needs may be based on "council wisdom" and goal setting may be ad hoc and reactive, there is a clear preference for a rational approach based on information gathering, openness, and analysis.[72] Great emphasis is placed on the policy-making role. The oversight function is frequently mentioned, and evaluation is stressed as the council's most important responsibility in implementation. In the *Handbooks*, there is discussion of the supervisory role with respect to hiring and evaluating the chief administrator and productivity improvement. Council members are urged to work together as a team and to fully utilize the contributions of city staff.

These publications do not give much explicit attention to the representational role. Some decisions are made with a concern for allocational responsiveness rather than programmatic goal attainment, yet the guidebooks do not address this issue nor distinguish between what we have called universalist versus separatist approaches to allocating services to constituents. Still, there is recognition of the usefulness of complaints for feedback to administrators, complaint handling is covered as part of constituent–council member interaction, and methods are provided for maintaining good communication between the council member and the public.[73]

In sum, these associations serving city officials emphasize the governance and supervisory roles of council members and emphasize the positive contributions they can make. The advice offered to council members is useful as a specification of techniques that can be used in handling a large number of tasks. They do not discuss the characteristics of the governmental process in which council members work and the constraints that may limit council contributions. They also gloss over the difficulties in using rational approaches and in maintaining cooperation. They provide an idealized picture of the council's contributions through the governance and supervisory roles but fail to tie these roles to the members' basic representational responsibilities. The advice must be joined with a realistic assessment of the council's performance.

Council Performance in Governance and Supervisory Roles

Despite the positive potential, the actual performance of councils often falls short. There are a number of criticisms of the council, including self-criticism by council members themselves. A composite list of these shortcomings, drawn from interviews in the five large cities in North Carolina, is presented in Table 5–5. The criticisms do not represent the dominant view of the city council in any of the five cities. Rather, they are problems that some council members or some councils experience some of the time. Taken together, however, they indicate the difficulties that council members have in matching the idealized view. Councils are prone to provide too little leadership in the mission and policy dimensions and become excessively involved in some aspects of administration and management, although there are omissions in these dimensions as well.

In some of the North Carolina cities, there was confusion among many respondents about whether councils made any positive contribution. Some officials felt that the best thing the council did was to stay out of the way of staff, but could not identify any positive contributions. These council members manifested "a vague sense of malaise" about their role.[74] In other cities, the council was assessed positively and satisfaction was high. The difference appears to be a failure in the former cities to discern the full range of actual and potential contribu-

Table 5–5. Criticisms of Council's Performance[a]

Formulation of Mission

1. Fails to set direction or provide overall leadership

Policy Making

2. Rejects staff recommendations arbitrarily
3. Is overly suspicious of staff in assessing recommendations
4. Is unable to decide
5. Ignores and/or rubber-stamps proposals

Administrations

6. Interferes in administrative affairs through complaint handling
7. Obstructs implementation through excessive oversight and approvals
8. Imposes a heavy workload of inquiries and reports (especially in the period preceding elections), "clogging the machinery of government"

Management

9. Damages morale by criticizing staff publicly
10. Sends negative message to staff with pay freeze or cut
11. Interferes in contracting
12. Imposes organizational or procedural changes on manager

[a]Responses based on interviews with sample of council members, department heads, and community leaders in Charlotte, Durham, Greensboro, Raleigh, and Winston-Salem. These are the negative responses to the question, "What are the greatest contributions of the city council to the performance of city government in this community?"

Source: Svara (1986a), used with permission of *Popular Government*.

tions the council can make, in particular the significant direction it provides (at least implicitly) through the mission dimension.

Perceived deficiency in the formulation of mission is not uncommon. In a national survey of council members, establishing long-term goals received the lowest effectiveness rating among a list of council functions. As indicated in Table 5–6, only half considered council performance to be very or usually effective. The contrast between the governance and representational roles of council members is evident when this finding is contrasted with the 93 percent who feel that councils are effective at responding to citizen needs. Dealing with the specific and immediate needs of citizens is easier than handling the abstract and long-term needs of the community as a whole.

In another national study of council decision making, members allocated 100 points among the various decisions they made according to how important the decisions were. They separately estimated how much

Table 5–6. Self-Assessment of Council's Effectiveness

Question: How would you rate the effectiveness of your city council in performing
the following functions?

		City Size		
	Total	*Small*	*Medium*	*Large*
Responding to Citizens' Needs	760 (93.3)*	434 (92.5)	210 (94.6)	116 (93.6)
Enacting Legislation	733 (90.2)	418 (88.5)	200 (92.2)	115 (92.7)
Coordinating Council Meetings	706 (86.5)	405 (85.9)	191 (86.8)	110 (88.0)
Budget/Financial Mgmt.	680 (83.9)	401 (86.1)	177 (81.2)	102 (80.9)
Overseeing Program Performance	566 (69.6)	332 (70.7)	155 (70.8)	79 (63.2)
Overseeing Admin. Performance	548 (67.6)	325 (69.6)	152 (69.4)	71 (56.8)
Establishing Objectives and Priorities	507 (62.1)	285 (60.5)	143 (64.7)	79 (63.2)
Establishing Long-term Goals	412 (50.4)	237 (50.2)	115 (52.3)	60 (47.6)

$N = 836$

1979 survey conducted for the National League of Cities.

*Percentage reporting "very" or "usually" effective.

Source: National League of Cities (1980: 29), used with permission of the National League of Cities.

of their time is spent on different kinds of decisions. Major choices about future development received 80 percent of the points for importance but account for only 5 percent of the time spent by the council.[75] Most of the San Francisco Bay Area councils—particularly in small cities—were oriented toward maintaining conditions as they are or making marginal changes to adapt to new circumstances.[76] Less than 40 percent of the city councils considered "programming the city's future" to be their leading purpose. All councils depend heavily on the executive for advice and analysis regarding the formulation of mission.

Still, the major decisions—and nondecisions—by the council over the years create the framework within which specific policy choices are made. Major shifts in council composition can result in a fundamental reorientation of city government.[77] The task, however, is a difficult one. Cities have a wide range of purposes and potentially conflicting priorities. Because the future is unknown, it is natural that officials will sometimes focus on continuing to do what they have always done and respond to crises when they occur. The short time perspective of council members reinforces this tendency.[78]

Once goals are established, they are not easily translated into policies and priorities. This difficulty befuddles a simple linear rational policy-making approach. Cities do not confront a single problem and pursue it until it is resolved. The complexity and interrelatedness of problems produce conditions in which impacts of one policy on another may not be predictable. There are policies without purpose. Some policies outlive the purpose that spawned them or emerge independent of the formulation of goals. "Policy" may be, as Lynn has observed, "*ex post* interpretations of governmental activities based on the consequences as perceived by those with a stake in the action."[79] Rather than reflecting prior intent, some public policies are, "in effect, 'second-hand hindsight'." Goal setting may occur in reverse as an inference from existing activities. The long-range implications of actions in the present are likely to be obscure. The impact of each incremental deviation from a general policy seems insignificant. One more spot zoning decision doesn't make a big difference, but a pattern of approving spot zonings over time does.

In their policy-making activities, many councils fail to provide the direction expected of them and that they expect of themselves. The council is perceived to mishandle recommendations from staff in some instances either by rejecting them arbitrarily, ignoring them, or accepting them without question, as indicated in Table 5–5. The second lowest rating in the NLC survey, reported in Table 5–6, was assigned to establishing objectives and priorities; 38 percent of the council members did not consider their council's performance to be effective as a usual thing. Achieving the appropriate level of deliberation in review of recommendations and providing clear guidance in decisions is not easy.

Councils are interested in how policies are translated into programs and how services are delivered. Councils are usually informed by the manager (probably less so by the executive mayor) about the development of program "regulations," such as definitions of eligibility for a program, and have the opportunity to accept, reject, or revise these recommendations. They make specific implementing decisions, for example, the design and placement of a facility that is part of a larger project. Indeed, councils frequently get bogged down in making specific choices.

Furthermore, council members frequently intervene on behalf of constituents in the form of requests for information, complaints about service delivery, discussions of regulations, or requests for specific services or benefits.[80] For the most part, administrators view councilmanic interventions as negative, resulting in a distortion of priorities (reported by 32 percent of the department heads surveyed by Abney and Lauth), partiality in service delivery (21 percent), and lack of strict adherence to departmental regulations (18 percent). On the positive side, most of the department heads (70 percent) felt that councilmanic contacts provided the opportunity to educate council members about their programs. The managers interviewed by Mundt and Heilig supported the councilmanic involvement in complaint handling "because it reduces citizen frustration with the channeling of complaints."[81] Still, administrators prefer citizen to council member contact and report that they respond more favorably to the former than the latter.[82]

In contrast to the extensive amount of complaint handling, councils make little use of formal evaluation or systematic oversight. There is tension between the evaluative aspect of council review and the involvement in specific aspects of program design and service delivery. Although council members in the NLC survey rate their effectiveness in program and administrative oversight higher than their performance in setting goals and objectives, 30 percent did not consider effectiveness to be high in these areas. In addition, almost half expressed the opinion that program evaluation was the aspect of the budgeting process most needing improvement. Council members prefer a substantially higher level of involvement in evaluation.[83]

There are few complaints about direct interference in management activities and more about the general tone set by the council through its actions. Bureaucracy baiting was not common in the North Carolina cities, yet some complained that council members were insensitive to staff morale in their public criticisms. Resonating to citizen dissatisfaction with "bureaucrats"—an example of symbolic responsiveness—with public criticism that could have conveyed through the appropriate administrative official creates resentment among staff. This kind of open scolding of staff is not the same as consistent examination of the work of staff. In a survey of North Carolina city managers, two-fifths felt that the council's appraisal of their performance was not satisfactory in its depth or frequency.[84] Although the *Handbook* outlines the procedures for appraisal of the manager in detail, it appears that relatively few councils in the council-manager form are engaging in managerial appraisal. Only 22 percent of the North Carolina councils do it very well. In mayor-council cities, councils have little opportunity to formally appraise elected executives.

One final factor affecting council performance is the developmental cycle suggested by Wolf and Wolf.[85] The recurring stages are "becoming a council" after each election, "implementation and fulfilling promises" during which the goals established by the council are acted on or "brought to closure," and "preparing for exit or re-election" during

which council members become self-centered seeking to look good
going into the election or to secure a legacy for their tenure in office.
Common attention and cooperative efforts to establish and implement
goals, strengthen the council group process, and interact effectively
with administrators through oversight and appraisal are likely to be
confined to the middle stage in the cycle. Council members are not as
likely to be in the proper frame of mind for rational team-oriented
approaches in the other two stages. Other events that fragment the
council would have the same effect.

Thus, despite the idealized view of council members as rational,
detached governors and merit-minded supervisors, in actuality many are
befuddled policy makers, overly engaged implementors, and near-
sighted overseers who ignore their supervisory role. To improve performance, it would be useful for council members to have a more realistic
target that takes into account the full range of council roles and the
pressures under which they operate. We shall use the dichotomy-duality
model as a guide to specifying those responsibilities. In the next section, we shall examine how the form of government affects the council's performance.

Revised View of Council Contributions

The goal for the council performance is satisfactory accomplishment of
their governance and supervisory roles in a way that is compatible with
their representational tasks. The council's contributions, organized in
terms of the governmental dimensions, are presented in Table 5–7. The
guidelines are appropriate to the conditions of the council-manager form
of government. In this setting the contributions of the council can be the
greatest without deviating from either the norms of democratic control
or administrative insulation. Which of these contributions the council in
mayor-council cities can accomplish and how it will do so depends on
the council's resources and relations with the mayor.

With respect to mission, councils need to structure their activities to
provide opportunities and time for goal-setting, (e.g., through annual
council retreats). They should expect support from the executive or their
own staff in developing an ongoing process of reviewing and revising
their goals. They can draw upon interactions with constituents during
and between campaigns to frame the general concerns that contribute to
a citywide agenda.

In policy making, the council's most common activity is reviewing

Table 5–7. Responsibilities of the City Council in Governance
and Management

Mission

1. Clearly formulate the mission of the government. Consider the needs of the entire community and future trends in determining the purpose, scope of services, and direction of city government.

Policy

2. Clearly formulate goals, objectives, and service priorities as guidelines for the manager. Acknowledge and expect substantial policy contributions from the manager through recommendations and the exercise of discretion consistent with mission and goals.
3. Review recommendations from staff with respect and care. Be aware of the implications and consequences of decisions.

Administration

4. Generally oversee and assess the effectiveness of policy implementation and service delivery.
5. Set high expectations for staff's responsiveness to citizens. Help constituents to know how to make complaints to the appropriate administrative staff. Review general patterns of complaints and responses.
6. Avoid getting entangled in specific implementing decisions for projects and programs which come to the council for approval by stressing assessment of consistency with mission and policy.

Management

7. Respect the manager's right to exercise executive responsibilities within the city governmental organization. Avoid interfering in operational decisions.
8. Periodically appraise the performance of the manager and the organization. Encourage and support the manager in improving organizational performance and productivity.

Source: Svara (1986a), used with permission of *Popular Government.*

the proposals of others. It needs a good process for giving careful consideration to them. Acknowledging the shared responsibility for policy making with the executive lightens the load, if proposals reflect the council's thinking and are supported by complete information. Having good oversight procedures also eases the task of making policy decisions. When information about policy implementation and impact is received, the council can determine whether its intent is being accomplished and fine tune the policy as necessary. Policy adjustments can also be made through the budgetary process. The key concern is clear expression of purpose, because it links a policy to mission and provides the basis for evaluation.

Improving the council's performance in administration requires shifting emphasis from the specific to the general. "Checking" activities such as specific inquiries, pursuing individual complaints, and making random probes are important for keeping the council member informed of what is going on in city government. Service responsiveness—an aspect of the representational role—reinforces oversight, but council members need not directly intervene if complaints directed to staff receive the same treatment as those referred by a council member and if the council member receives a follow-up report of the response from staff, as well as information about general patterns of complaints.

Assessing the impact of policies and programs, however, requires systematic oversight and evaluation. Hughes suggests that oversight be accomplished through "regular performance reports to the council on departmental operations to highlight results in relation to agreed-upon objectives."[86] The objective of council members and administrators alike should be to improve the policy-administration linkage to insure that the process of administration clearly and faithfully translates policy into action. Periodic review and program revision buttress the council's policy making; they also provide opportunities for constituents and interested groups to provide comment. In a highly selective way, councils should also identify areas for which evaluation studies should be conducted.

Distinct from oversight and evaluation is appraisal of the manager's performance and the productivity of the organization. This activity is possible in the council-manager form and advocated by the ICMA. In elected executive forms, the council should work out with the mayor the arrangements for review of organizational practice or seek to extend its oversight function into issues of organizational performance. Rather than relying on unsystematic checking activities or scheduling an evaluation only when problems are suspected, appraisal should be organized as a separate activity on a regular basis.[87]

The council has four responsibilities in productivity improvement.[88] It should (1) set the tone for staff so that the importance of productivity is recognized and (2) set priorities. The council should (3) make sure the government is equipped to undertake improvements and provide support—"both moral and financial." Finally, the council should (4) follow up on the program and review progress. Encouraging and monitoring improvements of organizational performance are an important council contribution to the management dimension. When councils have members elected from districts and stress accountability, productivity improves.[89]

The council, then, should strengthen its governance and supervisory performance. In doing so, the approaches suggested in practitioner guidebooks will be helpful, but council members must be aware that none of these tasks is easy to accomplish because of the conditions of city government. For the council to perform well in these areas, it must draw upon the resources of the executive and staff. There must be attention to the process and the relationships among officials as well as the adoption of procedures for governance and supervision. The task of governance is as much interpersonal as it is procedural. The division of responsibility needs to be monitored and adjusted in order to permit the fullest contribution of both council and the executive and staff. The extent to which the council is able to adjust the relationship depends in part on the cohesion among council members, internal leadership on the council, the form of government, and the pattern of interaction among officials in the governmental process.

Variation in Council Contributions

The ability of councils to perform in the representational, governance, and supervisory roles that have just been described varies with the form of government. The theoretical and empirical differences between the council in the strong mayor-council form and the council-manager form will be emphasized in this discussion. It is difficult to generalize about the council in the weak mayor-council form. It may be extensively involved in administration and act as manager of departments. On the other hand, it may experience frustration in establishing its role in mission formulation and policy making because of the formal dispersion of authority in this form. The council is not likely to collect enough influence to establish integrated control over city government. In fact, a mayor with extensive informal resources may overshadow the council. Thus, despite its formal role in administration and management, it is likely to be one of many competing claimants for influence over policy making or constricted to a limited role as in the strong mayor-council form. The weak mayor council will approximate the council in the strong-mayor or manager form, depending on the scope of its jurisdiction, its direct control over administrators, and the influence of the mayor.

The council in the strong mayor-council form is a counterweight. Members emphasize the representational role, particularly allocational and service responsiveness, to the detriment of the governance role.

Mayors encourage and reinforce this orientation. The mayor of Montgomery used "an open strategy of rewarding council supporters with city facilities and services to maintain a council majority" that backed his policy agenda.[90] Policy decision making is reactive, ratifying or checking mayoral initiatives. The mayor is supported by the staff expertise in the administration and can assemble experts from outside to develop proposals, and there is no restriction on using information in a strategic way to advance his or her own position and weaken that of opponents. The mayor can restrict the council's access to expertise and can decide the extent to which requests from the council for additional information will be met. The dependence on the mayor for benefits or positive treatment from administrators puts the council member at a distinct disadvantage in policy disagreements. A mayoral aide in a city with generally positive mayor-council relations indicated that council members know that opposing the mayor means that they will get little help from administrative staff on their requests.

Opposition to proposals from the mayor may also provide leverage for obtaining additional benefits to be dispersed to constituents. In this case, however, the council members' opposition to the mayor may be more symbolic than real and used to secure support in other areas. Mayors are presumably happy when council members become fixers and patrons because the means to resolve conflict with these council members are concrete and within the mayor's control. The council member who opposes a development project until he is assured that jobs will be given to constituents is easier to satisfy than one who objects to the adverse impact on traffic patterns and environmental conditions. In the former case, the governance role has been fused with the representational role. In the latter, it has not. One is left with the conclusion that council members in the mayor-council form are strong as representatives but weak as governors. They serve to check to mayor, but make few positive contributions to governance.

Despite receiving largess from the mayor, council members are likely to be dissatisfied with their performance and role in this form. A report on the National League of Cities Council Policy Leadership Program conducted in the late seventies noted that three of the four mayor-council cities used the program to improve the council's organization and procedures. The purpose of these efforts was "to develop the council's capacity to compete more effectively with the mayor and the executive branch for influence in the city's policy making process (the councils in these cities usually had been subordinate to the mayor)."[91]

These councils sought to create the capacity to collect information and conduct analysis in order "to evaluate executive branch initiatives." The approach reflects the conflictual relationship with the mayor rooted in the separation of powers and the limited resources the council has to deal with the mayor.[92] It is hard for distrust among officials to be reduced sufficiently to allow the council to expand its contribution. Thus, the council's only recourse appears to be increasing its own power resources.

In the council-manager form, the council has a stronger and more secure position. In the Council Policy Leadership Program, two council-manager cities were among the three cities that emphasized improving council decision making and interpersonal communications among each other and with staff. The relationship is fundamentally different and based on the formal authority of the council over the manager. As a rule, managers adjust to councils, whereas the council adjusts to the executive mayor. It is interesting to note that the changes in the council's activity reported in the LBJ School report occurred in council-manager cities. Only in these cities can the council unilaterally alter its contributions to the governmental process. It is possible for the council to play a larger role in the governmental process than in strong mayor-council cities, and this higher involvement is supported by the manager. This happens not because of coercion but because managers value strong councils and because they are potentially benefited when the council is more involved.

The council, therefore, occupies the position of senior partner in the governmental process. The typical relationship with the manager is neither that of a master and servant nor that of two equal partners. With its formal power, the council may dominate the manager but by doing so it loses the contributions of a true professional administrator. It may also defer to the manager to the extent that de facto policy control passes to the appointed executive. Although this council retains the power to dismiss the manager at any time, they may be too dependent to exercise that option. Observers who suspect managerial domination, however, should determine whether there is actually extensive delegation of authority to the manager to carry out policy goals that originated with the council.

The council in the council-manager form defines its own course and sets the terms of relations with the executive unless it chooses not to do so. The council can play a larger role in the formulation of mission and policy making. It is able to instruct the manager about its preferences, if necessary, although anticipated reaction by the manager is to be expected. It has greater opportunity for access to information and staff within the organization. The potential for complaint handling, oversight, and evaluation are greater because the manager is in a weaker position than the executive mayor to block council inquiry.

The greatest difference lies in the exercise of the supervisory role, most obviously in the appointment of the executive but also in the potential for appraising the executive. The prescriptions of the reformers that politicians should stay out of management were necessitated by the council's potential power over management activities. That such interference is uncommon reflects self-restraint on the part of council members as well as the weight of values and statutes that prohibit it. The manager is recognized as an expert in organizational leadership by the council and given freedom to act as the executive officer. Still, the council must be capable of being the catalyst for change in organizational practices, when the manager is reluctant to act, and the agent of change which replaces the manager who will not act. In contrast, the council can not choose the executive mayor, assess his or her performance, nor effect corrective action. The executive mayor will typically demand freedom of operation in the management realm. The council can—in the absence of agreement with the mayor for more extensive involvement—simply investigate and seek to secure change through exerting leverage with the mayor (e.g., the trade-off of budgetary support for organizational change).

As earlier chapters have stressed, however, it would be a mistake to analyze the council-manager relationship simply in power terms. The structural characteristics permit a cooperative relationship between the council and the manager in which the responsive and compliant behavior of the manager is not compelled but rather a normal expression of the interpersonal dynamics of the form. In the conflictual interactions that characterize the mayor-council form, on the other hand, power is a major resource and the council has less of it than the mayor.

The similarities and differences in how the council views itself and is viewed by department heads are evident in the responses presented in Table 5–8, from officials in the six council-manager cities and five strong mayor-council cities from the six pairs of comparison cities with similar demographic characteristics but different form of government described in Chapter 2 and Appendix A. (Selected differences in the one weak mayor-council city will be noted but are not included in the table.) Council members and department heads reacted to a series of statements

Table 5–8. Council Roles in Council-Manager (C-M)
and Strong Mayor-Council (SM-C) Cities

	Percentage Agreeing			
	Council Members		Dept. Heads	
	C-M	SM-C	C-M	SM-C
Representational Role				
A major part of council members' job is doing services for people	61.5	83.3	50.8 *	72.9
Council members should devote less time to providing services to citizens	26.9	37.5	47.0 *	25.0
Citizens should refer complaints directly to staff rather than through council	46.2	62.5	88.1	81.3
A major responsibility of council members is to see to it that citizens are treated fairly	92.3	91.7	74.2	77.1
Council members should try to get special benefits for their constituents	34.6	20.9	10.6 **	41.6
Governance Role				
The council is more of a reviewing and vetoing agency than a leader in policy making	30.7 **	70.8	40.9 **	70.8
The council understands its role in administration	69.2 *	37.5	52.3 **	27.1
The council deals with too many administrative matters and not enough policy issues	45.8	58.3	46.9 **	75.0
The council does not have enough time to deal effectively with important policy issues	42.3	66.7	37.3 *	56.3
Supervisory Role				
The council's appraisal of the manager's (or) mayor's administrative performance is satisfactory in depth and frequency	73.9 *	39.1	68.4 **	33.4
6 C-M and 5 SM-C cities (1 weak M-C excluded): N =	26	24	67	48

*p < .05 based on chi-square for comparable officials by form of government.
**p < .01.

about the roles of the council and its relationship with the executive.
Virtually all the council members agree that councils stand up for citizens and insure that they are treated fairly. The council in the mayor-
council cities is overwhelmingly viewed as a service-providing entity,
an opinion shared by the council and administrative respondents. Service responsiveness is also important in the council-manager cities—
another indication of the universality of this aspect of the representa-

tional role. Substantially fewer of the council members, however, agree that this is the primary role, and only half of the department heads do so. Against the reality of a heavy service emphasis, the mayor-council council is slightly more inclined to devote less time to services and to route citizen complaints directly to staff. There is little difference among council members in agreeing to a separatist view of allocation, although the elected officials in council-manager cities are somewhat more inclined to try to get special services for constituents.[93] With respect to each indicator of the orientation to the representational role, however, staff in council-manager cities are more likely to oppose service involvement by the council than their counterparts in mayor-council cities. Of the latter, only 25 percent, as opposed to 47 percent of the council-manager department heads, recommend less attention to services by the council. Over 40 percent, as opposed to 11 percent, approve of getting special benefits for constituents. In short, the staff of council-manager cities resist the dominance of the service orientation, whereas that of mayor-council cities support it. Presumably, these attitudes by staff do not signify an antipathy to service delivery in council-manager cities but rather a preference for greater council attention to other roles. The one aspect of the service orientation on which the council members from the weak-mayor cities differ is a higher separatist view, expressed by 43 percent of the council members.

In the governance role, the council is likely to be seen as a reviewing and vetoing agency rather than a leader in policy making in strong mayor-council cities—over 70 percent express this opinion—although a significant minority hold that view in council-manager cities as well. More of the council members from mayor-council cities—two-thirds— feel that they lack sufficient time to deal effectively with important policy issues as opposed to just over two-fifths of the elected officials in the council-manager cities, despite the similarity of the comparison cities in size and complexity. Respondents in the mayor-council cities are more likely to feel that the council deals with too many administrative matters and not enough policy issues, even though these councils have a lower involvement rating in administration and management decisions than their counterparts in council-manager cities. This attitude is especially prevalent among department heads in mayor-council cities. Consistent with these findings, it is much more common for respondents in council-manager cities to feel that the council understands its role in administration. The council in the elected executive form, then, is defined by its service responsiveness with negative assessments for its contributions to policy. With its emphasis on services, it becomes more concerned with administration rather than with policy.

The council members in the weak-mayor form, in contrast, reject the view that they are a reviewing agency (only 14 percent agreed) and feel that they understand their role in administration (71 percent did so). In the other measures of the governance role, they are similar to the other mayor-council respondents.

The supervisory role as manifested by appraisal of staff is more commonly perceived to be filled in council-manager than mayor-council cities. Over two-thirds of the council members and department heads agree that evaluation is adequate in depth and frequency, whereas less than 40 percent of the strong mayor-council officials hold this view. The majority of weak-mayor council and staff respondents (57 percent) rate appraisal as satisfactory.

The relationship among officials and differing contributions of the council are further illuminated through examination of the opinions of council members and department heads concerning the involvement of officials in the governmental process in cities with different form of government. As discussed in Chapter 3, the actual level of council involvement in all dimensions of the governmental process is higher in council-manager than in strong mayor-council cities, although lower than in weak mayor-council cities. There is great divergence in the preferred levels of involvement from one form of government to another. Since council members and staff in council-manager cities are generally satisfied, they neither seek to enlarge their own contribution nor restrict that of the other. Council members in the strong mayor-council cities, however, would like to be substantially more involved in all dimensions. They would also prefer that the mayor and staff be somewhat less involved across the board than is currently the case. Department heads are happy with the council role as it is. In the weak-mayor city, the mayor is likely to feel disadvantaged by the opinions of both the council and the department heads who prefer that his involvement be relatively low. Council members want a large role for themselves; department heads would prefer that it be reduced.

These findings along with the other indicators of a restricted role reinforce the conclusion that the council is a counterweight in strong mayor-council cities and restricted to a comparatively low level of involvement in all dimensions of the governmental process. It is hard for this council to actively fill all aspects of the governance role, and it is largely excluded from the supervisory role. The council in council-

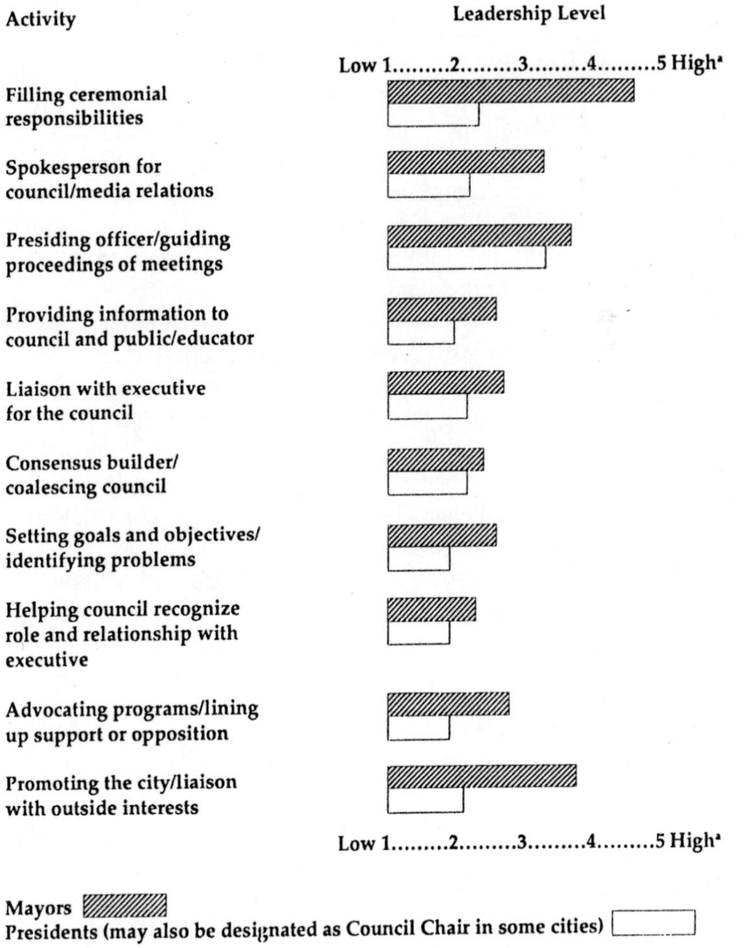

Activity	Leadership Level

Low 1.........2.........3.........4.........5 High*

Filling ceremonial responsibilities

Spokesperson for council/media relations

Presiding officer/guiding proceedings of meetings

Providing information to council and public/educator

Liaison with executive for the council

Consensus builder/ coalescing council

Setting goals and objectives/ identifying problems

Helping council recognize role and relationship with executive

Advocating programs/lining up support or opposition

Promoting the city/liaison with outside interests

Low 1.........2.........3.........4.........5 High*

Mayors

Presidents (may also be designated as Council Chair in some cities)

*Leadership scale based on combination of the extent of activity (low=0/medium=1/ high=2) and effectiveness (low=0/medium=2/high=3).

Data from six pairs of council-manager and mayor-council cities.
N: Council-manager = 88; Mayor-council = 90.

Figure 5-1. Level of Leadership Provided by Mayor in Council-Manager Cities and Council President in Mayor-Council Cities.

manager cities is the senior partner even though its actual and preferred involvement is less than that of the appointed administrator in all dimensions except mission formulation. It makes greater contributions to governance and management than the council in strong-mayor cities, while not containing the contributions of the executive. The council and manager maintain positive relationships. The council in weak-mayor cities may play a dominant partner role and be drawn extensively into administrative and management concerns. It is hazardous, however, to generalize from one case. The council in this form may feel as powerless as other official actors in a fragmented system, rather than manifesting the high involvement and positive self-assessment of the one council included in this research.

There is one final difference between cities with different governmental forms. The council in the council-manager form is more likely to have internal leadership that attends to group needs. The mayor in the council-manager cities may be compared with the council president (also called chair or vice mayor) in mayor-council cities. Although the former is a visible public leader who has already been analyzed as the political head of government, he or she is also the council leader. The council president is largely an internal leader and not a very strong one at that. Measures of the extent and effectiveness of activities by these officials are presented in Figure 5–1. The council president is most active in the position's obvious responsibility—the presiding role at meetings. For all others, the average rating that combines involvement and effectiveness is below the medium level. The mayor makes a greater contribution than the council president in every activity. The council in cities with an elected executive does not have its own visible leader who engages in team building, liaison with the executive, goal setting, or advocating programs as effectively as the council in cities with an appointed manager. Thus, the former council faces a more powerful and independent executive with less effective leadership of its own. It is not surprising that this council feels that it is at a disadvantage. The council-manager council benefits not only from its collective advantages but also from the potential contributions of the facilitative mayor.

Conclusion

In some respects, all city councils are alike. The leaders that constitute them provide a bridge between citizens and city government. They differ in how they define their representational role, but they are likely to view their linkage function as a major obligation and reason for holding office. Council members may also uniformly aspire to be the governors of their communities, but they differ in their ability to fill this role effectively. Councils that must compete with an executive mayor for control of governance activities are likely to lose out, although the council may be able to displace the weak mayor from the primary place in governance and also exert supervisory control over certain departments. The council-manager council has the potential of handling governance and supervisory functions with support and reinforcement from the manager. This council may, but does not necessarily, fall under the sway of the manager's considerable informational and organizational resources, although this outcome is possible.

Changes in the methods of electing council members are producing some convergence among councils. With the increased use of districts, more council members will define the representational role—and potentially the governance role as well—differently from the detached universalist trustee presumably typical in the past in the council-manager form. The ombudsman orientation may become the dominant representational perspective along with a universalist or separatist approach to allocations. At the same time, there may be more activists joining councils who are programmatic delegates representing a distinct policy-oriented group and who are less interested in constituency service or the full range of policy issues. These council members are less likely to be induced to confine themselves to a representational role by a mayor who wishes to exchange constituency services for policy support and to be more suspicious of the manager's proposals. If these changes continue—and some officials contend that the "future is now"—all councils will find it harder to direct attention to the long-term, general policy problems of the city.

It is possible that council members like congressmen dedicated to the constituency service will lose the capacity to deal effectively with social problems in their desire to satisfy the "individual needs of ordinary citizens." Although responsiveness is a good thing, "without constraint . . . such behavior can corrode the conduct of democratic government by undermining the ability of that government to act in ways that improve the lot of citizens."[94] The activist council member who speaks for a "single-issue" group may avoid the service trap but not be able to escape an overly narrow view of public affairs.

In order to improve the performance of the council in both major forms of government, unfavorable or unrealistic views of the council need to be altered. The role of the council is diminished in mayor-council cities by the mayor's comparative powers and by indulging the council members' service orientation. This council needs a more extensive governance role and more opportunities to oversee and appraise. These councils need more resources to strengthen their position in a conflictual relationship with the mayor. The council in the council-manager form, on the other hand, has great potential in all roles. The members must not be viewed, however, as an extension of the professional staff who should neglect their representational responsibilities and approach policy problems with the same perspectives and methods of staff. The representational role of the council may need to be strengthened.

In all cities, council members should be supported and encouraged in the challenging task of being representatives and governors of their communities.

6

Administrators: Servants, Knaves, or Responsible Professionals?

The final group of officials to consider are those who occupy appointed positions as administrators in local government. Administrators—managers, professionals, and highly skilled staff—in government have substantial influence over policy both through the recommendations they make and through their decisions about distributing services and implementing policy, their manipulation of information and expertise, and their discretion in the discharge of their duties. Administrators also determine how productively the resources of city government—staff, funds, equipment, property—are applied to accomplishing the city's purposes.

Some argue that public "servants" with their knowledge, their command of the routines, and their control over resources have become their own masters. The bureaucracy in major departments of large cities represent new political "machines," that is, entrenched, self-centered concentrations of power impervious to control from superiors.[1] To the extent that political and administrative leaders are unable to have general policy transmitted through the managers and staff of government and converted into services for citizens that are consistent with policy intent, democratic control of local government is not being achieved. The notion that elected officials make all policy can be dismissed as simplistic. The existence of "bureaucratic power," however, can lead to a countermisconception, that administrators are uncontrolled and uncontrollable. It is indisputable that administrators exert tremendous influence over both the content and delivery of public policies, but it does not follow that this influence is necessarily used to subvert democratic principles nor that administrative independence (as opposed to administrative autonomy) has negative consequences.

Indeed, excessive control of administrators is not always positive. Advocates of "good government" have long argued that administrative staff need to be shielded from outside interference to insure efficient and consistent government and must have the freedom to make choices required to implement policies and adapt to changing conditions.[2] Political control in the form of interference with service delivery or hiring decisions may diminish fairness and obstruct sound management. The tightly controlled and fully accountable agency may be the most rigid and clogged with red tape, since every action is done "by the book" with no exceptions to established procedures. Insulation does not mean that the agency is impervious to outside control just as tight control does not automatically produce responsiveness.

There is a divergence in orientation that impedes the exchange of ideas regarding issues in urban administration. When reformers talk about separating administration from politics, traditionalists react negatively to what they perceive to be a rationalization for bureaucratic autonomy. When traditionalists or "new reformers" advocate greater political control through strengthening elected officials or increasing the representativeness of governing boards, reformers may interpret this as an effort to politicize urban administration and encourage interference and demands for special treatment. These contrasting views may be linked to differing perspectives on administrators themselves. The issue is whether administrators are responsible or domineering contributors to the governmental process along with mayors and council members.

This chapter examines perspectives on urban bureaucracy and the characteristics and roles of administrators. The value preferences of urban administrators reveal how they view their position and their relationship to elected officials and the public. Administrators are and prefer to be active participants in all aspects of the governmental process, and their behavior is not fully controlled by external sources. The internal controls in the form of administrators' ethical commitments are, therefore, critical in preserving democratic government and responsible performance. The ethical codes of administrators are examined to determine whether they specify the criteria for behavior that is both responsible and professional. Throughout the chapter, the impact of the form of government on administrators' characteristics, values, and ethical standards is considered. In contrast to previous chapters, the conclusion is that administrators are more alike than different in mayor-council and council-manager cities. They make adjustments, however, to their own institutional context and the patterns of conflict and cooperation in which they work.

Perspectives on Urban Bureaucracy

It is not hard to find derogatory things said about the administrators that inhabit city hall or government offices generally.[3] The familiar image is of bloated bureaucrats feeding at the public trough, rigid and unbeatable, insensitive to the public at best and cruel and destructive at worst, mired in red tape yet prone to make exceptions as favors, attentive to the power brokers, inefficient and ineffective. We seem to be more comfortable with this stereotype than with positive descriptions of how the permanent staff of city government works. Still, there are other models. Dvorin and Simmons have argued that public administrators have been characterized not only as pariahs—the negative view just described—but also as technicians and saviors.[4] The application of expertise and technology to the solution of social problems is a central theme of the urban reform movement and the rise of the city manager.[5] The illusive appeal of removing politics from administration was intended to allow administrators as technicians to do their work unimpaired. Administrators as dedicated and capable public servants who save society from natural or man-made calamity may seem to be an image that does not fit the urban experience. Still, the administrative change agents of the late sixties may have seen themselves in this way and have been perceived for a time as quasi-saviors by disadvantaged groups.[6]

This classification does not offer much help, however, in characterizing the attitudes and behavior of urban administrators. The "pariah" image is more negative than the administrator typically deserves. Even if one is critical of bureaucrats, they are hardly social outcasts. Administrators have largely dispensed with the notion that they are purely technicians, although technical expertise is a part of a broader competence that administrators claim to bring to their positions. After flirtation with the savior role in the "New Public Administration," administrators (or public administration theorists) have abandoned the contention that they must solve the economic and social problems of the society.

Another approach to characterizing our ambivalent views of administrators is to see them as either servants or knaves, on the one hand, or as professionals, on the other. The perspective conveyed by the first two labels is that administrators are good if controlled and unprincipled and crafty if not. As a servant, the administrator can make a positive contribution, but if autonomous the administrator becomes the knave—seeking to advance personal and agency interests as far as possible. This distinction is compatible with the conflictual orientation to urban politics since it assumes that power will be used for selfish aims unless checked. The alternative view stresses the knowledge, expertise, and group standards of administrators. These attributes are indicators of professional status.[7] Professionalism implies a commitment to serve along with an insistence on sufficient independence to be able to follow the prescribed methods and values of the group. Conceptually, the professional is distinct from either the servant or the knave. If deference to outside forces is carried to the point of abandoning the standards of the profession, then the professional becomes a servant.

Conversely, public professionals become knaves when they refuse to acknowledge outside control or seek to subvert it. Although professionalism is traditionally associated with autonomy and peer review rather than accountability to nonprofessional superiors, public administration is a "dependent" rather than independent profession. The professional practice of public administration is embedded in public linkages. The nature of the endeavor makes accountability an unavoidable professional requirement. Even when accountability is trivialized or resisted, it is recognized as a requisite of public service.[9] Thus, there is a conceptual link between accountability and professionalism for public administrators. [10] Administrators are not necessarily accountable, but if they are not, neither are they professional.

To be sure, the norms of the group may be used as a mask to hide the exercise of bureaucratic power. The evidence that other independent professional groups use allegiance to each other and reference to established professional practice to hide incompetence, wrongdoing, preference for high-status clients, manipulation and control of low-status clients, and excessive charges creates apprehension about relying on professionalism in public administration.[11] Levy, Meltsner, and Wildavsky are illustrative of prevailing *assumptions* about the attitudes and behavior of professional bureaucrats.

> Our bureaucrat is, like all of us, concerned with his own welfare. He views his agency's policies as affecting that welfare. He is interested in the

agency's clients primarily as they affect the agency and, through the agency, his own welfare. While others may be directly concerned with the distribution of an agency's resources in the city, our bureaucrat is not. To him, the shape of the resource distribution is a byproduct of pursuing his own objectives.[12]

Established urban agencies are content to maintain a steady state in order to preserve the agency's welfare and tranquillity. "Professionalism, in the garb of standards for service to existing clientele," provide a rationale for avoiding new customers or changing services.[13] "Doing his job in the 'right' or professional way" is a shield against new methods and demands to improve performance. Professional standards produce a disjuncture between the preferences of staff and favored clienteles, on the one hand, and those of citizens who do not fit the administrator's view of who needs to be served, on the other. Elitist outcomes result. Administrators may not actively challenge elected officials, but their interests are in conflict with those of other officials. They use "professional" standards to advance their own position and to resist outside control. The Oakland Library was a case in point.

Another line of criticism that stresses the antagonism between professionalism and the public interest is Lipsky's examination of "street-level bureaucrats."[14] Officials such as teachers, policemen, social workers, and inspectors have extensive contact with the public, exercise considerable discretion, and have substantial potential impact on (but little control over) the citizens served. In effect, they make policy in their discretionary actions "on the street." Street-level bureaucrats operate alone with inadequate resources and ambiguous expectations and often experience physical or psychological threat. These officials may develop coping mechanisms that devalue the status of the citizen.[15] They tend to act in ways that are sanctioned by their peers, superiors, or professional groups rather than in ways that are responsive to clients. The profession can be more important as a referent group than the citizen or client and reinforce the alienation of administrators from the public.

These expectations are consistent with the conflictual orientation to city government which presumes that self-interested behavior is universal. Managers will try to dominate elected officials and citizens and will use their influence to promote policies that are compatible with bureaucratic interests. In mayor-council cities, this orientation seems to virtually preclude the possibility of public-serving professionalism. Administrators are either aloofly committed to preserving the professional norms of the agency and are not responsive, or they are responsive in order to win favor with elected superiors or to build their own or a party constituency but not professional.[16] In either case, the assumption seems to be that they are dedicated to bureaucratic aggrandizement. Self-interest supplants professionalism. In council-manager cities as well, Sparrow has argued that city managers are committed to growth policies because the expansion of city size augments the resources of city government and enhances the stature of the manager.[17] Ferman asserts that when power is "captured by the bureaucracy"—likely with weak mayors and in council-manager cities—policy is based on "the internal needs of the organization rather than on clients' concerns."[18] Bureaucrats are more isolated, unaware of citizen concerns, and unlikely to compromise. They respond to the segments of society that participate at high levels, and, therefore, distribution of services is likely to favor business interests and the middle-class. Their "decision-making criteria tend to produce inequitable distribution patterns." The logic of this orientation is that, unless bureaucrats are controlled, they will use professionalism as a guise or a weapon to control city government and to distort its policies and service distribution.

There are dissenters to this view. Abney and Lauth advocate incorporating the "positive aspects" of professionalism into government rather than the "negative effects," such as protecting turf, stressing survival over performance, insisting on managerial control for its own sake, and refusal to coordinate efforts with other departments.[19] They conclude from a survey of department heads that a concern for equity is stronger in cities that support professionalism and rationality in decision making. "Equality in service delivery is apparently pursued more in reform cities than in nonreform cities."[20] Kearney and Sinha argue that professionalism is an "antidote to many of the commonly recognized dysfunctions of bureaucracy"—especially hierarchical control, inertia, and lack of creativity—and "makes bureaucracy more democratic."[21]

Viteritti has attacked the premise that professionalism is antithetical to responsiveness and that political control promotes it. "Politics" leads to inequality because of unequal political influence and rates of political participation. Within bureaucracies, other factors affect decisions. Efficiency—the primary managerial value—is not incompatible with effectiveness. The orientation of urban service-providers is to act in terms of service need (as opposed to specific preferences or demands): "a distribution of goods and services among communities that is not consistent with their particular social needs is not only inequitable but also *managerially indefensible.*"[22] The social and political characteristics that "tend to hinder the poor in a distributive process governed by politics can work to the advantage of the poor in a decision-making environment based on sound management." Equity in the delivery of a service is most likely when the direct political pressure exerted on an agency is low, although response to particularistic demands is reduced. Professional qualities in an agency "complemented by an external environment that allows agency operations to remain relatively free of political interference" reinforce the commitment to equity.[23]

The study of service delivery in Detroit and Chicago—both mayor-council cities—by Jones further supports the view that professionalism promotes equity whereas direct political pressures may distort it.[24] The distribution of services is largely the result of the application of agency rules reflecting professional values. These rules translate the goals of the agency—established externally—into fair, effective, and efficient procedures for responding to the needs and demands of those intended to receive the service.[25] When agencies begin to respond to specific requests for services that deviate from normal service-delivery patterns, they are likely to curtail "routine search" of need among potential clients who are less active.[26] Political responsiveness decreases fairness and consistency in the distribution of services, although it may produce "special attention" to the needs of politically favored areas.[27] There is little evidence that the preferences of street-level bureaucrats shaped in dealings with clients undermine the operation of general rules formed by the department.[28] Indeed, it was patronage jobholders who activated "attention" rules that departed from the agency's decision rules in Chicago. Housing enforcement in Chicago confirms the importance of administrative mechanisms for making distributional decisions based on need, but this case also illustrates that a political mechanism can coexist with administrative neutrality.[29]

These alternative views of professionalism and empirical studies indicate that (1) professionalism does not always produce uncontrolled bureaucratic power, and (2) professionalism is possible in mayor-council cities because administrators are not necessarily dominated by elected officials and political appointees. To be sure, staff in mayor-council cities will have more difficulty acting as professionals because of the greater likelihood of conflict and attempts to manipulate administration and management for political advantage, but they can do so. Even when professionals are immersed in conflict, they may act in terms of a different set of rules than political officials. Their specialized talent or expertise allows them to maintain their independence.[30] Professionalism also serves a pragmatic purpose in these cities as well as being valued for its own sake. When taking sides among competing actors, "the manager needs 'money in the bank'—stored up goodwill from a track record of professionalism, fairness, and success."[31]

Cities with the council-manager form of government are even more likely to stress professionalism than mayor-council cities. The positive consequences of professionalism, therefore, should be more fully realized. The Oakland Library case suggests the opposite, but a more appropriate conclusion appears to be that stressing agency over professional standards and agency autonomy produced the negative consequences. The national standards for library service and staffing prevailing at that time (1965–1966) were *not* being met by the Oakland libraries.[32] Since that time, there has been a transformation of professional values to make them more attentive to client needs and more accepting of citizen participation. "Many municipal professions," Thomas observes, "—in areas ranging from housing and development to police protection to highway engineering—now favor incorporation of community opinions into what had previously been exclusively professional decisions."[33] Compliance with the current standards in these professions is likely to produce decisions that serve the public well.

The reason why the library could act so irresponsibly and use selected professional norms to justify self-serving actions was that "it was left alone. For many years, the library was an organizational isolate, free to be its own client."[34] Such autonomy is, however, a departure from normal operation in a council-manager government. The council-manager form promotes democratic control, and managers accept accountability in principle and in practice.[35]

City managers as general administrators are not necessarily servants or knaves, although they can be either. To proponents of council-manager government, knavish behavior is reprehensible. If the manager usurps the policy-making authority of the council and runs city government, this manager has also violated professional norms and become a politico—if overtly political—or an administrative dictator who operates behind a protective professional screen. That managers are dedicated to public service and to enhancing "effective and democratic local government by responsible elected officials" has always been a basic tenet of the profession.[36] Indeed, from the reform perspective, the risk is not that managers will overreach the proper bounds of activity, but rather that managers will not achieve or be able to sustain professionalism. Far from being entrenched, the city manager is still at risk of being relegated to the nonprofessional or political status of "hired hand" rather than that of professional.[37] If the council either refuses to utilize the knowledge and judgment of the manager or uses its authority and power to invade the administrative and management dimensions of the governmental process, the manager's position is undermined.

Despite the temptation to wield power and the risk of being victimized by the council, the manager can maintain the middleground between subservience and self-serving autonomy and still sustain a positive relationship with the council. The manager's unique role entails providing professional leadership without independent political power resources, on the one hand, or political dependency on all elected officials or the mayor, on the other. These conditions make the manager a true professional public administrator, because he or she is not autonomous but has sufficient independence to exercise discretion in defining and filling the role. Managers are not likely to have an independent political base in the community, unless they are "locals" with deep roots in the city served.[38] They develop direct ties with a wide range of groups and organizations in the community. This community support does not enable the manager to stand alone in defiance of the council or dictate to it, although it may reinforce the distinct perspective the manager brings to city government. Thus, the manager can be professional and political at the same time.

In sum, administrators must be viewed from multiple perspectives. The servant—the "hired hand"—is not the same as the professional, because he or she has abandoned or been deprived of independent judgment and discretion. The professional who is bound by standards of responsible behavior and responds to the needs of the public is not a knave. The knave may have professional qualifications or be unqualified, but by definition the knave is unprincipled in the sense that personal, agency, or party interests take precedence over the broader public interest. The notion that administrators who operate in a conflictual governmental process are always knaves must be rejected. The pattern of interaction among officials may require them to act in a self-protective/self-promoting manner. "Shrinking violets" may be able to preserve existing resources by avoiding risk and change, but they lose out to more aggressive participants in the political process.[39] In this setting, actions in defense of the public purpose the agency serves are not irresponsible. The permanent staff in mayor-council cities—presumably nonsubservient—can vary in the degree to which it is insulated and self-serving, responsive to specific demands in order to establish a political base, or universally public serving guided by fair service-delivery rules. Similarly, the city manager can be knavish—a politico or dictator—or responsibly professional.

Thus, the three kinds of administrators can be found in cities with and without separation of powers, although each is manifested by slightly different types as suggested in Table 6–1. First, the servant in the mayor-council system is the appointee of the mayor, for example, a chief administrative officer, an unofficial chief of staff, and other political appointees or "political bureaucrats" whose first concern is the agency and the mayor rather than the party organization.[40] In these cases, the administrator's loyalty is clear. Hogan concluded that chief administrative officers—despite their professional attributes of education and experience—"are the good servant, apparently sensitive to the 'political situation' of the mayor, and always eager to please."[41] Similarly, the hired hand or administrative assistant in council-manager cities is dominated by the council.

Second, the self-seeking and control-avoiding administrators are more likely to be politically assertive in the mayor-council city—rulers of fiefdoms, power brokers, or empire builders—but "shrinking violets" protect their position with a low profile and passive aggressive behavior. In the council-manager form, the politico may emerge if he or she has a strong local base, but the administrative dictator who claims to remain above politics by asserting that his or her "professional" judgment cannot be challenged is probably a more common political type.[42] The "organizational isolates" are left alone by neglect and bureaucratic pseudo–professionals secure autonomy because their demands to be insulated from "politics" undermine oversight. These administrators may pervert and selectively apply professional standards to their own benefit. Even if they perform competently, they are acting outside the bounds of democratic control.[43]

Finally, in either form administrators or departments can act in a responsibly professional manner, accepting control as part of their definition of responsibility but asserting an obligation to be independent and exercise discretion. The conditions in cities with separation of powers cause professionals to emphasize the public interest as perceived by their own agency or area of expertise. Administrators in cities without separation include not only these agency-oriented and specialist administrators but also generalists who act in terms of a broadly inclusive definition of the public interest.

Table 6–1. Types of Local Government Administrators

| Municipality | | |
Separation of Power	Nonseparation of Power	Characteristics
Servant Types		
Chief administrative officer Chief of staff Political appointee/ political bureaucrat	Hired hand Administrative assistant	High level of dependency on officials who make appointment. May be trained, but not necessarily. Promoting interests of superiors takes precedence over demands of other actors or professional standards.
Knave Types		
Rulers of fiefdoms Entrepreneur Power broker Shrinking violet Organizational isolate Bureaucratic pseudo-professional	Politico Administrative dictator Organizational isolate Bureaucratic pseudo-professional	Independent political base gives these administrators considerable autonomy from nominal "political" superiors. Training and expertise are used to gain advantage over amateurs. Promoting agency or personal interests takes precedence over directives from superiors or professional standards. Responsiveness to demands used to maintain and expand political base or to avert risk to status quo. Professional standards may be used to advance agency interests and as a shield from outside control.
Professional Types		
Professional administrator (specialist and agency oriented)	Professional administrator (specialist, agency oriented, and generalist)	Expect and accept democratic control. Insist on independence in order to exercise professional judgement, but subject to internalized controls that include commitment to public interest and standards of efficiency, effectiveness, and equity. Promoting the agency's or a "comprehensive" definition of the public interest takes precedence over complying with specific demands and produces resistance to directives from superiors that are incompatible with public interest.

Administrators may play a subservient role, a self-directed role, or an influential but contained role in the democratic process. True professional administrators can make an independent contribution to democratic governance rather than obstructing it.

Characteristics and Roles of Urban Administrators

The top-level administrators and many of the staff involved in specialized functions are likely to have training designed to give them special competence to handle their responsibilities. General managers—city managers and chief administrative officers—increasingly have training in administration and management as their professional field of expertise, whereas administrators of departments have training appropriate to that field and have usually been recruited from within the ranks of professionals in that area. There is a higher level of professionalism in council-manager cities, although differences should not be overdrawn. It is a mistake for reform supporters to dismiss mayor-council administrators as unqualified political appointees.[44] Professionalism is signified in part by formal training, mobility, and role definition. Other attributes—distinctive values regarding the nature of the position and ethical standards—are examined in the following sections.

City managers in the early years of this profession usually had technical training in engineering and often moved into city management laterally from a managerial position in business or some other governmental agency; they were more likely to be "administrative generalists" who moved from one administrative position to another rather than "careerists" who were committed to municipal administration. In addition, there was a group of "local appointees" often without training or experience but selected because of strong local ties and support.[45] Increasingly, however, managers have been trained for this field, as Table 6–2 indicates. Most now have college degrees and studied government or administration rather than engineering, and the majority have graduate degrees as well. Even if they started work in government with a specialized functional knowledge, almost all specialized in management, administration, or planning in their graduate training. Presumably, the proportion of careerists is increasing at the expense of both generalists and local appointees. These trends will promote the further development of a self-aware profession of public management, be-

Table 6–2. Change in Educational Background of City Managers, 1934–1984

	1934 (%)	1971 (%)	1980 (%)	1984 (%)
Highest Educational Attainment				
Masters or advanced degrees	13	27	51	58
BA or BS degree	51	42	32	30
Some college	N/A	26	12	10
High school	21	3	3	2
Grade school	15	2	1	0
College Majors[a]				
Engineering	77	33	13	N/A
Liberal arts	6	39	N/A	
Political science/government/history	N/A	N/A	43	
Management/administration/planning[b]	3	26	33	
Other/no information	14	2	11	
Master's Degree Specialization[c]				
Management/administration/planning	N/A	N/A	85	N/A

[a]Major of those with BA or BS degree.

[b]For 1970, the proportion represents those who majored in public or business administration, but does not necessarily include planning, which was not separately identified in the 1971 survey results. The 1934 proportion is based only on those with public administration, since the other two majors were not identified.

[c]Specialization of those with master's degree.

Sources: Data for 1934 and 1971 are from Stillman (1974: 77), 1980 data are from Stillman (1982), and 1984 data are from Schellinger (1985).

cause, as Stillman argues, careerists are likely to be more cosmopolitan, to have stronger ties to the national professional organization, and to be concerned with advancing the prestige and status of the profession.[46] They are also more likely to keep informed about developments in municipal administration elsewhere and to introduce new methods in their communities. Local government managers, therefore, have become a professional group with common training and a national professional association in which practitioners are active.

In comparison to the chief administrative officer (CAO) found in many mayor-council cities, the city manager is more professional. Whereas the manager reports to the entire council, the CAO is usually responsible to the mayor. The CAO is appointed by the mayor in 85 percent of the cities, with council approval in 53 percent.[47] Over half the managers had masters or other advanced degrees (in 1980) in comparison to 29 percent of the CAOs. In 1984, 58 percent of the managers reported having a graduate degree. CAOs tend to be "locals" (45 percent of whom had resided in their cities for over sixteen years) whereas city managers increasingly are nonlocals.[48] In addition, CAOs are more likely to be appointed from another post within the same government (38 percent) than are managers (24 percent in 1984.)[49] Almost all the CAOs have prior experience in administrative posts in city or county government and in private business. The average tenure for CAOs is two to three years and is greatly affected by how long the mayor stays in office. Only 38 percent of the CAOs who served a mayor in his or her first term had a tenure that exceeded three years. In contrast, 62 percent of the CAOs whose mayors had been reelected three times or more had over four years and 43 percent over seven years in office. The average tenure of managers has fluctuated from 7.8 years in 1974, to 4.2 years in 1980, and by 1984 back to 5.4 years.[50] Most CAOs (82 percent) have at least some desire to remain in their present post, but few wish to obtain a CAO position in a larger city (33 percent) or to become a city manager in the same size (25 percent) or larger city (32 percent). In comparison to managers, CAOs are not as upwardly or geographically mobile.[51] Thus, the general administrator in mayor-council cities is more likely to be experienced in government and business within the city in which he or she serves and is selected by the mayor for reasons other than professional qualifications, although the CAO may have extensive training as well as experience. City managers are careerists who increasingly have advanced training in public affairs, have served in other cities, and aspire to move to "better" positions elsewhere.

There are similar differences in the characteristics of the heads of police, public works, and fire departments in cities of over 50,000 population surveyed by Abney and Lauth. In cities they characterize as the "most reformed" with council-manager form, at-large elections, and little party activity, 27 percent had worked in another city before they assumed their current position, in contrast to 10 percent of the department heads in the "least reformed" cities with mayor-council form, district elections, and active parties.[52] Furthermore, only 22 percent of the department heads in the former cities lacked a bachelor's degree, whereas 37 percent of those from the least reformed cities did not have a baccalaureate.

Managers are better trained and more professionally oriented than CAOs. The difference in these general administrators' roles illustrates the contrast between the servant and professional types.

City Manager Roles

City managers have been assuming a leadership role with independence that they acknowledge and others recognize. Managers have long been pulled between the two roles as technician and agent of the council, on the one hand, and "politician,"[53] "development administrator,"[54] and policy leader,[55] on the other. The emerging role is not that of the "politico" or "administrative dictator," which we identified in the last section. Rather, the manager's professionalism is being redefined to accommodate a broader range of leadership activities. Newell and Ammons report that the "policy" role—policy development and council relations—accounts for 32 percent of the manager's time, and the "political" role—community leadership and relations with officials outside government and the city council takes up 17 percent. The "management" role consumes 51 percent of the time.[56] A continuing shift toward the policy and political roles is likely since younger and professionally trained managers are likely to devote more time to them and less to the management role.

These roles appear to be taking hold of the profession, although there is ambivalence among managers as they think about the future. Stillman found that managers responding to an ICMA survey in 1981 were evenly divided between a "Back-to-the-Fundamentals School" and a "Forward-to-the-New-Horizons School."[57] Turning back the clock and reverting to a more narrowly defined role is unlikely. Browne reports that almost three-quarters of the managers in a Michigan survey considered their leadership to be very necessary in policy initiation; only three percent considered it to be unnecessary or inappropriate.[58] They had high rates of acceptance of their proposals, and nearly all the managers felt that their relationship with the council was excellent or good.

The role is more "political," in the sense that the manager participates in the give-and-take of policy formation—the "professional diplomat" activities suggested by Stillman[59] and the brokering role forecast by the ICMA.[60] Newell and Ammons identified a dramatic increase (from 22 percent in 1965 to 56 percent in 1985) in the proportion of managers who report that the policy role including council relations is the role most important to job success.[61] The increase in the "policy" role was offset by a decline in the proportion choosing the "political" or community and intergovernmental leadership role as most important from 33 percent to 6 percent. It would seem that this finding does not signify that the broader "political" leadership activities are less important but that the council relationship has become more highly critical to managerial success. Such a role makes the manager more visible and vulnerable. This change would presumably make the manager's tenure more uncertain and less stable but also make the manager more accountable.

Despite a larger role in policy, the manager's prerogatives in implementation and management are no longer universally accepted as absolute. Council members and citizens want to be aware of and seek to shape the work of staff. Managers appear to be concerned about elected officials' incursions into their traditional roles. Stillman quotes a manager to illustrate this new frustration: "It is possible that the 'golden age' of city management may be on the way out. Politicians continue to assert themselves and whittle away the manager's authority."[62] As we discussed in Chapter 5, council members are likely to continue to be concerned with delivering services as they increasingly take on the ombudsman role. Thus, managers are being integrated into the governmental process more fully. They are more active in policy making at the same time that they are less insulated in their administrative performance.

Chief Administrative Officer (CAO) Roles

The CAO faces different circumstances in determining his or her role. The CAO's position may be secure, producing independence from the mayor (e.g., San Francisco), or the CAO may serve both the mayor and the council (e.g., the "city coordinator" in Minneapolis.) Typically, however, this administrator derives influence from the mayor. Mayors and CAOs in Hogan's survey responded to a series of statements about the status of the CAO, clearly establishing the extent to which the CAO operates within the mayor's orbit. (See Table 6–3.) Almost all agree that the CAO is the agent of the mayor and has power proportionate to his or her responsibility to the mayor. The CAO is valued as the mayor's most active troubleshooter. There is a modest difference of opinion about the stability of the CAO's duties; two-thirds of the administrators agree that they expand or contract as the mayor determines—presumably one-third feel that the duties are more fixed—but 80 percent of the mayors feel that they determine the duties. Only a third of the respondents see much possibility of conflict between the mayor and the CAO.

Table 6–3. Chief Administrative Officers' and Mayors' Perceptions
of CAO's Role

Statement	% Agreeing CAO	% Agreeing Mayor
The CAO increasingly has been made more clearly the manager-agent of the mayor. As the manager is made more responsible to the mayor, he tends to be given more power, to approach more nearly the status of second in administrative command.	84	92
The CAO and related staff have become the most fully realized assets of the mayor's office. They have become the mayor's most active problem solvers.	90	92
The CAO's duties generally expand or decrease as the mayor may determine.	67	80
There is an invitation to conflict in the position of the CAO. If he or she acquires enough influence to be effective, and thus has a certain standing with other officials, it may be difficult for the CAO to remain loyal to the mayor when they disagree.	35	32
The CAO idea encounters one of its severest tests in an effort to give the manager sufficient power to provide him with adequate leverage to infuse values of professional management into the administration of city government.	78	81
The problem with many CAO cities today is finding a mayor who is willing to delegate responsibility for administrative detail to a CAO and finding a CAO who can secure the confidence of the mayor.	63	63
In CAO cities it is possible that department heads cannot be persuaded to report to the CAO rather than to the mayor, or that the mayor will not deal with department heads through the CAO.	57	54

$N = 151$ cities

Source: Hogan (1976: Table 5.2), used with permission of the University of Arizona Press.

The ambiguity of the CAO's status comes through in the questions about independence and authority over other staff. Most agree that it is difficult to give the CAO sufficient power to bring professionalism to the administration of city government. Over 60 percent felt that mayors had difficulty delegating sufficient authority to the CAO and, conversely, that CAOs had difficulty winning the confidence of the mayor. Finally, over half of the CAOs and mayors agreed that department heads and the mayor bypass the CAO in their dealings with each other. Thus, the CAO's subordination to the mayor compromises the former's policy and executive leadership.

Department Head Roles

Department heads occupy the middle ground between the executive—mayor or manager—and staff. In mayor-council cities, the head's relationship to the mayor will either be very close if appointed by the mayor or somewhat distant and reserved if not. The mayor may have difficulty establishing control over departments with "permanent" heads, and departments are likely to compete with each other. In council-manager cities, the manager and department heads are more likely to relate to each other as professionals with shared values. The structure promotes recognition of the manager's executive authority and division of labor among departments. As we have observed previously, a central authority and shared goals induce cooperation.

The relationships in the mayor-council city are likely to be conflictual. The atmosphere is described by Gordon Chase, who commented on his orientation to the mayor as a new "political appointee" heading a department:

> My credit there [in city hall] was very important to me. That was where I'd got my job and that was where I was going to keep it. Moreover, I knew . . . that I would need their help. An administrator in New York City who has City Hall one hundred percent behind him has at least a chance of getting something done. Without that support, he doesn't have a prayer. The overhead agencies [budget, personnel, etc.] alone would eat you alive—to say nothing of the vested community interests in town.[63]

There are also struggles with line or operating departments over policy priorities, jurisdiction—who gets control over a program or avoids unwanted assignments—and resources. In these disputes, political appointees are "outsiders" to their departments, lack their own constituency, and, consequently, are more dependent on the mayor, whereas career heads are more likely to have the backing of staff and those served. All heads, however, compete for support from the mayor, the council, the media, and community groups. On the complex battlefield of mayor-council governments, it is not always easy to identify friends and enemies. All department heads must look out for themselves. The question is whether the department head is able to maintain professional integrity in the process.

The task is made more difficult by the differing perspectives of the mayor and the department head regarding management principles. Mayors usually have little administrative experience, and it may take them some time to realize the importance of effective administration and sound management.[64] Handling personnel matters may be an ongoing source of friction.[65] If the mayor controls appointments, he or she will often choose people who advance the mayor's political aims but obstruct or undermine the head's capacity to manage the department. The head and the department may deal with the mayor on a political level—actively or passively protecting themselves—or stress qualities of competence and performance. The latter approach is "the only basis for a solid professional relationship."[66]

These problems in the relationships between the department heads and the executive and with each other are contrary to the norms of council-manager government and less likely to occur in cities with this form. Managers do have administrative background and respect sound management practices. Use of staff appointments for patronage—by either council or manager—is rare. Managers and department heads are likely to approach the problem from the same perspective—some approximation of a goal-oriented problem-solving approach and commitment to efficiency and effectiveness—although they may have different policy priorities. Departmental perspectives may collide, and the manager or council must arbiter the resolution,[67] but these instances are less common than in mayor-council cities and the resolution is more likely to be achieved by administrative officials alone. Rational principles and professional criteria shape internal relationships and provide the criteria for solving problems.

Similarities and differences in relationships in mayor-council and council-manager cities are found in department heads' perceptions of the objectives of the executive and what factors the council considers important in making departmental appropriations. From Abney and Lauth's survey of department heads, attitudes toward the mayor in "least" or the city manager in "most" reformed cities may be compared.[68] Managers are perceived to place much greater emphasis on efficiency, effectiveness, and equity than are mayors. The elected executives, in turn, are thought to emphasize maintaining and expanding services more than managers. The at-large, nonpartisan council is expected by 53 percent of the department heads to give the city manager's recommendation greatest weight among all factors that affect budget decisions. Only 32 percent of their counterparts in mayor-council cities feel that the district, partisan council would place most importance on the mayor's recommendation. If the weight of the executive's recommendation is set aside and the importance of other factors compared, the council in the most-reformed cities is perceived to rank quality of information, effectiveness in accomplishing objectives, and reputation for efficiency more highly than does the council in the least-reformed cities. The latter gives greater weight than the former to strength of clientele and services for constituents, although neither of these factors is nearly as important in either type of city as the "rational" factors.

The picture that emerges from these data is that the department heads in unreformed cities see themselves in competition with elected officials. They can play the mayor off against the council since they perceive that the council does not usually give the greatest weight to the mayor's recommendation. They can use support from their own clientele and channeling services to the council members' constituents as ways to secure appropriations. In the cities with managers and other reform institutions, in contrast, department heads feel that making good use of resources, getting results, and promoting equity in service delivery are important to the manager as well as to the council. The quality of information provided to the council is viewed as a very important factor in appropriations by most of these department heads; 75 percent rank it first or second if the executive's recommendation is removed from the rankings as opposed to 52 percent of the department heads in mayor-council cities. These attitudes reinforce each other to produce a professional orientation in the most reformed cities in comparison to the mix of professional and political in the least reformed cities. When institutional features are mixed—some reform and unreformed structures used together—the attitudes of department heads fall between those in the cities that use either reform or traditional structures.

Gruber infers from interviews with top and midlevel managers in three departments of a medium-sized mayor-council city in the Northeast that administrators consider themselves to be relatively free of democratic control. Furthermore, they "do not perceive much need for it."[69] They are insulated from elected officials, do not relate to the purposes of their department, and have negative attitudes toward the mayor and the council. Elected officials are perceived to make contact with them only to lodge complaints and to get special treatment for constituents. Administrators acknowledge the authority of elected officials over policy making, but they define policy to mean a vague and nonconstricting purpose (e.g., "educating children" as the "policy" for the schools). They include in "administration" everything else done in pursuit of that goal and stress their responsibility for it.[70] Although Gruber generalizes about the weakness of democratic control for "bureaucrats" in local government generally, the characteristics she describes are generally consistent with Abney and Lauth's findings for unreformed cities but not for reformed cities.[71] In contrast to Gruber's results, Nardulli and Stonecash find that the manager and police administrators in a council-manager city (Champaign, Illinois) have a "strong sensitivity to the climate of public opinion" and to the council's views on administrative actions.[72] Officials evidence a "concern for both rationalistic and political considerations."

An "exchange theory" of bureaucratic control propounded by Gruber is also more appropriate to the mayor-council setting. In this approach, which is compatible with the conflictual pattern, elected officials must use things administrators want—like financial resources—to "exchange" for control.[73] When Nardulli and Stonecash use this concept, however, control and responsiveness are not in doubt: "in exchange for the acceptable delivery of the desired type and quality of a particular service, agency officials attempt to secure financial and political support." Although one must be careful generalizing from comparisons of two case studies, in the council-manager city, adequate services that respond to council preferences precede the effort by administrators to secure resources. In the mayor-council city, responsive service delivery must be achieved by withholding resources and inserting elected officials and the public into insulated administrative processes. Abney and Lauth's data point in the same direction. It would appear that administrators in mayor-council cities have a tendency to perceive the council to be operating in a manipulative way and to be relatively uninterested in good quality information and departmental effectiveness and efficiency, whereas control by the manager and council is expected in the council-manager cities. The impact of structural features of city government need to be considered before concluding that all local "bureaucrats" resist control. Indeed, the distancing of elected officials may be the protective—but not necessarily knavish—behavior that administrators pursue to protect their programs and services from interference in mayor-council cities.

In sum, administrators are significant policy actors in addition to filling administrative and management roles. We have slighted the management roles to emphasize activities that require extensive interaction with elected officials.[75] Administrators as actors in the dimensions of governance may place varying degrees of emphasis on political and professional factors. This difference reflects the institutional setting in which the manager works and how the tension among servant, knave, and professional orientations is resolved. If the council or mayor expect administrators to be knaves and take measures to undermine their power, administrators are likely to fulfill the expectation and act in self-protective ways. In view of the extensive contributions the administrator makes to policy making and the extent to which administrators determine their own role by their attitudes and behavior, further exploration of the values of administrators is needed.

Values of Urban Administrators

In their attitudes and values, professional administrators and other highly trained specialists such as planners or social workers tend to be service oriented and committed to helping the public, at least in the abstract. By training and orientation, they are likely to place a premium on rational approaches, the orderly management of affairs, and reasonable resolutions of conflict. They will blend various quantities of idealism and realism in their proposals but have an openness to change and new ideas.[76] They take a long-term perspective and recognize that changes often take time to show results. Nalbandian and Edwards report that Master of Public Administration students and recipients—many of whom in their sample are or will be city managers—share with those trained in business administration a positive orientation to values associated with management, planning, and professionalism.[77] They share with social workers a preference for innovativeness and the public interest that is greater than that of business administrators. Public administrators are less empathic than social workers but more so than business administrators.

Several studies of city managers and a single survey of chief administrative officers offer insights into the value preferences of general managers regarding their role in the governmental process. The results have been compiled in Table 6–4. Most managers believe they should take an active part in policy leadership, and the chief administrative officers tend to agree. Most of the city and county managers in a North Carolina survey feel that they should promote equity both through advocating new services and through delivery of existing services. These

Table 6-4. Value Commitments of City/County Managers and Chief Administrative Officers (CAOs)

Value Commitments	N. C. City Mgrs.[a]	N. C. County Mgrs.[b]	Okla. City Mgrs.[c]	Calif. City Mgrs.[d]	CAOs[e]
Policy and Administrative Initiatives					
A manager should advocate major changes in policies	81	79	85	81	77
A manager should assume leadership in shaping municipal policies	80	88	89	88	N/A
A manager should advocate new services in order to promote equity and fairness for low-income groups and minorities	88	90	N/A	N/A	N/A
A manager should promote actively equity and fairness in the distribution of existing city services	100	100	N/A	N/A	N/A
Political Involvement					
A manager should facilitate the expression of citizen opinions even if they counter council views	77	67	N/A	N/A	N/A
A manager should maintain a neutral stand on any issues on which the community is divided	47	48	36	24	46
A manager should advocate policies to which important parts of the community may be hostile	59	28	24	55	37
A manager should work through the most powerful members of the community to achieve policy goals	N/A	N/A	47	53	51

(continued)

Table 6–4. (*Continued*)

Value Commitments	N. C. City Mgrs.[a]	N. C. County Mgrs.[b]	Okla. City Mgrs.[c]	Calif. City Mgrs.[d]	CAOs[e]	
Relations with the Council						
A manager should consult with the council before drafting his own budget (CAOs-consult with mayor)	62	75	40	31	85	(consult with mayor)
A manager should act as an administrator and leave policy matters to the council (CAOs-leave to mayor and council)	52	54	53	22	56	(leave to mayor and council)
A manager should make it clear to council when they are intruding in administrative areas	93	88	N/A	N/A	N/A	
A manager should insist on having a free hand in directing the internal operations of city government	90	84	N/A	N/A	N/A	
Electoral Politics						
A manager should encourage people whom he respects to run for city council	N/A	N/A	58	44	N/A	
A manager should give a helping hand to good councilmen who are coming up for reelection	N/A	N/A	35	25	N/A	
N =	131	59	55	59	151	

[a]Svara (1988a).

[b]Svara (1988a).

[c]Hirlinger and England (1986: 27); data from 1983.

[d]Loveridge (1971: 49); data from the Bay Area, 1966–1967.

[e]Hogan (1976: 46–47).

respondents indicate high support—particularly in cities—for citizen participation. This finding suggests that the pattern observed in Cincinnati where managers became not only supporters but initiators of citizen participation measures is widespread.[78] The measures of political activism are mixed across the studies. The California managers were the least likely to feel that they should remain neutral, and the North Carolina managers and the CAOs were the most cautious. When the issue, however, is advocating policies in the face of substantial opposition, the city managers in North Carolina and California are similarly adventuresome; the county managers, Oklahoma city managers, and CAOs disagree with advocacy in this situation. Approximately half of the managers would work through powerful members of the community to achieve policy goals.

In their relations with the council and, in the case of the CAO, with the mayor, there is considerable variation across the surveys in opinions about whether the manager should consult with political superiors before drafting the budget. Almost all CAOs feel that consultation is necessary, as do three-quarters of the county managers and two-thirds of the city managers in North Carolina. Most of the Oklahoma and Bay Area managers develop the budget independently of the council. Actual practice of city managers conforms more closely to the attitudes expressed in North Carolina than in Oklahoma or the Bay Area. In a national survey, Green reports that in practice 90 percent of the managers always or sometimes consult with the council before drafting the budget (56 percent always do so), 81 percent regularly consult the council before appointing department heads (46 percent always), and 85 percent consult the council before removing department heads (54 percent always).[79] Elected officials—the council in council-manager cities and the mayor in mayor-council cities—have the opportunity for involvement in executive functions through consultation, although managers differ in the degree to which they feel this should be happening.

The attitudes of the Bay Area managers most strongly depart from the traditional precept than the manager should concentrate on administration and leave policy to the council. A majority of the managers in the other studies and the CAOs agree with this position, even though it contradicts their own opinions regarding policy advocacy and leadership. Perhaps the orientation of the Bay Area managers reflects a level of training and emphasis on the social sciences that was unusual for the mid-sixties and the activism among professionals during this time.[80] The majority opinion in favor of emphasizing administration in the other studies may indicate that most managers are more comfortable with administrative matters, where their expertise is recognized. Indeed, the North Carolina managers overwhelmingly agree that they should steer the council away from intrusion in administrative matters and should insist on having a free hand in internal operations. These attitudes appear to be consistent with the ambivalence about future roles reported by Stillman.[81] In practice, 66 percent of city managers report that they sometimes "act as an administrator, and leave policy matters to the council" and 19 percent always do so.[82] The Bay Area managers' opinions from twenty years ago seem to be atypical in their insistence on independence in policy formation and discharging executive functions and their disdain of the administrative role.

Since administrative roles interact with those of elected officials, the views of elected officials about managerial values are also important. The contrast between the attitudes of California managers and their council members—their "nearly mutually exclusive conceptions of the policy role"[83]—has been the foundation for the generalization that administrators and elected officials in council-manager government are at odds with each other. In contrast to what Hogan characterizes as "open hostility between city managers and their councils" regarding the manager's policy role, the mayor and the CAO have a high degree of consensus on role definitions.[84] This interpretation appears to counter the thesis that in mayor-council governments officials are likely to experience conflict, and in council-manager governments, cooperation. Data from the council-manager cities in the six pairs of cities I have studied help to clarify the nature of attitudes and relationships among officials. Findings reported in Chapter 3 indicated that the council's preferences regarding managers' involvement in all dimensions of the governmental process corresponded quite closely to their actual involvement, but this acceptance of the manager's contributions may mask a divergence in attitudes.

Examination of the opinions of administrators and elected officials regarding the administrator's role from Loveridge, Hogan, and the six case-study cities with council-manager form of government is instructive. Two major conclusions emerge. First, council members in the six cities more often agree with department heads on definitions of the manager's policy role than Loveridge found. This occurs because the council members accept a broader role for the manager than the Bay Area council members did or because the department heads view the manager's position to be somewhat more restricted than did the Bay

Area managers. As indicated in Table 6–5, the council members in the six cities overwhelmingly agree that the manager should (1) assume leadership in shaping pol cies, (2) advocate major changes in policy, (3) advocate new services to promote equity, (4) actively promote equity in service delivery, and (5) foster citizen participation. On the first two items, the Bay Area council members were split—tending to oppose a leadership position for the manager but strongly supporting the manager's advocacy of policy changes.[85] The attitudes of all respondents is quite similar with regard to the manager's taking sides in community controversies. Managers and council members are almost evenly split about whether the manager should advocate policies if there is significant opposition. About three-fifths of the council members want the manager to remain neutral when the community is divided, but three-

Table 6–5. Policy Roles of City Administrators: Perceptions of Administrators and Elected Officials in Three Studies

| *Perceptions* | *Loveridge[a]* | | *Six C-M Cities* | | *Hogan[b]* | |
	City Mgrs.	*Council Members*	*Dept. Heads*	*Council Members*	*CAO*	*Mayor*
A manager should advocate major changes in policies	88	82	69	77	77	61
A manager should assume leadership in shaping municipal policies	88	43	84	81	N/A	N/A
A manager should maintain a neutral stand on any issues on which the community is divided	24	63	25	62	46	68
A manager should advocate policies to which important parts of the community may be hostile	55	47	49	48	37	23
A manager should work through the most powerful members of the community to achieve policy goals	53	15	40	36	51	50

(continued)

Table 6–5. (*Continued*)

Perceptions	Loveridge[a]		Six C-M Cities		Hogan[b]	
	City Mgrs.	Council Members	Dept. Heads	Council Members	CAO	Mayor
A manager should consult with the council before drafting his own budget (CAO consult with mayor)	31	49	50	62	85	87
A manager should act as an administrator and leave policy matters to the council (and mayor for CAO)	22	87	62	72	56	77
A manager should facilitate the expression of citizen opinions even if they counter council views	N/A	N/A	75	96	N/A	N/A
A manager should advocate new services in order to promote equity and fairness for low-income groups and minorities	N/A	N/A	85	92	N/A	N/A
A manager should promote actively equity and fairness in the distribution of existing city services	N/A	N/A	97	100	N/A	N/A
A manager should make it clear to council when they are intruding in administrative areas	N/A	N/A	94	89	N/A	N/A
A manager should insisit on having a free hand in directing the internal operations of city government	N/A	N/A	96	89	N/A	N/A
N =	59	353	68	26	151	151

[a]Loveridge (1971: 49, 86).

[b]Hogan (1976: 46–47).

quarters of the administrators do not agree. The council members interviewed in the case-study cities are more tolerant of the manager's working through powerful members of the community,[86] and department heads are more likely to feel that managers should consult with the council on the budget. Council members in the six cities want to be informed when they are involved inappropriately in what they recognize to be the manager's sphere of activity.

As Loveridge found, most council members feel that the manager should act as an administrator and leave policy matters to the council, even though the council members recognize and accept the manager as a major contributor to policy. The difference in findings is that most department heads agree, as we observed in North Carolina and Oklahoma surveys, whereas managers in the Bay Area rejected this notion. In contrast to the "mutually exclusive conceptions" of the manager's policy role, the findings from the six cities indicate highly similar views with only one exception: councils are more cautious than department heads about the manager's getting involved in controversy. This difference may occasionally be the source of tension but hardly "open hostility."

When the attitudes of officials in mayor-council cities are compared, a second conclusion emerges. The CAO's position is usually defined more narrowly than the manager's, and the mayor's attitude tends to be more negative or restrictive than the council's. The CAO and mayor are close in their perceptions of the administrator's role, although not necessarily closer than the council and the manager. If simple differences in percentages are compared, they are much closer than the manager and council in the Bay Area cities (as Hogan emphasizes) but slightly less close than in the six cities. The mayors are least supportive of the administrators' advocating major changes in policy and countering hostility of segments of the community, and CAOs are less inclined than managers to do so. The mayors are most likely to feel that the administrator should remain neutral on controversial issues and consult on the budget, and CAOs are more likely to agree than managers. Finally, three-quarters of the mayors accept the idea that the CAO should confine himself or herself to administration, and a majority of CAOs agree (although the proportion is slightly lower than among the department heads in the six council-manager cities.) Although half the mayors and CAOs feel that the CAO should work through powerful members of the community to achieve policy goals, one presumes from other opinions that the CAO would be acting as the agent of the mayor.

In conclusion, the manager expects and is given a broader scope of responsibility than is the CAO. There is some tension in the relationship between the council and the manager produced by role definitions that occasionally diverge, but apparently not the sharp disparity reported by Loveridge. CAOs are close to the mayors who appoint them, but more constrained in their participation in the policy process than are managers. These findings provide further evidence that the CAO is subservient—the "good servant" as Hogan concludes—whereas the city manager has the blend of accountability and independence required to be a politically responsible professional.[87]

If one moves below the level of general managers to compare the attitudes of department heads in different governmental settings, other differences emerge. If the CAO is more "political" than the manager in the sense of being an extension of the political will of the mayor, the department heads in "unreformed" governments are more "political" in other ways. They are less committed to rationality and equity as objectives for their departments and slightly more concerned about preserving or expanding resources.[88] Whereas service effectiveness was ranked first by 51 percent of the department heads in the "most reformed" cities and efficiency was ranked first or second by 76 percent, the percentages in the "least reformed" cities were 41 percent and 61 percent, respectively. Conversely, maintaining traditional services was among the top three objectives of 25 percent of the department heads and increasing service levels was ranked first or second by 29 percent in the least reformed cities. The comparable proportions were 19 percent and 16 percent in the most reformed cities.

Thus, the value preferences of administrators are consistent with accountability to the council and the public and the preservation of managerial freedom. These values imply an independence that is appropriate to professionalism but without the desire for autonomy that is often associated with it. These characteristics are more strongly present among city managers and department heads in the council-manager form than among administrators in mayor-council cities. The CAO is very attentive to the mayor, whereas department heads in mayor-council cities are more likely to promote their own interests and manipulate political factors to win advantage vis-à-vis the mayor and council. The difference, however, is one of degree rather than kind. Permanent staff in mayor-council cities are also likely to be professionals who stress competence. They operate, however, within a conflictual process in which a broader range of objectives—including agency protection and advancement—must be pursued.[89] There is a greater likelihood that values which emphasize self-seeking behavior or insulation will displace a commitment to political responsibility.

There is, however, in all cities the potential for autonomous behavior by administrators that deviates from the direction of elected officials or public opinion. To reduce the likelihood of abuse of office by administrators, it is desirable to elaborate what constitutes politically responsible behavior. Stronger affirmation of support by administrators for ethical standards based on responsibility is needed in order to reduce public distrust of administrators.

Ethical Obligations of Urban Administrators

Administrators are and prefer to be contributors to policy making, to have extensive discretion in administration, and to be free from interference in management. They are and want to be engaged in the political life of their community. For citizens to be comfortable with this kind of administrator and for administrators to have guidance in handling their activist roles, standards for behavior which make clear how administrators handle their responsibilities are needed. The concept of "responsibility" combines obligation and choice, duty and external control along with independence and self-restraint.[90] If administrators are to be "politically responsible" and "responsibly political" as Mayer and Harmon contend they should be,[91] they must be guided by standards that are realistic and reflect both the extensive resources possessed by administrators and the full range of contributions they make to the governmental process. At the same time, these standards must be consonant with democratic theory.

To begin this discussion, standards are elaborated for the city manager. Many of the same standards will apply to "political" appointees and career staff in departments of mayor-council governments. Their need, however, to advance the values and preferences of the mayor as well as the council (and possibly another reviewing board) produces some additional complications that are addressed later in the section. Studying the appointed executive has certain advantages. The manager's contributions to policy are clear, since the manager does not channel proposals through the mayor who may block them or make additions and deletions. The question of organizational impacts on behavior is less salient for the leader of the organization, and the problems of defining responsibility for officials several steps removed from political authorities are not present. Presumably, the manager takes orders only from the council and confronts directly the ethical implications of following or not following the directions of elected officials. Having developed standards for the city manager, alterations that need to be made for appointees and permanent staff in mayor-council cities will be considered.

Such standards are not currently available, despite three statements of ethical values available to city managers.[92] These are the Code of Ethics of the International City Management Association (formulated in 1924), its recently developed Declaration of Ideals (1984), and the Code of Ethics of the American Society for Public Administration (developed in 1984). These statements do not fully address the counterpressures and normative issues confronted by administrators who are leaders in city government, yet are simultaneously subject to political control. They fail to incorporate responsibilities of the manager that have been enunciated in other professional publications in the past decade.[93] Furthermore, the statements do not specify the behavior expected of city managers. Bowman has argued that a meaningful code of ethics must be operationalized.[94]

Responsibilities of City Managers

In view of the pervasive criticisms of administrators, managers should be explicit about the nature of their professional responsibilities. City managers have obligations that extend beyond mere "correct" behavior. The Codes and the Declaration acknowledge these responsibilities but say little about how to perform in a proactive, public serving manner. In order to fill gaps in the existing statements, an expanded list of responsibilities for the manager is presented in Table 6-6. To insure comprehensive coverage, the provisions have been arranged according to the four dimensions of the governmental process (i.e., mission, policy, administration, and management).

MISSION

The manager should respect democratic control and advance the goals and purposes established by elected officials. Cooper, who stresses multiple sources of responsibility and control—internal and external, subjective and objective—concludes that, "the fallacy of the politics-administration dichotomy notwithstanding, the constitutional authority of elected officials ultimately must be maintained."[95] The manager should help the council resolve questions related to mission through

Table 6–6. Responsibilities of the Local Government Manager

Mission

1. Respect democratic control, strive to accomplish the established purposes of the government.
2. Defend and promote the basic values of American society and of the community served.
3. Actively assist the governing board to understand the needs of the community and to anticipate the future in formulating mission goals.

Policy

4. Encourage and support the governing board in its development of clear policy that reflects mission, popular concerns, and professional judgment.
5. Provide complete, unbiased information concerning proposals and fully elaborate potential alternatives.
6. Advance the government's goals in recommendations and exercise of discretionary authority.
7. Explain the implications that recommendations and actions may have on the distribution of resources and in respect to values in the community.
8. Be sensitive to the need for change and advocate alteration in policy when appropriate.
9. Ensure that the process of making policy is open, information is available, and participation of all citizens is encouraged. Provide access and respond to all individuals and groups fairly and impartially, while recognizing that affirmative efforts are required to involve individuals who have fewer political resources.

Administration

10. Faithfully translate policies into programs and services and administer them with effectiveness, professional competence, and responsiveness to citizens.
11. Promote equity in program administration and service delivery.
12. Support the governing board in systematic assessment of program results.

Management

13. Maintain high standards of personal conduct, support employees' development, promote merit and affirmative action, and foster a positive organizational climate.
14. Support the accomplishment of organizational goals with optimal use of resources; promote savings and improved productivity.
15. Assert the right to manage the organization without interference and support the governing board in its appraisal of managerial and organizational performance.

Source: Svara (1986c), used with permission of *Popular Government*.

planning and anticipating future needs. The formulation of mission is not necessarily attended to with care and may be shaped as much by "nondecisions" as by positive ones. The manager should provide council members with the information, and perhaps as important, the encouragement they need to chart a course for the jurisdiction.

The manager must also have a broader commitment than merely

supporting the current majority on the city council, as important as that is. The manager should be "cognizant of the dominant societal values."[96] Rohr urges administrators to support the values of the "regime," which for the United States means "the fundamental political order established by the Constitution of 1789."[97] Hart asserts that "public administrators have the professional obligation to transcend administrative neutrality in any cases in which public policy conflicts with the regime values."[98] Frederickson and Hart argue further that the "primary moral obligation" of administrators is the "patriotism of benevolence: an extensive love of all people within our political boundaries and the imperative that they must be protected in all of the basic rights granted to them by the enabling documents."[99] Managers have a special opportunity to act on this obligation in their interactions with the council over the definition of broad purposes and goals for the government.

Implicit in this obligation is the potential for conflict with elected officials or powerful forces in the community. Yet, the obligation to obey the council—Weber's requirement that the administrator display "moral discipline and self-denial" in following orders of superiors—is also an ethical responsibility, not an avoidance of morality, which is consistent with the value of political supremacy.[100] The tension between the two requirements can not be wished away. Administrators cannot be their own masters, and equally important, "honorable bureaucrats cannot administer unjust programs."[101] The codes, however, are for the most part silent on the responsibility to support "higher" values in the formulation of mission.[102]

Managers as active participants in formulating mission should seek to insure that changes in the scope of services, shifts in the burden of supporting service cost, or alterations in institutional arrangements promote these values and do not harm disadvantaged groups. Local values are important but may not take precedence over those core values of the larger society. The manager, therefore, has the obligation to defend and promote values of the nation and the community served.

POLICY

In policy, advancement of mission, complete information about alternative recommendations and their implications, and advocacy for change should be expected of the manager. Managers ask to be partners with the council in handling the affairs of the community. Standards for policy activity, therefore, should be explicit. Managers should be forthright about their commitment to full and fair provision of information and to promoting the city's goals through their recommendations and discretionary actions. The manager should so explicate the implications of proposals and actions that the value and distributional consequences are clear to the council and to the public.[103] Many managers—half in a national sample—make a considerable effort to shift the priorities of the council in a direction that reflects the manager's value preferences.[104] In a study of city planners, Howe and Kaufman found that 69 percent of the respondents ranked high on a scale that measured political orientation, including policy activism; 27 percent of the respondents ranked high on a technical scale but low on a political scale.[105] City managers as well feel they should foster change. Managers should be honest about their policy biases to themselves and to the council. They must assess their own proposals critically.

The manager also has responsibilities with respect to the policy-making process. Encouraging the participation of all groups in the policy process, however, and trying to assist those less likely to participate are not explicitly mentioned. The codes are also silent on the issue of fairness and impartiality in dealing with citizens and providing information. The survey of planners suggests that such guidance is needed. Among the planners, releasing reports or leaking information to business groups, developers, or white homeowners is more likely to be considered unethical than helping environmental or low-income groups, although unauthorized leaks were viewed as unethical by a majority of respondents in all cases, as was distorting information for whatever purpose.[106] Concern for honesty and impartiality, then, should accompany the commitment to openness, participation, and affirmative efforts to involve less powerful groups in the community.

ADMINISTRATION

In the administrative dimension, the standards stress effectiveness and responsiveness; they also give explicit attention to the obligation to translate faithfully the intentions of elected officials into operational programs. When programs and services are created by the council, the manager is obliged to ensure that they are delivered equitably. This obligation, a major concern of the New Public Administration, is rooted in regime values as interpreted in recent Supreme Court decisions concerning the application of the equal protection clause to access to services.[107] The manager should go beyond advocating equitable regulation and service delivery and should *promote* these qualities. This professional obligation—despite political pressures to the contrary—makes the manager a protector of the interests of minorities and the poor in the delivery of existing services.

The manager should also respect the council's and the public's interest in knowing how the government is doing by providing usable information concerning program results. In order to reduce the possibility that staff, particularly the "street-level bureaucrats," will ignore or dehumanize citizens and clients, Lipsky suggests that practices should be simplified and made more understandable to clients, accountability increased and outside investigations facilitated, and involvement of clients in program administration expanded.[108] The manager is responsible for insuring that the administrative process is responsive, not simply by answering inquiries and handling complaints fairly but also by encouraging staff to pay attention to citizen opinions in delivering services. As an extension of the obligation to insure effectiveness, the manager needs to provide to the council information that supports evaluative oversight.[109] Doing so promotes comprehensive assessment of services by the council, an aspect of political control that is needed to counterbalance the extensive discretion exercised in the policy and administrative dimensions by the manager and staff.

MANAGEMENT

The manager should maintain high standards of personal conduct, support the development of employees, maintain a balanced commitment to merit, affirmative action, and equal opportunity, and foster a positive organizational climate. The manager should constantly seek to improve economy and productivity in resource use. Surprisingly, there is no reference to efficiency in the ICMA statements. Balk calls for public administrators to develop a "solid productivity ethic."[110] Managers need to acknowledge their obligation to save money within the array of programmatic objectives shaped in mission, policy, and administrative decisions, but not as a programmatic objective in itself.[111] If savings are produced by changes in the level or distribution of services, these should be treated as policy and handled accordingly. This emphasis on economy is not the reassertion of a narrow accounting mentality and tight control. Ammons finds that high productivity comes when good control data are available and used for self-guidance and group problem solving rather than punishment in a participative organization.[112]

Interference by elected officials in operations impairs effective management, and the manager should insist on insulation. The ICMA code obliges the manager to "resist any encroachment on professional responsibilities." The tenet has been viewed by some elected officials, however, as a screen that prevents them from seeing "areas about which they have a legitimate right to know."[113] A new guideline for this tenet, approved by ICMA in 1987, indicates that the manager "should openly share information with the governing body" while striving to maintain the full extent of the manager's responsibilities as provided in the charter. The responsibility can be carried still further. Managers should not only provide information but also encourage appraisal of their own performance and that of the organization. The manager should invite the council to be a critical reviewer of the performance of the whole organization so as to expand support for improved management and to strengthen his or her prerogatives in this area.

To summarize, the manager should respect democratic control and advance the goals and purposes established by elected officials. The manager fosters democratic government by affirming the responsibility to promote the goals established by the council and to assist the council in formulating goals.

In policy, the manager should be faithful to the overall goals of the government yet advocate change when needed. Managers should be forthright about their commitment to the full and fair provision of information and to promoting the city's goals through their recommendations and discretionary actions. The manager should also insure that all citizens can participate meaningfully in the policy-making process.

In the administrative dimension, the standards stress effectiveness and responsiveness. Once programs and services are created by the council, the manager is obliged to ensure that they are delivered equitably. The manager should also respect the council's interest in knowing how the government is doing. He or she is responsible for supplying the council (and the public) with usable information concerning the impact of a program if the duty to execute policies faithfully is to have full meaning.

In management, the manager should observe high standards of personal conduct, support the development of employees, and foster a positive climate in the organization. The manager should constantly seek to improve economy and productivity in resource use and support the council in its appraisal of the organization. To do less invites encroachment that the manager is obliged to resist.

These ethical responsibilities are appropriate to the unique status of the city manager as a policy leader, implementer, and organizational director who operates under the control of elected officials within the value system of a democratic society. The obligations complement and reinforce the responsibilities of the council, specified in Table 5–7 in Chapter 5. The responsibilities blend the traditional concerns of public administration for democratic control, neutrality, expertise, efficiency, and economy with the manager's policy leadership and obligations to the public. They build on the ICMA and ASPA codes of ethics and ICMA's Statement of Ideals. Finally, they are consistent with an emerging "ethics in practice" implicit in work of the ICMA and Urban Institute concerning effectiveness and productivity improvement. These responsibilities presume a cooperative pattern of interaction in which the manager is able to blend his or her leadership with that of the council. Meeting these responsibilities in turn fosters that cooperative spirit and inspires trust.

Administrators in Mayor-Council Cities

There are important distinctions and greater complexities when administrators serve both a legislature and elected executive within a conflictual pattern of relationships. Whereas city managers have a clear line of accountability to political superiors and the public "above," and unified authority over the organization "below," the administrator in the strong mayor-council city is answerable to the mayor and his or her appointees as well as to the council. In the weak-mayor city, the administrator may be more closely accountable to either the mayor or the council or to another elected official or policy-making board. Definition of accountability is complicated when one set of elected officials seeks to promote different ends than the other. The administrative style as set by political appointees may be overtly partisan and particularistic rather than professional and universal. Consequently, the values of professional administrators may be at odds with those of the mayor and his or her appointees. Conflictual interactions depress ethical considerations. The ethical obligation, however, remains. The administrator is a moral agent, who cannot escape individual responsibility for actions by claiming a neutral role, deferring to executive control, or being viewed as subject to organizational forces.[114]

The major responsibilities are the same in a government with separation of powers, but they will be accomplished with a different style. For example, Gordon Chase's reflections on public management offer a rough-and-tumble ethics based on the implicit premise that responsible professional behavior is sound politics. In the conflictual setting, there is greater secrecy and reticence and heavier reliance on brokering and bargaining. Despite the distractions, however, the values of professional responsibility must be affirmed.

The overall orientation to responsibility is more agency centered in mayor-council cities. Rather than being subservient, administrators must transcend specific and short-range demands that counter the accomplishment of the agency's purpose. In their "manifesto," Wamsley and others assert that administrators stand above the political process (in part) as arbiter and balance wheel.[115] The distinctive feature of the "agency perspective" is reliance on the "agency" as the expression of a consensus about the public interest in a given area of policy and as the repository of established values and practices in that policy area. Administrators, while they are accountable to elected superiors in office at any given time, also have an obligation to protect the public interest as it has been determined over time with regard to the work of their agency. Administrators cannot be responsible if they amorally sacrifice their mission in order to protect their resources and autonomy, or if they pursue their own mission insulated from controls. Administrators must respect democratic control but at the same time strive to accomplish the established purposes of the government or their department. The "agency perspective" on the purpose of programs and services may well be the guiding light for an administrator when pressured by mayor or council to alter course without formal change in policy. Independence makes political sense as well. "Loyalty is not a great deal of help to a chief executive," Chase and Reveal observe, "if it is not coupled with integrity. In fact, blindly loyal aides have pulled down a great many more chief executives than have managers who found it necessary to resign on principle."[116] For their part, mayors or party organizations act on expediency as well. The Chicago machine, for example, "tolerates professionals because it has to," Jones concludes. "A modern service-delivery organization will not work without them."[117]

In the mission dimension, administrators are obligated to defend societal values and should help elected officials to understand the needs of the community and to anticipate the future in formulating mission goals as city managers do. The mayor, however, may wish that certain issues not be raised with the council, and the council may ask for more assistance than the mayor will allow. In this situation, politically responsible behavior may require transmitting information through nongovernmental actors (e.g., through the media or supportive constituencies) when the mayor would block direct communication with the council or the public.[118]

All of the responsibilities in the policy dimension potentially put career administrators at odds with political appointees and the mayor, unless one is willing to presume that the administrator should only communicate with the mayor. This is not possible—even though the administrator's "obligation is first and foremost to the chief executive"—and there is inevitable tension.[119] The policy standards may require providing more information to the council than the mayor prefers or be seen as offering potentially damaging information to opponents on the council or in the public. As we noted in the discussion of council-mayor relations in Chapter 3, most council members and almost half the department heads in the strong mayor case-study cities did not agree that the mayor provided them with sufficient policy alternatives. Thus, offering more and fuller information will both require a change in behavior and may also encounter resistance from the mayor. Dealing with the council can either be made "tolerable or catastrophic" by the administrator's actions: "Good information, professionalism, and a willingness to propose reasonable alternatives to meet legislative goals will aid immeasurably in public managers' relationships with legislators."[120] In order to promote the government's goals in recommendations and exercise of discretionary authority, administrators must seek to understand what the goals are and how departmental programs relate to them. They should not define the council's policy directives so broadly that they do little to constrain behavior.

Efforts to insure that the process of making policy is open, information is available, and the participation of all citizens is encouraged can be disturbing to other officials and subject to misuse and misinterpretation. Since administrators, as well as mayors and council members, establish ties to supporters in the population, elected officials may view citizen participation efforts as constituency building. Since conflict in the governmental process puts a premium on having supporters, it is harder for administrators to provide access without co-opting and controlling citizens. They may give favored access to "friends" and erect barriers to critics of a department.[121] It is particularly important, therefore, that administrators in mayor-council cities be fair and impartial in their dealings with citizens. Active efforts to involve those who view the department negatively are also important.

The administrative standards regarding implementation and service delivery are virtually identical for council-manager and mayor-council staff. The difference is the obligation in mayor-council cities to resist "political" bases for distribution which are incompatible with equity and effectiveness and to refuse to punish citizens because of the "misbehavior" of their district representative. The tension between consistency and favoritism can lead to "powerful job stress" for administrators.[122]

There is an obligation to provide information to the mayor and governing board to assess program results. Whether permanent staff are or should be sufficiently forthcoming with information to be "supportive" or "provide assistance" to elected officials—as one expects of the city manager—is problematic. The adversarial relationships in mayor-council cities and accountability to two "masters" alter the expectation for staff. They should regularly provide accurate information on program results, be open and responsive to inquiries, and cooperate with the reviews undertaken by the mayor or the council. Administrators must be wary, however, of special investigations for political purposes. "Investigation was war," Chase notes, and the way that council members come out as "stars" before the media is "to make you look bad."[123] Administrators are not expected to invite this kind of inquiry.

The responsibilities in the management dimension are the same in both forms of government with one major exception. Although administrators have a "right" to manage the organization without interference, it is circumscribed by the executive power of the mayor and the appointment of political department heads. Consequently, there will be more incursion by noncareer officials. Personnel matters will be particularly sensitive. When there are top-level vacancies, administrators should anticipate what kind of appointment the mayor will find acceptable. "If you consistently ignore the chief's interests with respect to geographic, ethnic, and political distribution," Chase and Reveal warn, "you deserve to have strangers rammed down your throat."[124] The administrator should fight back if the mayor is making inappropriate appointments, but not draw upon the reservoir of good will too often. When the mayor wants to make low-level appointments, there is "no point in losing sleep" or weakening the relationship with the mayor, "but a carte blanche for political patronage is untenable." Some rules are to insist that the department pick the position to be filled, demand minimal qualifications and performance, and reserve the right to fire employees if they do not make the grade. The basic demand of the administrator is that he or she must have the kind of people needed to do the work of the agency.[125] Another approach is to clearly demarcate the merit from the patronage positions ahead of time and not tolerate deviation. Administrators must assess the situation in their department and city before deciding what the division should be.[126]

In sum, administrators should strike a balance between maintaining professional integrity and responsiveness to directives and demands from political leadership. Skepticism about the survivability of administrators who observe the standards for responsible behavior in the conflictual setting of mayor-council government can be laid to rest. Indeed, they have advantages as well as disadvantages in meeting the standards in comparison to city managers operating in a cooperative setting. They must be somewhat guarded about getting caught between the mayor and the council. Openness and sharing of information make the administrator vulnerable in a situation dominated by conflict. The clientele or constituency support that an agency can develop, on the other hand, may provide a firmer foundation for resisting the imposition of change than the relatively defenseless city manager has.

It is possible for administrators to adhere to standards of responsibility that do not ignore the realities of the governmental process but that promote, at the same time, a higher level of honesty, accountability, responsibility, and professional integrity than would result from following amoral values of political survival. In many specific choices regarding behavior, the administrator can be guided by an agency perspective on how the public interest is to be attained. This perspective encompasses the mission and policy decisions that have been made over time in that government and the tradition of service in that agency. Relying on this perspective implies a segmentation of city administration into functional orientations, but it insures that the public will continue to receive the programs and services that have developed political support over time in the community.

Administrators in a council-manager government are less likely to experience political incursions from individual council members to alter policy goals, divert implementation, or obtain special treatment in hiring. They are less vulnerable to attack as a result of volunteering complete information, providing a broad array of alternatives, or assisting elected officials in thorough oversight and appraisal. Accountability is achieved without conflict in this setting. Managers and career administrators can be less cautious about being open and responsive. A more open participative governmental organization can be maintained with less segmentation by departments.[127]

Conclusion

Urban administrators are neither pariahs nor saviors, and they are much too involved in politics to be mere technicians. Many administrators are either tightly constrained and subservient in their behavior or beyond the control of elected officials. In neither case are these administrators true professionals, despite their level of training and competence. It is likely that the division of staff into the categories of servants and knaves is more common in mayor-council government with its emphasis on power and control to resolve conflict. The council-manager form, however, also has managers who are administrative assistants or hired hands and administrative dictators. More common in both forms—and prevalent in council-manager cities—are professional administrators who act in a politically responsible way.

Administrators have increasingly taken on a policy leadership role as well as implementing programs, delivering services, and managing the resources of the organization. City managers, though still somewhat ambivalent about this new role, indicate strong support for administrators who provide policy leadership and attend to the needs of the public. Department heads in council-manager cities reflect the orientation of the manager with a greater commitment to rational criteria in decision making and to effectiveness, equity, and efficiency in service delivery. The CAO in a mayor-council city assists the mayor but is less independent and has less clearly established administrative authority than the city manager. Department heads in mayor-council cities tend to use the same criteria as those in council-manager cities but to a lesser extent and with somewhat greater attention to maintaining and increasing service levels and to providing services for particular constituencies. They are not unprofessional but tend to be less professional.

A set of standards has been proposed that goes beyond the existing statements of professional ethics and values by the ICMA and ASPA. The standards link public-interest concerns to professional criteria for performance, rather than viewing professionalism and public service as contradictory. In addition, the responsibilities establish the legitimacy of "political" activism for administrators within a framework of controls. The standards can provide the basis for reducing the mistrust of administrative officials and enabling them to fill their diverse roles in the governmental process. No less will be required if public officials are to increase their capacity for effective governance and constructive management. Administrators in mayor-council cities may not speak about their obligations with the same idealism as their counterparts in council-manager cities, but they endorse similar value commitments when they conclude that ethical administration is good politics.

7

Conclusion: Improving the Quality of Urban Governance and Management

There are great differences in the governmental process between city governments of different forms. At the most fundamental level, there are likely to be different patterns of interaction among officials. The mayor-council form of government often experiences conflict, whereas council-manager governments typically are cooperative. Within these patterns, official leaders in city government develop roles and orientations that are shaped by the form of government. These roles in context are not better or worse when judged against each other, but rather they are more or less complete and appropriate in terms of the characteristics of the form and the particular city served.

The differences in "style" among cities have long been observed, but the cooperative pattern has not been recognized by political scientists as a distinct alternative that rests on conditions that depart from those promoting conflict. Cooperation has been treated as a deficiency, an illusion, or an aberration from the normal politics of the city. In the first view, city governments, like cities, should have conflict. To avoid conflict deprives government of a quality needed to insure democracy. In the second, city governments are not actually free of conflict (unless the city has none because of its small size or homogeneity.) Rather, conflict has been suppressed by excluding those who would challenge the prevailing arrangement of power. In the third view, cooperation does not fit and, therefore, is not investigated in its own right. For example, Eulau and Prewitt decided to "not pay much attention" to the "nonpolitical" benevolent and pragmatic styles displayed by over three-fourths of the councils they investigated "because our major interest is in council *political* behavior."[1] The politics of cooperation has not been accorded legitimate status by scholars. To be sure, practitioners have proclaimed cooperation as a hallmark of reform government. They too have often been unwilling to accept the political character of the governmental process.

With the cooperative and the conflictual patterns to guide inquiry into the behavior of officials, it is possible to identify a wider array of roles than has been the case in previous research. Two separate typologies are needed to understand performance of mayors in mayor-council and council-manager governments. Council members can be examined in terms of the same roles, but the legislators in the council-manager government are likely to fill more of these and to approach them differently than their counterparts in the strong mayor-council city. Administrators differ as well, but the orientation to administrators shifts if conflictual behavior is not assumed in all circumstances. The professional behavior of administrators necessarily rests on certain attitudes that characterize cooperation, for example, rationality, goal orientation, fairness, and commitment to public service. Despite our negative stereotypes of administrators, administrators can act in a responsible manner. This is obviously the case in council-manager governments, since the characteristics of the governmental process reinforce responsible professional performance. It is also true in mayor-council governments to an extent that we have only rarely acknowledged. Administrators must reconcile professionalism with conflict conditions. Although it is difficult, they are often able to do so.

This concluding chapter will review the major points and findings from earlier chapters. These have tended to emphasize the differences among cities. The remaining sections will seek synthesis and interchange across the divergent patterns and between the alternative forms of government. First, we shall consider how to decrease conflict and promote cooperation. Second, we shall look for ways to transfer constructive practices and behaviors from one type of city to the other. Finally, we shall consider the implications of the discussion for assessing the effectiveness of city officials and their city governments.

Summary of Major Points

The initial task was to develop a framework within which the characteristics and behavior of mayors, council members, and administrators could be examined. The governmental process was defined as the behavior of officials within the formal institutional structure of city government and was distinguished from the larger political process in cities. Elected and administrative officials make decisions in the four dimensions of the governmental process: mission—goals and purpose; policy—programs and plans to accomplish goals; administration—the implementation of policies and delivery of services; and management—coordination and control of resources to accomplish the purposes of the organization. The pattern of interaction among officials can be based on conflict or cooperation. In the conflictual pattern, officials attempt to block each other because of incompatible goals and competing interests. There is no central authority to police the situation. In the cooperative pattern, officials have compatible goals and complementary interests. The prospects of cooperation are enhanced when there is a central authority that can resolve conflicts and remove the source of the disturbance.

The separation of powers in mayor-council governments typically produces the conflictual pattern because officials have opposing interests. The conflicts of the larger political process are pulled into the governmental process when mayors, council members, and staff mobilize support from groups in the community. There is an inclination to respond to demands for services, programs, or recognition from groups in order to secure support. Conflict is moderated by a tendency toward compromise and accommodation among competitors. Positive reciprocity may emerge within the conflictual pattern and keep conflict in check.

In council-manager cities the interactions among officials are likely to be characterized by cooperation because of the presence of central authority in the council, the integrated organizational authority of the manager, and the greater tendency for officials to share values. The insulation of the council from direct pressures reduces the transfer of community conflicts into the governmental process. Conflict can arise in council-manager government when participants perceive that they have incompatible goals. It is more common for these cities to experience incomplete cooperation based on failures to coordinate their efforts and differences in the interpretation of goals and priorities. Cooperation is not impossible in mayor-council cities if goals are shared, but it is difficult to achieve and maintain when structural factors reinforce conflicting interests.

These differences between mayor-council and council-manager governments have commonly been attributed to characteristics in council-manager cities which tend to produce less community conflict and use of electoral institutions that reduce dissension within the council and weaken linkages to the public. Survey results from council members and department heads in six pairs of similar cities with different form of government indicate that differences in the pattern of interaction among officials result from the governmental structure. Council members in council-manager cities are much more likely to have a positive relationship with the manager and to feel that the manager provides sufficient alternatives for policy decisions than do council members in strong mayor-council cities. Furthermore, elected officials in the council-manager cities studied draw on the expertise of professional staff, trust staff to handle citizen complaints without council intervention, and provide appraisal of the administrative performance of the executive to a greater extent than do the council members in the strong mayor-council cities. Council members from the one weak mayor-council city in the research have a generally positive assessment of their relationship with the mayor and their use of staff.

The impact of the cooperative pattern and council-manager government, on the one hand, and the conflictual pattern and mayor-council government, on the other, on outcomes of the governmental process are negligible, despite the commonly expressed view that council-manager governments are less responsive. There does appear to be a greater insulation of governmental officials from political forces in the community and a greater tendency to respond to needs, whereas in mayor-council cities the governmental process is more permeable to the larger political process and responsiveness to articulated demands is more likely. There is little difference between forms in responsiveness to racial minorities and persons of lower socioeconomic status.

Administrators do not have more autonomy in council-manager government, although they do make substantial contributions to all dimensions of the governmental process. Council members as well have a larger role than their counterparts in strong mayor-council cities, although the councils in weak mayor-council cities take an active part in administration and management as well as mission and policy making. In council-manager governments, the council is freer to define the terms of their involvement in administration and management, for example, the level of oversight review and organizational appraisal they will conduct. Executive mayors, on the other hand, constrict the amount of activity by council members in their cities. The absence of conflict often observed in council-manager cities cannot be interpreted as the suppression of elected officials by bureaucrats. The norm is active cooperation resulting from high levels of involvement by both council and staff. The contributions of officials are consistent with the dichotomy–duality model identified in earlier research in council-manager cities. Council involvement is highest in mission and recedes across the other dimensions. In the strong mayor-council city, the division is closer to the dichotomy model since council participation is largely restricted to broad policy matters with involvement limited to advising or reacting in the other dimensions. The weak mayor-council city, on the other hand, approximates a duality model with division of all dimensions among the council, mayor, and permanent staff.

The patterns of interactions are evident in assessments of the contributions of officials. The division of responsibilities in council-manager cities is satisfactory to both sets of officials; neither elected officials nor department heads prefer much change in involvement for themselves or the others. Council members want a substantially greater role in strong mayor-council cities, but department heads prefer that they continue their limited activity. In the weak mayor-council city, the council members want to expand their contributions, whereas department heads would prefer the same or less involvement on their part. Neither want to see the mayor's role enlarged.

The theoretical discussions, literature review, and analysis of data from the surveys provided the background for examining the roles and behavior of mayors, council members, and administrators. In each case, new perspectives were offered to highlight aspects of the office which have been overlooked or disregarded in previous research.

Mayors provide political leadership in their cities in distinctive ways depending on the form of government and pattern of interaction in which they operate. In mayor-council cities, the executive mayor is the driving force in city government and has at least some formal power resources to support this position. In council-manager governments, on the other hand, the facilitative mayor is potentially a guiding force who helps the council and manager to achieve a high level of performance. This mayor does not need power resources to support performance if the relationships are cooperative. The executive leadership model is not necessary for leadership and can damage the cooperative relationships in the council-manager form. Facilitative leadership is not likely to be effective as the dominant mode in the conflictual conditions in mayor-council cities, although mayors who must function in a context of conflict might usefully employ more techniques that do not depend on power over other officials.

Mayors display certain major types of leadership in the two institutional settings. In mayor-council cities, it has been common to identify several types of mayors: the caretaker, who is weak in both policy initiation and implementation; the reformer, who is strong in policy initiation; the broker, who is strong in policy implementation; and the innovator, who is strong in both aspects of the policy-making process. In council-manager governments, the mayor can make a special contribution to coordination of actors, on the one hand, and to policy guidance, on the other. The symbolic head is weak in both areas, handling only the ceremonial and presiding dimension of the position. The coordinator helps to build consensus within the council and offers liaison with the manager, whereas the activist or reformer stresses policy guidance to the exclusion of enhancing relationships. The director type of facilitative mayor is strong in the areas of coordinating the efforts of other officials and of guiding policy making.

To be effective, all mayors must display personal resourcefulness and drive and offer a vision for their city. The mayor in the mayor-council form, although possessing formal resources that define an executive role, must use existing resources skillfully and generate more in order to gain the upper hand in conflicts with the council and permanent staff. The council-manager mayor may utilize opportunities for coordination and policy guidance present in the form. The facilitative mayor seeks to strengthen rather than to dominate other participants in the governing process. The executive mayor has long been recognized as the key leader in the mayor-council form. Council-manager mayors as well can contribute substantially to the performance of their governments and the betterment of their communities. The position is not a pale imitation of the executive mayor's office in mayor-council city, but rather a unique leadership position that requires distinctive qualities.

City councils fill similar roles regardless of the form of government. Members are representatives who speak for citizens and link them with city government. Council members also act as the governors of their communities, but they differ in their ability to fill this role effectively. Councils are at a disadvantage in competition with the strong mayor in making policy, guiding its implementation, and overseeing results whereas the council in the council-manager form provides more leadership and has a better working relationship with staff in the governance role. This council also has a real supervisory role in the selection of the city manager and periodic appraisal of the manager's performance. In weak mayor-council cities, the council may be able to play a substantial role in governance and also to exert supervisory control over certain departments.

There is a related difference in the way the executive views the council. City managers discourage council members from placing a dominant emphasis on constituency service and support the council's governance and supervisory activities. The council can strengthen its performance in all areas to fill its responsibilities more fully, but it need not overcome resistance from the manager and staff to do so. The strong mayor, on the other hand, encourages council members to focus on the representational role and exchanges constituency services for policy support. For these councils to fill all their roles, they need more resources to strengthen their position in a conflictual relationship with the mayor. The mayor also needs to be willing to include the council in a fuller range of decisions. The council in council-manager cities is likely to benefit from having a visible, multifaceted leader in the mayor, whereas the president of the city council in mayor-council cities is a low profile, narrowly developed position.

Changes in the methods of electing council members are likely to make councils more similar. District elections are being used extensively, especially in larger cities with substantial minority populations. The representational role will be given more emphasis, and council members are more likely to see themselves as ombudsmen. Whether council members will also become separatists rather than universalists in their attitudes on service distribution and programmatic delegates representing single-purpose interest groups remains to be seen. Council members elected from districts do not ignore citywide concerns despite strong interest in their neighborhood nor do they see themselves as representing different constituencies than at-large members. The challenge to council members will be to counter the pressures for even greater constituency orientation to the detriment of addressing the needs of all citizens and the problems of the community as a whole.

Some urban administrators are either under close control and subservient in their behavior or beyond the control of elected officials. From the perspective of democratic government, these administrators are servants and knaves. In either case, they do not meet the criteria of public administration professionalism despite their level of training and competence. Professionalism requires both respect for political supremacy and sufficient independence to exercise expert judgment. There are probably more administrators who fall into the categories of servant and knave in mayor-council government, which emphasizes power and control to resolve conflict. The council-manager form, however, also has managers who can be categorized in the same way. Administrative assistants are servants, and administrative dictators and politicos are knaves. More common in both forms—particularly in council-manager cities—are professional administrators who act in a politically responsible way.

Administrators, who implement programs, deliver services, and manage the resources of the organization, are also major contributors to policy formation. City managers, though still somewhat ambivalent about their policy role, generally accept their obligation to provide policy leadership and to consider the needs of the public as well as the directives of council members in their actions. Department heads in council-manager cities accept the manager's leadership and are committed to using rational criteria in decision making and to seeking effectiveness, equity, and efficiency in service delivery. The CAO in a mayor-council city is closely linked to the mayor and consequently has less independence and less clearly established administrative authority than the city manager. Department heads in mayor-council cities differ in degree from department heads in council-manager cities in their decision-making criteria. They do not stress the rational and public service factors quite as strongly and place somewhat more emphasis on maintaining and increasing service levels and providing services for particular constituencies. They are less professional rather than unprofessional in filling their duties.

City managers have extensive responsibilities that link public interest concerns and professionalism. Managers should be active in policy within a framework of controls. Administrators in mayor-council cities have similar obligations but fill them with a different style. In trying to deal fairly and consistently with mayors, council members, and citizen groups who pull in different directions, administrative officers can justify responsible behavior as pragmatic behavior. Their responsibilities are essentially the same as those of city managers. With a common concern for public service professionalism, administrators are more alike than different across cities.

Decreasing Conflict / Promoting Cooperation

Conflict is common in many city governments. Given the structural characteristics of mayor-council cities, it is unavoidable but can occur in any setting when the goals of participants are incompatible or when rewards are perceived to be zero-sum in character. Conflict, however, can be more or less contained, depending on the behavior of officials.

Axelrod offers four suggestions based on analysis of strategies in winning games in an experimental setting.[2] His advice for promoting accommodation can be adapted to the conditions of city government. First, "don't be envious." If the division of rewards is shared rather than zero-sum, the key is not to compare your resources with other participants and be envious if you have less. Mayors and councils often become locked in battles for preeminence. Superiority as the sign of success is not a good test "unless your goal is to destroy the other player." The best approach is to consider how to improve your own position, even if it means that the other participant will also be better off by your actions. Conversely, a role for one official that diminishes the roles of others will necessarily produce conflict. Officials must take into account the needs and interests of those with whom they interact. Second, it does not pay to be the first to take advantage of the other participant. The short-term gain is offset by long-term losses. Third, reciprocity is the norm: one should "reciprocate both cooperation and defection" in proportion to the other participant's behavior. When one actor blocks the other, the injured party must respond in kind or invite exploitation. To seek revenge, however, by continuing to punish the other actor after a change in behavior invites endless recrimination. Avoiding superiority and responding to only the last act balances self-protection with forgiveness. Finally, officials should not try to be "too clever," to discern deeply hidden motives behind actions. A variant in city politics is an avoidance of excessive cynicism. If officials get trapped into believing that no action is what it seems to be, it becomes difficult to develop a stable pattern of accommodation. If officials want to promote a constructive working relationship, they should clearly signal their intentions rather than hiding or obscuring them.[3]

In a similar vein, Yates devotes considerable attention to ways of managing conflict in organizations, some of which may be applied to relationships among officials.[4] Certain preconditions should be established. These include setting norms of civility and mutual respect in interactions. Seeing other officials as enemies should be avoided. The basis for common action is established by identifying mutual problems. Officials should seek to include all affected parties in order to prevent those excluded from undermining accommodation, to provide full access to information, and to keep lines of communication open. These conditions are assumed to be present in the cooperative pattern, but also help to prevent conflict from flaring out of control. To have an effective relationship, a sense of mission to which all officials relate can be established, even though officials retain other goals that are incompatible. Avoiding negative symbolic politics, on the one hand, and seeking out winning issues, on the other, will help to sustain accommodation. Taking an incremental approach and focusing on concrete issues can help to reduce the constraint of conflicting goals among officials; it may be easier to secure agreement about a specific action than it is to obtain unanimity about the purposes of that action. Finally, elected officials should take into account the needs of implementers. Sometimes, administrative resistance is produced by having to contend with programs that cannot be implemented or laws that cannot be enforced.

Both approaches have in common the premise that conflict is not handled by preparing for battle and seeking to vanquish the foe. Mayors, council members, and administrators in mayor-council cities have to work together, even though they do not fully trust or agree with each other. Accommodations that reflect separate and collective interests can be achieved and sustained. When conflict characterizes relationships in council-manager cities, these same guidelines may be useful depending on the source of conflict. It is also possible that changing the city manager will remove the source of tension and permit all officials to reestablish cooperation. Council members in this form have a choice not available in mayor-council cities; they can replace the executive. They should be honest, however, in deciding whether to exercise this choice. If infighting among council members or deficiencies in the mayor's performance are the cause of conflict, the manager should not be made the scapegoat. Indeed, firing the manager may simply fuel the conflict among others.

In council-manager governments with essentially cooperative relationships, a common problem is the decline of cooperation. Here, methods for goal clarification and consensus building are in order.[5] Workshops and retreats, often run by outside expert group-process facilitators, are used in many cities to identify problems, set goals, and determine strategies and priorities. Communitywide strategic planning efforts are increasingly common.[6] The focus of efforts can be the internal relationships on the council, council-manager interaction, and government-community dialogue. Periodic appraisal of the manager's performance, which occurs in many council-manager cities, can be the occasion for assessing relationships and the council's performance as well. For these methods to work, officials must enter the discussions with a high level of trust. They can come out with a clearer understanding of mutual preferences and intentions and increased ability to communicate.

Insofar as efforts to improve relationships among officials ignore established patterns of interaction, they will be inefficient or ineffective. If relationships are cooperative, one need not start laying the groundwork for more positive relations. On the other hand, to use goal setting and team building in a conflictual setting without first establishing the necessary foundation is to invite disaster. The participants do not have the trust that is required to make those approaches successful. Officials are not locked into conflict nor do they automatically experience cooperation. Properly assessing the nature of interactions among officials helps determine the appropriate starting point for efforts to strengthen relationships.

Transfer of Constructive Practices Between Forms of Government

The discussion of differences among cities is not intended to provide a rationale for substantial changes in the governmental structure. Few cities will abandon their form of government. Rather they will adapt it to their needs and change their behavior and specific institutional features within the existing form. There is much of value in the governmental process of each form.

Many have observed that the council-manager form needs stronger political leadership and greater capacity for negotiating and brokering among contending interests. A cluster of activities that are associated with the strong mayor must be accounted for by the mayor, council, and manager in council-manager cities. The mayor's office needs to be recognized for the contributions it can make in these areas, as observed in Chapter 4. In particular, the facilitative mayor needs to do a better job of mobilizing popular and official opinion. Since leadership is and should be collective in the council-manager form, cities need to make use of group approaches to goal setting. The manager also has potential as a community leader who helps to forge partnerships between government and the community, forms coalitions to address community problems, and fosters effective citizen participation.[7]

Executive mayors need to rely less on power and confrontation and more on inclusive leadership. They will not have enough power to command and could usefully consider the coordinative approaches used by the facilitative mayor to improve mayor-council relations. Councils in strong mayor-council cities need to expand their contribution to policy making, oversight, and appraisal of administrative performance.

Mayors and administrators may fear that expanded council contributions would impede effective governmental performance. One mayoral aide agreed in an interview that the staff would prefer to "let sleeping councils lie." The mayor and council would need to move cautiously into new roles and relationships observing the suggestions for containing conflict mentioned earlier. It seems unlikely, however, that the council will fill a broader range of responsibilities until it is permitted to expand its activities. The rule of reciprocity would apply if the council abused its enlarged role in policy and administration. Council presidents or chairs could increase their team building and liaison roles and be recognized by the mayor as a key agent of communication with the council. The chief administrative officer could provide greater organizational integration if the position were less clearly tied to the succession of the mayor. Even though this official could be accountable to and removable by the executive, incumbent CAOs would be more likely to span turnover in the mayor's office if the position were not seen as being linked to the mayor's electoral success. The tension between the mayor and department heads could be reduced with greater continuity of professional leadership.

Finally, administrators need to enunciate their professional judgments and convictions more fully in council-manager cities, particularly as elected officials become more assertive; and they need to be more broadly responsible in the separation-of-powers cities.

Consequences of Patterns of Interaction for City Government

Assessing the consequences of conflict depends in large part on whether and to what extent conflict is controlled. In most situations a working arrangement emerges among the contending parties so that the business of government can proceed. There will usually be constraints on conflict, both to conserve resources and to enhance the prospects of favorable outcomes in future encounters. In cases of bipolar cleavage dominated by zero-sum calculations of benefits and losses, each combatant will "keep fighting until he gets what he wants—or is defeated," as Royko described the battle between the mayor and council in Chicago before former Mayor Harold Washington gained majority support on the city council.[8]

To characterize the motives of political actors as self-serving is not a condemnation. To many, the political process depends on individuals asserting their self-interests. Ambition prompts candidates and office holders to run for office and to be accountable. The argument that the public good is generated from the competition among parties with conflicting incentives can be traced back to James Madison in *The Federalist*, No. 51. Harnessing conflict to limit abuse of power is the purpose of constitutional checks and balances, a hallowed constitutional principle. Separation of powers presumes and engenders conflict and, therefore, promotes accountability.

The positive consequences of the conflictual pattern arise from developing solutions that both satisfy the claims of the contending parties and also advance the collective public interest. Conflict is positive because it signals the need for change and stimulates participation from citizens and groups. Under certain circumstances, some contend, a conflictual decision-making process produces superior results. If all the opposing positions are out on the table and if agreement can be secured, then the outcome may be better than that which results from a more orderly decision-making process with restricted participation. Since the human mind cannot absorb all information relevant to a decision, cannot know all possible solutions, and cannot overcome parochialism, a decision that emerges from mutual adjustment among the parties will be "better" than one arrived at in a more rational fashion.[9] This is the central normative claim of pluralistic democratic theory.[10] When considering the relationship between government and the public, some conflicts may actually be alleviated by the give-and-take process of conflict resolution. Government can be more effective at dealing with real problems when conflict is drawn out and resolved, rather than being content with the efficient provision of routine services. In sum, when conditions approximate the conflictual pattern in the governmental process, the outcomes can be superior to those that could be achieved without conflict, on the condition that conflict can be resolved within government and between government and the citizenry.

The negative consequences occur when this condition is not met. Governments become essentially reactive, shifting attention rapidly from one crisis to another. Problems become an indispensable cuing mechanism in the absence of direction and control. Mayors and council members are at loggerheads, and elected officials and their appointees cannot control the bureaucracy. Administrative agencies fold in upon themselves, unresponsive to political superiors, other agencies, or the public. There is a standoff between upper and lower levels within the organization, and there is tension between the officials and citizens, neither able to control or secure the desired response from the other. Thus, every division is a line of cleavage, direction and purpose are impossible, and government actions consist of providing habitual services and making frantic attempts to put out fires.

Decisions do not reflect the balancing and blending of divergent views but rather are political resultants. An outcome arrived at through bargaining may be a deal struck to promote the interests of the competitors rather than a creative solution. It is also possible that exclusion will be used to aid agreement by limiting that number of participants and that opponents will be coerced into support or silence. Implementation is problematic. There is no reason to expect this chaotic process to be self-correcting, and in fact the conflicts engendered over decision making and implementation feed future disputes. Stability comes in the form of a "cease-fire" and the retreat into separate official and bureaucratic enclaves.

The conflictual pattern, in conclusion, describes how things are— good and bad—within certain city governments. Occasionally, it develops normative overtones, as in the claimed superiority of decision making through partisan mutual adjustment and the expected higher levels of participation associated with it. The disputes and dissension can become, however, permanent, self-perpetuating, and uncontrollable; and the potential positive conditions associated with the positive resolution of conflict are undermined.

There are numerous positive results that one can expect when the cooperative pattern is found. Governments are capable of planning and maintaining a proactive stance in assessing needs and meeting problems. Governmental performance can be characterized by effectiveness, efficient management, and commitment to productivity. Governments can be public serving and address needs in the community. Officials, despite differences in perspective and duties, can be extensively involved in complementary roles, each making distinct contributions with synergistic effects.

There are potential negative consequences, however, that arise if the concern for cooperation produces a tendency to avoid controversy, unduly emphasizes the maintenance of order, and excludes disruptive intrusions from the governmental process. City governments may limit the scope of services to exclude expensive and controversial areas of policy. Reformed governments have been criticized for valuing economy and efficiency to such an extent that they avoid complex problems.

In policy making, administration, and management, there may be an excessive reliance on rationality and a tendency to defend policy-making systems and implementation procedures without recognizing their limitations. An absence of controversy within the governmental process may extend to discouraging or ignoring expressions of divergent views by citizens. Governmental leaders may smother opposition. The political style of the community may delegitimize dissension to the extent that any critical opinions are branded as extreme. This tendency is reinforced by an antagonism toward criticism and defensive reactions from those who are attacked. A diminution of spontaneous participation may result, and officials may come to rely too heavily on sponsored participation and solicited input. These conditions can lead to a state of conformist, uncritical, and passive cooperation.

Experience of the past decade, however, suggests that some cities can accommodate substantial changes in institutions (e.g., the introduction of districts and direct election of mayor), in scope of services, and in expanded minority and neighborhood participation, all without undermining cooperative characteristics. The logic of the cooperative pattern leads to inclusiveness and fairness. Accountability can be achieved by commitment to service and clear lines of control in the absence of checks and balances and conflict. Still, cooperation creates two dilemmas for officials. One, they may have difficulty handling controversial issues, if a common basis for action cannot be found. Criticism, accusation, strident advocacy strain the system because the capacity for conflict resolution is weakly developed. Outside pressure may cause officials to close ranks, cutting off inputs. Two, it is also difficult for governments to be removed from the political strife of the city while still being responsive to it. Some governments may become aloof and play favorites behind the scenes, particularly if citizens pay little attention to the council and city government affairs.[11] Thus, the cooperative pattern is based on overarching values and central authority. Interactions are less competitive and more supportive. These characteristics differ from those of the larger political process and, therefore, some degree of insulation is required. The cooperative pattern of interaction may, but does not necessarily, lead to beneficial and effective styles of governance and management. The conditions associated with this pattern have great potential for positive consequences. Whether or not these are realized depends on the behavior of officials in the governmental process.

Cities are predisposed by their form of government to a different governing style and are likely to have different tendencies. One might speculate that council-manager cities if operating effectively would have more planning, a narrower scope of services, more concern about effectiveness, equity, and universalism in service delivery, more provisions for sponsored citizen participation, better developed and integrated management systems, and more efficient operations. Effective mayor-council cities, on the other hand, would have more large-scale developments, a wider range of services, more demand-responsive services, more spontaneous citizen participation, more internally cohesive but less integrated departments, and more highly mobilized staff.

Cities are different, and they can achieve success in different ways. Proposals to improve cities also proceed along two tracks. Just as structural reformers have been distinguished from the social reformers in the early stages of the municipal reform movement, one can distinguish those who advocate enhancement of linkage mechanisms and political organizations from the standard structural reform approaches. Many political scientists espouse what might be called the political reform tradition. Ferman advocates an even stronger elected executive and district elections and responsible parties to help insure that substantive policy problems are addressed.[12] Yates promotes even greater pluralism in city government.[13] Hawley and Jones support stronger parties, and Gruber recommends that elected officials and citizens develop greater political leverage over administrators and strengthen the position of political appointees.[14] Welch and Bledsoe advocate district and partisan elections because this combination provides the "fairest representation of all groups and serve[s] to structure political conflict and debate in the form most understandable to the average citizen."[15] Just as the structural reformers were willing to endorse indirect approaches to improving governmental performance and attacking the city's ills—unlike the social reformers who engaged in direct action under various institutional arrangements—the political reformers as well seek to achieve ultimate aims through changes in political structure and process. Their agenda emphasizes strong elected executives, active parties, and small constituencies as vehicles to improve urban governance. One might observe that they are more concerned with representation than with the governance of cities.

The structural reformers, active in revising the Model City Charter during the past five years, still endorse the basic principles of the reform movement. The structural reformers underemphasized representation in their concern for strengthening the governance and management of cities. They now accept the usefulness of district representation and direct election of the mayor but reaffirm their support for nonseparation of powers and integrated administrative authority in the hands of the city manager.[16] Cities with reform institutions have achieved administrative integration and accountability to elected officials that the political reformers attempt to achieve through stronger political leadership. Active leadership from elected officials and careful attention to maintaining the accountability of administrators is required. Administrators will not, however, necessarily resist control nor demand something in return for responsiveness. The structural reformers were comfortable in relying on professional administrators, and research summarized in this discussion vindicates that approach. Abney and Lauth conclude that reformed cities have succeeded in achieving "neutrality" without the oft-claimed "estrangement from clientele."[17] Public managers display greater responsibility and accountability than is normally expected of professionals. The structural reformers, therefore, advocate not only fuller contributions from elected officials but also a larger role and more professionalism from administrators. They do not view the expansion of activities by both sets of officials as incompatible. The roles of elected officials and administrators can be complementary.

In the future, there will be increasing convergence of official leaders in the major forms of government.[18] Mayor-council governments will continue to be more dependent on professional administrators. Council members are likely to become more articulate, engaged, and assertive. The decreasing insulation of the governmental process, particularly as district elections are more commonly used, will increase the likelihood of conflict in council-manager cities. Officials in this form will need to learn how to cope with it. It is possible that convergence in patterns of interaction will occur as well if council-manager governments come to experience real endemic conflict. Either a quasi-executive model with executive functions assigned to the mayor or a council that is highly responsive to particularistic demands would impair the professional leadership of the manager. It seems likely, however, that council-manager governments can respond to the challenge of offering stronger leadership and being more representative without losing the unique blending of democratic and professional leadership that it offers.

If so, distinct patterns of conflict and cooperation linked to form of government will persist. Greater appreciation of their differences will promote interchange and selective borrowing and adaptation of practices. All officials in all cities must seek to become more effective at meeting the needs of their communities. Leaders will be able to keep learning from each other because they operate in different contexts, while they continue to disagree about who has the superior form of local government. In various ways, official leaders can make a difference in the governance and management of their cities.

Appendix

Table A-1. Comparison of Paired Cities

City/State	1980 Population 000s	Change 70–80 (%)	Minority (%)	Less H.S. Ed. (%)	Bond Rating*	Council Size	Districts	Ballot Type	Comparison A**	B	C
New Haven, CT	138	-8	40	34	A	30	30	P	4	2	2
Hartford, CT	136	-14	54	45	Aa	9	0	P			
Knoxville, TN	183	5	15	33	A1	9	6	P	6	1	1
Greensboro, NC	156	5	34	28	Aa1	9	5	NP			
Akron, OH	237	-14	23	35	A	13	10	P	4	3	1
Dayton, OH	204	-17	38	37	A	5	0	NP			
Minneapolis, MN	371	-15	8	23	Aaa	13	13	P	3	2	3
Kansas City, KS	448	-12	30	29	Aa	12	6	NP			
Memphis, TN	646	-2	49	34	Aa	13	7	P	5	3	0
Charlotte, NC	314	14	32	29	Aaa	11	7	P			
Lincoln, NE	172	13	4	16	Aa	7	4	P	6	1	1
Raleigh, NC	150	22	28	20	Aaa	8	5	NP			
Measure of equivalence:	<20%	<10%	<10%	<6%	1 level	<4	<4	same	28	12	8
Row comparison: A**	4	5	0	4	6	4	3	2	28		
B	1	1	1	0	0	2	3	4	12		
C	1	0	5	2	0	0	0	0	8		

*In Moody's bond ratings, the "A" ratings are the highest of three bond classifications. From highest to lowest, the sublevels in this category are Aaa, Aa, and A ("1" indicates the best quality bonds within a level).

**A = comparison falls within measure of equivalence, e.g., if population difference between the two cities is less than 20%, the cities are considered to be equivalent on that characteristic.

B = observed difference should produce higher conflict in mayor-council city in pair (see chapter 3, note 79).

C = observed difference should produce higher conflict in council-manager city in pair.

Source: Data from *Municipal Year Book 1982* and *1984*. Appendix from Svara (1988b), used with permission of *Journal of Urban Affairs*.

Table A-2. Measuring the Level of Involvement by Officials
in Governmental Activities

Level of Involvement Index

1—Very Low: Not involved

Handled entirely by someone else, who may report on what has been done

2—Low: Minimum review or reaction appropriate to situation

Examples would be giving a routine OK to someone else's recommendations,
providing the opportunity to react as a courtesy, or making comments

3—Moderate: Advising or reviewing

Examples include making suggestions, reviewing recommendations, seeking
information or clarification, ratifying proposals

4—High: Leading, guiding, or pressuring

Examples are initiating; making proposals; advocating, promoting, or opposing;
carefully reviewing and revising a proposal

5—Very High: Handle entirely

No one else directly involved but others may be informed of actions taken

Activities for Which Involvement Is Rated*

Mission

16. Changing governmental institutions
    or revising the charter
17. Determining the level of taxes and
    fees
24. Determining the purpose and scope
    of city government
6. Deciding to undertake new or
    eliminate old services (not simple
    change in level)
1. Identifying problems, analyzing
    future trends for the city
8. Developing strategies for future
    development of the city

Administration

12. Investigating citizen complaints
10. Specific decisions about allocating
    services
13. Making specific decisions that are
    part of larger projects, site
    selection, facility design
7. Delivering services to citizens
23. Evaluating programs
29. Setting standards for employee
    treatment of citizens in service
    delivery
22. Developing operating procedures
    for programs: definition of
    eligibility, application methods,
    award criteria, etc.

Policy

25. Budget review and approval
5. Specific decisions concerning
    planning and zoning
19. Deciding to participate in federal
    aid programs

Management

14. Awarding large contracts
27. Determining wages and benefits for
    employees
18. Assessing organizational
    performance

(continued)

Table A-2. (*Continued*)

*Activities for Which Involvement is Rated**

Policy	Management
21. Initiating or cancelling programs	26. Proposing changes in management practices or organization
2. Developing annual program goals and objectives	28. Handling complaints from employees
9. Determining formula for allocating services	15. Routine contracting and purchasing
11. Formulating the proposed budget	3. Hiring decisions about department heads
20. Developing appliations for federal funds	4. Hiring decisions about other staff

*Number at left indicates the order of the activity in the questionnaire.

Notes

Chapter 1

1. John Shannon, "The Return to Fend-for-Yourself Federalism: The Reagan Mark," *Intergovernmental Perspective* 13 (Summer/Fall, 1987): 34–37.

2. A. Wuffle, "Reflections on Academia," *PS* 29 (Winter, 1986): 57.

3. David Easton, *The Political System* (Chicago: University of Chicago Press, 1963), p. 129.

4. Bryan D. Jones, *Governing Buildings and Building Government* (University, Ala.: University of Alabama Press, 1985), pp. 44–47, distinguishes between the substantive policy system and the management control policy system. Judith E. Gruber, *Controlling Bureaucracies* (Berkeley: University of California Press, 1987), pp. 13–14, distinguishes substantive constraint of the ends pursued by administrators from procedural constraint of methods used.

5. Wallace S. Sayre and Herbert Kaufman, *Governing New York City* (New York: Sage, 1960); Robert A. Dahl, *Who Governs?* (New Haven: Yale University Press, 1961); Edward C. Banfield, *Political Influence* (New York: Free Press, 1965); Allan Talbot, *The Mayor's Game* (New York: Harper & Row, 1967); James V. Cunningham, *Urban Leadership in the Sixties* (Cambridge, Mass.: Schenkman, 1970); John P. Kotter and Paul R. Lawrence, *Mayors in Action* (New York: Wiley, 1974); Charles H. Levine, *Racial Conflict and the American Mayor* (Lexington, Mass.: Lexington Books, 1974); Raymond E. Wolfinger, *The Politics of Progress* (Englewood Cliffs, N.J.: Prentice-Hall, 1974).

6. Kenneth Prewitt, *The Recruitment of Political Leaders* (Indianapolis: Bobbs-Merrill, 1970); Ronald O. Loveridge, *City Managers in Legislative Politics* (Indianapolis: Bobbs-Merrill, 1971); Heinz Eulau and Kenneth Prewitt,

Labyrinths of Democracy (Indianapolis: Bobbs-Merrill, 1973); Betty H. Zisk, *Local Interest Politics: A One-Way Street* (Indianapolis: Bobbs-Merrill, 1973); Eugene C. Lee, *The Politics of Nonpartisanship* (Berkeley: University of California Press, 1960); Willis D. Hawley, *Nonpartisan Elections and the Case for Party Politics* (New York: Wiley, 1973).

7. Gladys M. Kammerer, Charles D. Farris, John M. DeGrove, and Alfred B. Clubok, *City Managers in Politics* (Gainesville: University of Florida Press, 1962); John P. East, *Council-Manager Government* (Chapel Hill: University of North Carolina Press, 1965); Loveridge, *City Managers;* Richard J. Stillman II, *The Rise of the City Manager* (Albuquerque: University of New Mexico Press, 1974); Robert A. Caro, *The Power Broker* (New York: Random House, 1974).

8. Renewed interest in officials is signified by the appearance of a number of books including Harmon Zeigler, Ellen Kehoe, and Jane Reisman, *City Managers and School Superintendents* (New York: Praeger, 1985); Barbara Ferman, *Governing the Ungovernable City: Political Skill, Leadership, and the Modern Mayor* (Philadelphia: Temple University Press, 1985); Jones, *Governing Buildings;* Glenn Abney and Thomas P. Lauth, *The Politics of State and City Administration* (Albany: State University of New York Press, 1986); Gruber, *Controlling Bureaucracies;* and Susan Welch and Timothy Bledsoe, *Urban Reform and Its Consequences: A Study in Representation* (Chicago: University of Chicago Press, 1988).

9. For a review of the literature on service delivery, see Richard C. Rich, Ed., *The Politics of Urban Public Services* (Lexington, Mass.: Lexington Books, 1982).

10. Theodore Lowi, "Machine Politics—Old and New," *Public Interest* No. 9 (Fall, 1967): 83–92; Herbert Kaufman, "Administrative Decentralization and Political Power," *Public Administration Review* 29 (1969): 3–15; Peter Lupsha, "Constraints on Urban Leadership, or Why Cities Cannot Be Creatively Governed," in Willis D. Hawley and David Rogers, Eds., *Improving the Quality of Urban Management. Urban Affairs Annual Reviews*, 8 (1974): 607–623.

11. Albert O. Hirschman, *Exit, Voice, and Loyalty* (Cambridge, Mass.: Harvard University Press, 1970); John Orbell and Tory Uno, "A Theory of Neighborhood Problem Solving," *American Political Science Review* 64 (June, 1972): 471–489.

12. Rich, *Urban Public Services*, pp. 3–7, argues that critical theory tells us that officials support economic interests and offer basic services only to maintain order. Even if one accepts such an aggregate bias in the system, decisions by officials fill in the fine detail of urban policy and services.

13. Rufus P. Browning, Dale Rogers Marshall, and David H. Tabb, *Protest Is Not Enough* (Berkeley: University of California Press, 1984); and Welch and Bledsoe, *Urban Reform*, pp. 111–120, discuss changes that are altering the standard expectations about relationships and outcomes in urban politics.

14. This is a subjective distinction to be sure, but it is reflected in the contrasting perspective of books like Wayne F. Anderson, Chester A. Newland,

and Richard J. Stillman, *The Effective Local Government Manager* (Washington, D.C.: International City Management Association, 1983), and Douglas Yates, *The Ungovernable City* (Cambridge, Mass.: MIT Press, 1977).

15. For example, see Howard D. Tipton, "Promoting the C-M Plan," *Public Management* 67 (July, 1985): 10.

16. The sixth edition of the Model City Charter was adopted in 1963. The National Civic League undertook a study of the charter beginning in 1984 to prepare the seventh edition.

17. An exception is Douglas Yates, *Bureaucratic Democracy* (Cambridge, Mass.: Harvard University Press, 1982), p. 28, who classifies the strong executive as one—indeed, the "capstone"—of the values and structures which make up the "administrative efficiency" model of government. Also Lowi, "Machine Politics"; Bryan D. Jones, *Service Delivery in the City* (New York: Longman, 1980); and J. David Greenstone and Paul E. Peterson, *Race and Authority in Urban Politics* (New York: Sage, 1973) treat cities with strong mayors, weak parties, and administrative agencies organized in terms of modern administrative principles as reformed.

18. Joseph Zimmerman, *The Federated City* (New York: St. Martin's Press, 1972).

19. Daniel T. Rodgers, "In Search of Progressivism," *Reviews in American History* 10 (December, 1982): 113–132, and Martin J. Schiesl, *The Politics of Efficiency* (Berkeley: University of California Press, 1977) raise questions about historical criticisms of the reform movement such as that of Samuel P. Hays, "The Politics of Reform in Municipal Government in the Progressive Era," *Pacific Northwest Quarterly* 55 (October, 1964): 157–169, and Hays, "Political Parties and the Community-Society Continuum," in William N. Chambers and Walter D. Burnham, Eds., *The American Party System* (New York: Oxford University Press, 1967), pp. 152–181.

20. Hawley, *Nonpartisan Elections;* Welch and Bledsoe, *Urban Reform;* Russell D. Murphy, "The Mayoralty and the Democratic Creed: The Evolution of an Ideology and an Institution," *Urban Affairs Quarterly* 22 (September, 1986): 3–23.

21. John Higham, *Strangers in the Land: Patterns of American Nativism 1860–1925* (New York: Atheneum, 1966), p. 117.

22. Melvin G. Holli, *Reform in Detroit: Hazen S. Pingree and Urban Politics* (New York: Oxford University Press, 1969).

23. Otis A. Pease, "Urban Reformers in the Progressive Era," *Pacific Northwest Quarterly* 62 (April, 1971): 53.

24. David P. Thelen, "Urban Politics: Beyond Bosses and Reformers," *Reviews in American History* 7 (September, 1979): 406–412.

25. Frank Mann Stewart, *A Half Century of Municipal Reform* (Berkeley: University of California Press, 1950), pp. 73–74; and Stillman, *Rise of the City Manager*, pp. 15–16.

26. James Weinstein, "Organized Business and the City Commission and

Manager Movements," *Journal of Southern History* 28 (May, 1962): 180. On the characteristics of early reform cities, see Richard M. Bernard and Bradley R. Rice, "Political Environment and the Adoption of Progressive Municipal Reform," *Journal of Urban History* 1 (February, 1975): 149–175.

27. Pease, "Urban Reformers," pp. 54–55.

28. International City Management Association, *Make Policy—Who Me?* (Washington, D.C.: ICMA, 1977).

29. Melvin J. Stanford, *Management Policy*, 2nd ed. (Englewood Cliffs: Prentice-Hall, 1983), p. 14.

30. For examples of corporate mission statements, see Arthur A. Thompson, Jr., and A. J. Strickland III, *Strategy and Policy: Concepts and Cases* (Plano, Tex.: 1981); and William G. Ouchi, *Theory Z* (New York: Avon, 1981), appendix one.

31. The importance of goals does not mean that organizations are always goal directed in their behavior, in the sense that they rationally orient activities toward the accomplishment of goals. Organizations may be as much constrained by their goals, definition of purpose, and other elements of mission as positively guided by them. Private firms are, however, likely to have clearer, more coherent missions than general purpose governments.

32. John W. Kingdon, *Agendas, Alternatives, and Public Policies* (Boston: Little, Brown, 1984), pp. 3–4; Laurence E. Lynn, Jr., *Managing the Public's Business*. New York: Basic Books, 1981), pp. 143–151.

33. Randall B. Ripley and Grace A. Franklin, *Bureaucracy and Policy Implementation* (Homewood, Ill.: Dorsey Press, 1982), p. 32.

34. Thomas J. Peters and Robert H. Waterman, *In Search of Excellence* (New York: Warner Books, 1982), pp. 52–53.

35. Graham T. Allison, Jr., *Essence of Decision* (Boston: Little, Brown, 1971), p. 173.

36. Phillip M. Burgess, "Capacity Building and the Elements of Public Management," *Public Administration Review* 35 (December, 1975): 705–716, makes a similar distinction between program management and resource management—both of which differ from policy management, which is comparable to the policy dimension. Graham T. Allison, Jr. "Public and Private Management: Are They Fundamentally Alike in All Unimportant Respects?," in Barry Bozeman and Jeffrey Strassman, *New Directions in Public Administration* (Monterey: Brooks/Cole, 1984), pp. 32–45, also distinguishes between "managing internal components" of organizations, and developing "operational plans," which include both policy and administration.

37. Joseph L. Bower, "Effective Public Management," *Harvard Business Review*, 55 (March/April, 1977): 132.

38. Henry Mintzberg, *Power In and Around Organizations* (Englewood Cliffs, N.J.: Prentice-Hall, 1983).

39. For example, see Yates's conclusion (*The Ungovernable City*, p. 170) that business management practices will not work in city government. E. S.

Savas, *Privatization: The Key to Better Government* (New York: Chatham House, 1987), makes the case for the provision of municipal functions by private companies.

40. Emmette S. Redford, *Democracy in the Administrative State* (New York: Oxford University Press, 1969).

41. Gruber, *Controlling Bureaucracies,* pp. 16–23, has a similar test but uses more stringent grading requirements to determine whether control is democratic. "Mere congruence of bureaucratic action with citizens wants," unless dictated by citizens, is still bureaucratic autonomy. This position appears to require controls that are more explicit and direct than is often the case when administrators choose a curse of action that is consistent with general policy and public needs.

42. James H. Svara, "Dichotomy and Duality: Reconceptualizing the Relationship Between Policy and Administration in Council-Manager Cities," *Public Administration Review* 45 (January/February, 1985): 221–232. Party override of implementation of standard policy described in Jones, *Governing Buildings,* may violate both sets of principles, although it increases responsiveness to particularistic demands.

43. Svara, "Dichotomy and Duality"; William Browne, "Municipal Managers and Policy: A Partial Test of the Svara Dichotomy–Duality Model," *Public Administration Review* 45 (September-October, 1985): 620–622.

44. John K. Parker, "Administrative Planning," in James M. Banovetz, Ed., *Managing the Modern City* (Washington: International City Management Association, 1971), chap. 10.

45. John P. Crecine, *Governmental Problem-Solving* (Chicago: Rand McNally, 1969).

46. Glenn Abney and Thomas P. Lauth, "Councilmanic Intervention in Municipal Administration," *Administration & Society* 13 (February, 1982): 435–456; Kenneth R. Greene, "Municipal Administrators' Receptivity to Citizens' and Elected Officials' Contacts," *Public Administration Review,* 42 (July/August, 1982): 346–353.

47. Allen Schick, "Congress and the 'Details' of Administration," *Public Administration Review* 36 (September/October, 1976): 516–528.

Chapter 2

1. Edward C. Banfield and James Q. Wilson, *City Politics* (New York: Vintage Books, 1963), p. 5.

2. Interactions with many officials over the years in their cities and at meetings have contributed to these observations. In addition, systematic field research and interviews were arranged between 1984 and 1986 in six pairs of mayor-council and council-manager cities with similar characteristics. See Appendix, Table A-1 and note 80 (below) for a list of these cities.

3. Bryan D. Jones, *Service Delivery in the City* (New York: Longman, 1980), pp. 12–15, examines the "urban conflict model" as an explanation of the distribution of services in city government. Specifically, he considers whether the competitive struggle among groups explains who receives services. In Chapter 9, he distinguishes among "political" and "organizational" models of distributional decision making. In our discussion, some of his organizational models—in particular the "aggrandizing bureau" and the "street-level bureaucrat" models correspond to the conflictual pattern (and Jones notes that this are close to the political models.) Only his "Deliberate Policy" model corresponds to the cooperative pattern to be developed in this chapter, although his emphasis on the importance of formal authority within governmental bureaus is generally consistent with cooperation, whereas bureaucratic infighting would be an aspect of the conflictual pattern.

4. Harmon Zeigler, Ellen Kehoe, and Jane Reisman, *City Managers and School Superintendents* (New York: Praeger, 1985), p. 31.

5. Gordon Whitaker and Larry W. Davis, "Politics, Policy, and County Managers," paper presented at the 1986 Meeting of the Southern Political Science Association, observe that managers make more use of brokering and less use of rationality and persuasion when conflict among elected officials increases.

6. Judith E. Gruber, *Controlling Bureaucracies* (Berkeley: University of California Press, 1987), pp. 205–211, argues that the most effective strategy for control may be one in which administrators agree to accept controls in "exchange" for resources they need.

7. Robert A. Dahl, *Who Governs?* (New Haven: Yale University Press, 1961); Alexander L. George, "Political Leadership in American Cities," *Daedalus* 97 (Fall, 1968): 1194–1217; James V. Cunningham, *Urban Leadership in the Sixties* (Cambridge, Mass.: Schenkman, 1970); Barbara Ferman, *Governing the Ungovernable City: Political Skill, Leadership, and the Modern Mayor* (Philadelphia: Temple University Press, 1985).

8. Wallace S. Sayre and Herbert Kaufman, *Governing New York City* (New York: Sage, 1960), pp. 73–76; Theodore Lowi, "Machine Politics—Old and New," *Public Interest* No. 9 (Fall, 1967): 83–92; Peter Lupsha, "Constraints on Urban Leadership, or Why Cities Cannot Be Creatively Governed," in Willis D. Hawley and David Rogers, Eds., *Improving the Quality of Urban Management. Urban Affairs Annual Reviews,* 8 (1974): 607–623.

9. Douglas Yates, *The Ungovernable City* (Cambridge, Mass.: MIT Press, 1977).

10. Gerald Marwell and David R. Schmitt, *Cooperation: An Experimental Analysis* (New York: Academic Press, 1975), pp. 4–7.

11. It should be noted that the term is used in its literal sense of adjustment and compromise and not with the more restricted meaning that Kenneth W. Thomas and Ralph H. Kilmann, *Conflict Mode Instrument* (Tuxedo, N.Y.: Xicom, 1974), p. 12, give to it in their typology of modes of handling conflict.

Accommodation need not be passive and low in assertiveness. Furthermore, I do not intend for competition to be viewed as antithetical to cooperation, as Kilmann and Thomas suggest, as long as competition is carried out within a framework of common goals and avoids blocking actions. Zeigler et al., *City Managers and School Superintendents,* pp. 121–127, also use the Thomas-Kilmann terminology but with substantial modification.

12. Robert A. Dahl, *A Preface to Democratic Theory* (Chicago: University of Chicago Press, 1956); Charles E. Lindblom, *The Intelligence of Democracy* (New York: Free Press, 1965).

13. W. Graham Astley and Andrew H. Van de Ven, "Central Perspectives and Debates in Organization Theory," *Administrative Science Quarterly* 28 (June, 1983): 262.

14. Robert Axelrod, *The Evolution of Cooperation* (New York: Basic Books, 1984).

15. Ibid., chap. 4, describes how cooperation emerged among troops from opposing sides in the trenches in World War I during lulls between major battles. Hierarchy is treated as conducive to cooperation because it structures relationships and increases the likelihood of future encounters (pp. 130–131).

16. Ibid., p. 12.

17. Charles H. Levine, *Racial Conflict and the American Mayor* (Lexington, Mass.: Lexington Books, 1974), chap. 3.

18. Ibid., chap. 7.

19. Raymond E. Wolfinger, *The Politics of Progress* (Englewood Cliffs, N.J.: Prentice-Hall, 1974), pp. 402–404.

20. Zeigler et al., *City Managers and School Superintendents,* pp. 48–49, identifies this trait among school superintendents who are much more "obsessed with winning" than are city managers.

21. Banfield and Wilson, *City Politics,* p. 18.

22. Ibid. For example, the distinction was forcefully stated by Frank J. Goodnow, *Politics and Administration* (New York: MacMillan, 1914), p. 84. He asserted that municipal government "is almost exclusively a matter of administration."

23. Robert L. Lineberry and Ira Sharkansky, *Urban Politics and Public Policy,* 2nd ed. (New York: Harper and Row, 1974), pp. 102–104.

24. Bryan D. Jones, *Governing Urban America* (Boston: Little, Brown, 1983), p. 259.

25. Douglas Yates, *Bureaucratic Democracy* (Cambridge, Mass.: Harvard University Press, 1982), chap. 2.

26. Conflict would also be absent in small communities with homogeneous populations.

27. Yates, *The Ungovernable City,* chap. 1.

28. Graham T. Allison, Jr., *Essence of Decision* (Boston: Little, Brown, 1971), chap. 5; Jeffrey Pfeffer, *Power in Organizations* (Marshfield, Mass.: Pitman, 1981).

29. Timothy W. Costello, "Change in Municipal Government: A View from the Inside," *Journal of Applied Behavioral Science* 7 (May/April, 1971): 131, 132.

30. Jeptha A. Carrell, "The City Manager and His Council: Sources of Conflict," *Public Administration Review* 22 (December, 1962): 203–208; Anthony Catanese, *Planners and Politicians* (Beverly Hills: Sage, 1974).

31. Lowi, "Machine Politics"; David Rogers, "The Failure of Inner City Schools: A Crisis of Management and Service Delivery", *Educational Technology* 10 (September, 1970): 27–32.

32. Zeigler et al., *City Managers and School Superintendents*, pp. 50–51; Gruber, *Controlling Bureaucracies*, chap. 6.

33. Aaron Wildavsky, *The Politics of the Budgetary Process*, Fourth Edition. (Boston: Little, Brown, 1984).

34. Frederick M. Wirt, *Power in the City* (Berkeley: University of California Press, 1974), p. 345.

35. Gordon Chase and Elizabeth C. Reveal, *How to Manage in the Public Sector* (Reading, Mass.: Addison-Wesley, 1983).

36. Michael Lipsky, "Toward a Theory of Street-Level Bureaucracy," in Willis D. Hawley and Michael Lipsky, Eds., *Theoretical Perspectives in Urban Politics* (Englewood Cliffs, N.J.: Prentice-Hall, 1976), pp. 196–213.

37. Ferman, *Governing the Ungovernable City*, chap. 3.

38. Yates, *The Ungovernable City*, pp. 33–37.

39. Wirt, *Power in the City*, pp. 344–350.

40. Ferman, *Governing the Ungovernable City*, pp. 52–53.

41. Heinz Eulau and Kenneth Prewitt, *Labyrinths of Democracy* (Indianapolis: Bobbs-Merrill, 1973).

42. Charles F. Goodsell, *The Case for Bureaucracy* (Chatham, N.J.: Chatham House, 1983).

43. The International City Management Association has a long-standing code of ethics to guide the behavior of managers. The American Society for Public Administration has recently formulated a code of ethics, which though less vigorous in its support of certain values than some would have liked (e.g., Ralph C. Chandler, "The Problem of Moral Reasoning in American Public Administration: The Case for a Code of Ethics," *Public Administration Review* 43 (January/February, 1983): 32–39), is a start toward defining the responsibilities of administrative officials to elected officials and the public. Standards for responsible behavior by professional administrators are elaborated in Chapter 6.

44. Chester I. Barnard, *The Functions of the Executive* (Cambridge, Mass.: Harvard University Press, 1938); Rensis Likert, *New Patterns of Management* (New York: McGraw-Hill, 1961).

45. Charles Perrow, *Complex Organizations: A Critical Essay*, 2nd ed. (Glenview, Ill.: Scott, Foresman, 1979).

46. Allison, *Essence of Decision*, chap. 3; James G. March and Herbert A.

Simon, *Organizations* (New York: Wiley, 1958); Richard M. Cyert and James G. March, *A Behavioral Theory of the Firm* (Englewood Cliffs, N.J.: Prentice-Hall, 1963).

47. Some argue that views which stress the "loosely coupled" nature of organizations (e.g., K. E. Weick, "Educational Organizations as Loosely Coupled Systems," *Administrative Science Quarterly* 21 [March, 1976]: 1–19) or which even see them as "organized anarchies" using "garbage can" models of decision making (e.g. James G. March and Johan P. Olsen, *Ambiguity and Choice in Complex Organizations* [Bergen, Norway: Universitetsforlaget, 1976]), still make it possible for such an organization to fit into a cooperative framework. Although the loosely coupled organization is not a cohesive monolith, Astley and Van de Ven ("Central Perspectives," p. 252) argue that it is a collectivity in which strategic choices can be made, albeit with diffuse processes of choice and implementation.

48. Astley and Van de Ven, "Central Perspectives," p. 263.

49. Thomas J. Peters anc. Robert H. Waterman, *In Search of Excellence* (New York: Warner Books, 1982), pp. 15, 340.

50. Pfeffer, *Power in Organizations,* pp. 4–5. Douglas Yates, *The Politics of Management* (San Francisco: Josey-Bass, 1985), chap. 6, suggests that managers not overlook their formal authority in conflict management.

51. Emmette S. Redford, *Democracy in the Administrative State* (New York: Oxford University Press, 1969).

52. Gruber, *Controlling Bureaucracies;* Kenneth J. Meier, *Politics and the Bureaucracy* (North Scituate, Mass.: Duxbury Press, 1979).

53. A recent expression of this point of view along with advice on how to outmaneuver the bureaucracy is Michael Sanera's background paper for the second term of the Reagan administration, "Implementing the Mandate," in *Mandate for Leadership II* (Washington: Heritage Foundation, 1985), Part 4. For summary and commentary, see James P. Pfiffner, "Political Public Administration," *Public Administration Review* 45 (March/April, 1985): 353–356.

54. Herbert Kaufman, "Fear of Bureaucracy: A Raging Pandemic," *Public Administration Review* 41 (January/February, 1981): 1–9. Bryan D. Jones, *Governing Buildings and Building Government* (University, Ala.: University of Alabama Press, 1985), p. 83, notes that many bureaucrats are constrained in their behavior by a "generalized culture of obedience."

55. Charles R. Adrian and Charles Press, *Governing Urban America,* 5th ed. (New York: McGraw-Hill, 1977), chap. 7.

56. Banfield and Wilson, *City Politics,* p. 81.

57. John A. Rohr, *To Run a Constitution* (Lawrence: University Press of Kansas, 1986), pp. 18–19.

58. Haywood T. Sanders, "The Government of American Cities: Continuity and Change in Structure," *Municipal Year Book 1982* (Washington, D.C.: International City Management Association, 1982), p. 172. The complete breakdown is as follows:

Type	No.	%
Mayor-council	3,649	54.0
Council-manager	2,444	36.1
Commission	188	2.8
Town meeting	398	5.9
Representative town meeting	82	1.2
TOTAL	6,761	100.0

59. Thomas R. Dye and Susan MacManus, "Predicting City Government Structure," *American Journal of Political Science* 20 (May, 1976): 257–272.

60. Edward C. Banfield, *Political Influence* (New York: Free Press, 1965), p. 237.

61. Dahl, *Who Governs?*; Allan Talbot, *The Mayor's Game* (New York: Harper & Row, 1967); James V. Cunningham, *Urban Leadership in the Sixties* (Cambridge, Mass.: Schenkman, 1970)

62. Banfield, *Political Influence*, p. 241.

63. James B. Hogan, *The Chief Administrative Officer* (Tucson: University of Arizona Press, 1976).

64. Chester A. Newland, "Council-Manager Governance: Positive Alternative to Separation of Powers," *Public Management* 67 (July, 1985): 7.

65. Martha Wagner Weinberg, "Boston's Kevin White: A Mayor Who Survives," *Political Science Quarterly* 96 (Spring, 1981): 101.

66. Yates, *The Ungovernable City*, pp. 153–155; Clarence N. Stone, "Complexity and the Changing Character of Executive Leadership: An Interpretation of the Lindsay Administration in New York City," *Urban Interest* 4 (Fall, 1982): 29–50.

67. Chester A. Newland, "Public Executives: Imperium, Sacerdotium, Collegium? Bicentennial Leadership Challenges," *Public Administration Review* 47 (January/February, 1987): 53–54.

68. Weinberg, "Boston's Kevin White," 106.

69. Veto and election statistics from Charles R. Adrian, "Forms of City Government in American History," *Municipal Year Book 1988* (Washington, D.C.: International City Management Association, 1988), p. 10.

70. Jones, *Governing Urban America*, p. 368.

71. Newland, "Council-Manager Governance," p. 8.

72. Ronald O. Loveridge, *City Managers in Legislative Politics* (Indianapolis: Bobbs-Merrill, 1971), p. 163.

73. Alana Northrop and William H. Dutton, "Municipal Reform and Group Influence," *American Journal of Political Science* 22 (August, 1978): 707.

74. Richard J. Stillman II, "Local Public Management in Transition: A Report on the Current State of the Profession," *Municipal Year Book 1982* (Washington, D.C.: International City Management Association, 1982), pp. 161–173.

75. Edward H. Flentje and Wendla Counihan, "Running a Reformed City," *Urban Resources* 2 (Fall, 1984): 9–14.

76. Banfield and Wilson, *City Politics*, p. 177.

77. The 1986 population estimates for these cities are as follows: Dallas, 1,003,000; Phoenix, 853,000; San Antonio, 842,000; San Diego, 1,015,000; San Jose, 712,000.

78. Naomi Bailin Wish, "The Cost and Quality of Urban Life: A Matter of Governmental Structure or Regional Variation?" *Municipal Year Book 1986* (Washington, D.C.: International City Management Association, 1986), pp. 17–23.

79. The eight characteristics of the study cities—listed in Appendix, Table A-1—are discussed in James H. Svara, "Conflict, Cooperation, and Separation of Powers in City Government," *Journal of Urban Affairs* 10 (No. 4, 1988): 357–372. It is assumed that conflict is associated with higher population, less growth (as an indicator of economic conditions), higher proportion of minorities in the population, lower education, lower city government bond rating, larger councils, more district seats, and partisan elections. Of the 48 comparisons— eight characteristics in the six pairs of cities—28 are essentially equivalent, 12 predispose the mayor-council cities to more conflict, and 8 differ in the direction of producing higher expected conflict in council-manager cities.

80. The number of questionnaires distributed (D) and returned (R) were as follows:

	Council		Dept. Heads	
Type/City	D	R	D	R
Mayor-Council				
New Haven[a]	16	5	23	9
Knoxville	9	3	16	9
Akron	13	6	15	8
Minneapolis[b]	13	7	19	14
Memphis	13	5	15	14
Lincoln	7	5	15	8
TOTAL	71	31	103	62
Council-Manager				
Hartford	9[c]	4	22	11
Greensboro	9	6	12	8
Dayton	5	2	19	12
Kansas City	12[c]	4	17	12
Charlotte	11[c]	7	19	14
Raleigh	8	3	19	11
TOTAL	54	26	108	68

[a]From total council of 30 members, the council chair, party leaders, and half of the other members were given questionnaires.

[b]Weak mayor-council city.

[c]Mayor not included.

The research was conducted between 1984 and 1986.

81. Russell D. Murphy, "The Mayoralty and the Democratic Creed: The Evolution of an Ideology and an Institution," *Urban Affairs Quarterly* 22 (September, 1986): 3–23.

82. Willis D. Hawley, *Nonpartisan Elections and the Case for Party Politics* (New York: Wiley, 1973).

83. Jeffrey L. Pressman, "Preconditions of Mayoral Leadership," *American Political Science Review* 66 (June, 1972): 511–524.

84. Martin Shefter, *Political Crisis/Fiscal Crisis* (New York: Basic Books, 1985), pp. 230–232.

85. Jones, *Governing Urban America*, p. 368; Dennis R. Judd, *The Politics of American Cities*, 2nd ed. (Boston: Little, Brown, 1984), p. 114.

Chapter 3

1. Harold A. Stone, Don K. Price, and Kathryn H. Stone, *City Management Government in the United States* (Chicago: Public Administration Service, 1940), determined that unit prices for services were lower in council-manager cities and that graft and waste were reduced. E. S. Savas, "How Much Do Government Services Really Cost?" *Urban Affairs Quarterly* 15 (September, 1979): 23–41, finds that council-manager governments provide more accurate figures on the real cost of services than do mayor-council cities. Charles H. Levine, Irene S. Rubin, and George G. Wolohojian, *The Politics of Retrenchment* (Beverly Hills: Sage, 1981) find that the two council-manager jurisdictions in their study were more effective at handling fiscal retrenchment than the two strong executive systems, because of greater use of efficiency improvements and managerial controls over operations. For example, the council-manager cities reduced staff but increased salaries for those remaining, whereas the strong executive tried to retain staff while imposing general salary reductions. This evidence, however, is not conclusive with regard to greater efficiency in normal operations for a wide range of cities that differ in form of government. It appears that scholars have been willing to accept that reform brings greater efficiency without close scrutiny.

2. This is the case with commission government, which virtually requires a small at-large council since the commissioners are department heads in the city's government.

3. Haywood T. Sanders, "The Government of American Cities: Continuity and Change in Structure," *Municipal Year Book 1982* (Washington, D.C.: International City Management Association, 1982), p. 181; Tari Renner, "Municipal Election Processes: The Impact on Minority Representation," *Municipal Year Book 1988* (Washington, D.C.: International City Management Association, 1988), p. 17.

4. James H. Svara, "Unwrapping Institutional Packages in Urban Govern-

ment: The Combination of E ection Institutions in American Cities," *Journal of Politics* 39 (February, 1977): 172.

5. Sanders, "The Government of American Cities," p. 186.

6. Peggy Heilig and Robert J. Mundt, *Your Voice at City Hall* (Albany: State University of New York Press, 1984), p. 11.

7. Renner, "Municipal Election Processes," p. 16.

8. Theodore P. Robinson and Thomas R. Dye, "Reformism and Black Representation on City Councils," *Social Science Quarterly* 59 (June, 1978): 137. Renner, "Municipal Election Processes," p. 19, reports that there is a significant relationship between black representation and the method of election in cities that have more than 40% black population.

9. Robinson and Dye, "Reformism and Black Representation," pp. 138–140.

10. Albert K. Karnig and Susan Welch, *Black Representation and Urban Policy* (Chicago: University of Chicago Press, 1980); Richard L. Engstrom and Michael D. McDonald, "The Election of Blacks to City Councils: Clarifying the Impact of Electoral Arrangements on the Seats/Population Relationship," *American Political Science Review* 75 (June, 1981): 344–354.

11. Susan A. MacManus, "City Council Election Procedures and Minority Representation: Are They Related?" *Social Science Quarterly* 59 (June, 1978): 153–161.

12. Susan Welch and Timothy Bledsoe, *Urban Reform and Its Consequences: A Study in Representation* (Chicago: University of Chicago Press, 1988), p. 43.

13. R. Darcy, Susan Welch, and Janet Clark, *Women, Elections, and Representation* (New York: Longman, 1987), pp. 40–41.

14. For example, Terry N. Clark, "Community Structure, Decision-Making, Budget Expenditure, and Urban Renewal in 51 American Communities," in Charles M. Bonjean, Terry N. Clark, and Robert L. Lineberry, *Community Politics* (New York: Free Press, 1971), p. 304, found that decision making is more centralized (i.e., fewer major actors participate) in reform cities.

15. For a summary of alternative explanations of group influence, see Alana Northrop and William H. Dutton, "Municipal Reform and Group Influence," *American Journal of Political Science* 22 (August, 1978): 691–693. They conclude concerning the impact of reform generally that, although business and middle-class groups were advantaged, labor, minority, and lower-class groups were not necessarily disadvantaged. Theirs is one of very few studies that examine the separate impact of the council-manager form, and these are the results emphasized here.

16. William H. Dutton and Alana Northrop, "Municipal Reform and the Changing Pattern of Urban Party Politics," *American Politics Quarterly* 6 (October, 1978): 439.

17. Northrop and Dutton, "Group Influence," Table 2.

18. Peter K. Eisinger, "Black Employment in Municipal Jobs: The Impact of Black Political Power," *American Political Science Review* 76 (June, 1982): 380–392.

19. Peter K. Eisinger, "Economic Conditions of Black Employment in Municipal Bureaucracies," *American Journal of Political Science* 26 (November, 1982): 769.

20. Robert L. Lineberry and Edmund P. Fowler, "Reformism and Public Policies in American Cities," *American Political Science Review* 61 (September, 1967): 701–716.

21. R. J. Liebert, "Municipal Functions, Structure, and Expenditures," *Social Science Quarterly* 54 (March, 1974): 765–783.

22. Thomas R. Dye and John A. Garcia, "Structure, Function, and Policy in American Cities," *Urban Affairs Quarterly* 14 (September, 1978): 103–122.

23. Clark, "Community Structure," pp. 305–307, 310–311.

24. David R. Morgan and John P. Pellissero, "Urban Policy: Does Political Structure Matter?" *American Political Science Review* 74 (1980): 1005.

25. David R. Morgan and Jeffrey L. Brudney, "Urban Policy and City Government Structure: Testing the Mediating Effects of Reform," Paper delivered at the 1985 Annual Meeting of the American Political Science Association.

26. William Lyons, "Reform and Response in American Cities: Structure and Policy Reconsidered," *Social Science Quarterly* 59 (June, 1978): 118–132.

27. Karl F. Johnson and C. J. Hein, "Assessment of the Council-Manager Form of Government Today: Managers Meet the Challenge Through Balance," *Public Management* 67 (July, 1985): 4–6.

28. Dye and Garcia, "Structure, Function, and Policy," p. 117.

29. Ibid., Table 4, p. 116. In reformed cities, spending is positively related to the percent of nonwhite population (correlation = .37) and is inversely related to the percent of white-collar workers (−.23), whereas there is no correlation in unreformed cities (.02 and .06, respectively). In other words, council-manager cities, as compared to mayor-council cities, respond to higher minority or blue-collar populations by following a course of higher spending. Spending is not related to income in reformed cities (.02), but tends to go up as income rises in unreformed cities (.33). In both, there is a weak inverse relation between education level and spending (−.22 in reformed and −.28 in unreformed cities), and a strong inverse correlation between homeownership and expenditures (−.53 and −.55). Unreformed governments, on the other hand, spend more as the ethnic population increases (.62), whereas the relationship is weaker in reformed cities (.25).

30. Morgan and Brudney, "Urban Policy," pp. 17–18.

31. Albert K. Karnig, "Private Regarding Policy, Civil Rights Groups, and the Mediating Impact of Municipal Reforms," *American Journal of Political Science* 19 (February, 1975): 91–106.

32. Robert L. Lineberry and Ira Sharkansky, *Urban Politics and Public Policy,* 3rd ed. (New York: Harper & Row, 1978), pp. 162–164.

33. Richard C. Feiock and James Clingermayer, "Municipal Representation, Executive Power, and Economic Development Policy Activity," *Policy Studies Journal* 15 (December, 1986), pp. 211–229.

34. Ibid., 224. The "credit-claiming" explanation of behavior is from David Mayhew, *Congress: The Electoral Connection* (New Haven: Yale University Press, 1974), pp. 52–53.

35. Chester A Newland, "Public Executives: Imperium, Sacerdotium, Collegium? Bicentennial Leadership Challenges," *Public Administration Review* 47 (January/February, 1987): 53–54, notes that executive mayors need and are the target of large contributions from development interests. Welch and Bledsoe, *Urban Reform*, pp. 88–89, find that partisan councils are less opposed to unlimited development (44%) than are nonpartisan councils (51%), whereas district councils are slightly more opposed (50%) than at-large councils (48%).

36. Donald D. Rosenthal and Robert L. Crain, "Structure and Values in Local Political Systems: The Case of Fluoridation Decisions," in James Q. Wilson, Ed., *City Politics and Public Policy* (New York: Wiley, 1968), p. 227; see also Robert L. Crain and James H. Vanecko, "Elite Influence in School Desegregation," in Wilson, Ed., ibid., pp. 127–148.

37. Christine H. Russell and Robert L. Crain, "The Importance of Political Factors in Explaining Northern School Desegregation," *American Journal of Political Science* 26 (November, 1982): 791.

38. For example, Barbara Ferman, *Governing the Ungovernable City: Political Skill, Leadership, and the Modern Mayor* (Philadelphia: Temple University Press, 1985), pp. 210–211

39. Joseph P. Viteritti, "Bureaucratic Environments, Efficiency, and Equity in Urban-Service-Delivery Systems," in Richard C. Rich, Ed., *The Politics of Urban Public Services* (Lexington, Mass.: Lexington Books, 1982), pp. 53–68.

40. The quote is from Kenneth R. Mladenka, "The Urban Bureaucracy and the Chicago Political Machine: Who Gets What and the Limits to Political Control," *American Political Science Review* 74 (December, 1980): 996. Council-manager cities have been studied and reported on as follows: San Antonio, by Robert L. Lineberry, *Equality and Urban Policy* (Beverly Hills: Sage, 1977); Oakland, by Frank Levy, Arnold Meltsner, and Aaron Wildavsky, *Urban Outcomes* (Berkeley. University of California, 1974). And mayor-council cities as follows: Detroit, by Bryan D. Jones, *Service Delivery in the City* (New York: Longman, 1980); Houston, by Kenneth R. Mladenka and Kim Hill, "The Delivery of Urban Police Services," *Journal of Politics* 40 (February, 1978): 112–133, and by Mladenka, "The Urban Bureaucracy".

41. Frederick N. Bolotin and David L. Cingranelli, "Equity and Urban Policy: The Underclass Hypothesis Revisited," *Journal of Politics* 45 (February, 1983): 209–219. After controlling for crime rate and percentage black and after separating residential areas from business more carefully than has been done in previous studies, they found this political factor to be related to per capita police expenditures.

42. John Boyle and David Jacobs, "The Intracity Distribution of Services: A Multivariate Analysis," *American Political Science Review* 76 (June, 1982): 371–397. Police services are greatest in areas that have both high tax contributions and more poor residents, and "human" services—welfare, health, and elementary and secondary education—are distributed in a compensatory fashion with highest expenditures in areas that have lower income and larger nonwhite population.

43. Bryan D. Jones, *Governing Buildings and Building Government* (University, Ala.: University of Alabama Press, 1985), pp. 123–124.

44. Professionals may define need in ways that reflect their own biases rather than the characteristics of clients, as Levy et al., *Urban Outcomes*, pp. 231–232, show in the case of Oakland librarians. As discussed in Chapter 6, however, this detachment may have resulted from lack of accountability rather than professionalism per se.

45. Lineberry and Sharkansky, *Urban Politics*, 3rd ed., p. 164.

46. Theodore Lowi, "Machine Politics—Old and New," *Public Interest* No. 9 (Fall, 1967): 83–92.

47. James H. Svara, "Dichotomy and Duality: Reconceptualizing the Relationship Between Policy and Administration in Council-Manager Cities," *Public Administration Review* 45 (January/February, 1985): 221–232.

48. For information about the study, see notes 79 and 80 in Chapter 2.

49. Charldean Newell and David N. Ammons, "Role Emphasis of City Managers and Other Municipal Executives," *Public Administration Review* 47 (May/June, 1987): 246–252, find that mayors and managers fill similar roles.

50. Glenn Abney and Thomas P. Lauth, *The Politics of State and City Administration* (Albany: State University of New York Press, 1986), pp. 142–145, 192.

51. Ronald O. Loveridge, *City Managers in Legislative Politics* (Indianapolis: Bobbs-Merrill, 1971), pp. 93–95. This argument is discussed further in Chapter 6. Harmon Zeigler, Ellen Kehoe, and Jane Reisman, *City Managers and School Superintendents* (New York: Praeger, 1985), pp. 71–74, report that city managers estimate that they spend about a third of their time managing conflict. When asked later in the interview what percentage of their "communications" is "devoted to conflict resolution" in dealing with certain actors, the managers indicated that 65 percent or more of their "time" (sic, Table 4.1) is spent in conflict with the council, the community, their own administration, and representatives of state and federal governments. The latter findings are inconsistent with the overall estimate of conflict and are inexplicable.

Chapter 4

1. Haywood T. Sanders, "Governmental Structure in American Cities," *Municipal Year Book 1979* (Washington, D.C.: International City Management Association, 1979), p. 104.

2. A major issue in discussions concerning the revision of the Model Charter has centered on the selection of the mayor and definition of the role.

3. Robert A. Dahl, *Who Governs?* (New Haven: Yale University Press, 1961); Alexander L. George, "Political Leadership in American Cities," *Daedalus*, 97 (Fall, 1968): 1194–1217; James V. Cunningham, *Urban Leadership in the Sixties* (Cambridge, Mass.: Schenkman, 1970).

4. George, "Political Leadership," p. 1196.

5. Barbara Ferman, *Governing the Ungovernable City: Political Skill, Leadership, and the Modern Mayor* (Philadelphia: Temple University Press, 1985), p. 10.

6. Jeffrey L. Pressman, "Preconditions of Mayoral Leadership," *American Political Science Review* 66 (June, 1972): 511–524.

7. Robert L. Lineberry and Ira Sharkansky, *Urban Politics and Public Policy*, 3rd ed. (New York: Harper & Row, 1978), p. 194.

8. Pressman, "Preconditions of Mayoral Leadership," p. 523.

9. Glen Sparrow, "The Emerging Chief Executive: The San Diego Experience," *Urban Resources* 2 (Fall, 1984): 5.

10. Pressman, "Preconditions of Mayoral Leadership," p. 522.

11. Sparrow, "Emerging Chief Executive," pp. 5–6.

12. Robert Paul Boynton and Deil S. Wright, "Mayor-Manager Relationships in Large Council-Manager Cities: A Reinterpretation," *Public Administration Review*, 31 (January-February, 1971): 33.

13. Nelson Wikstrom, "The Mayor as a Policy Leader in the Council-Manager Form of Government: A View from the Field," *Public Administration Review*, 39 (May/June, 1979): 275.

14. Pressman, "Preconditions of Mayoral Leadership," p. 523.

15. Sparrow, "Emerging Chief Executive," p. 4.

16. Boynton and Wright, "Mayor-Manager Relations," p. 33.

17. Wikstrom, "Mayor as Policy Leader," p. 275.

18. Sparrow, "Emerging Chief Executive," p. 6.

19. Henry G. Cisneros, "The Quality of C-M Government," *Public Management* 67 (January, 1985): 3–5.

20. William Fulton, "Henry Cisneros: Mayor as Entrepreneur," *Planning* 51 (February, 1985): 4–9.

21. Wikstrom, "Mayor as Policy Leader," p. 275.

22. Sparrow, "Emerging Chief Executive," p. 8.

23. Billy George, "The Emergence of the Strong-Mayor, Council-Manager City: A Response to the Times," *Urban Resources* 2 (Fall, 1984): A1–A2.

24. This distinction is similar to that in David C. McClelland, "Two Faces of Power," *Journal of International Affairs* 24 (No. 1, 1970): 29–47. Leaders in organizations may be (1) directive and controlling or (2) stress strengthening subordinates and expanding their contributions.

25. Douglas Yates, *The Ungovernable City* (Cambridge, Mass.: MIT Press, 1977), pp. 153–157. Clarence N. Stone, "Complexity and the Changing Char-

acter of Executive Leadership: An Interpretation of the Lindsay Administration in New York City," *Urban Interest* 4 (Fall, 1982): 29–50, disagrees that the bureaucracy stymied Lindsay. When mayoral appointees were sensitive to needs in agencies, there was a positive response.

26. Ferman, *Governing Ungovernable City*, p. 120.

27. Sparrow, "Emerging Chief Executive."

28. Sanders, "Governmental Structure," pp. 103–104.

29. Ibid., for unlimited veto. For proportion with veto, Charles R. Adrian, "Forms of City Government in American History," *Municipal Year Book 1988* (Washington, D.C.: International City Management Association, 1988), p. 10.

30. Ferman, *Governing Ungovernable City*, p. 130; Martha Wagner Weinberg, "Boston's Kevin White: A Mayor Who Survives," *Political Science Quarterly* 96 (Spring, 1981): 97.

31. Bryan D. Jones, *Governing Buildings and Building Government* (University, Ala.: University of Alabama Press, 1985), pp. 149–150.

32. Ann Greer, *The Mayor's Mandate* (Cambridge, Mass.: Schenkman, 1974).

33. Ferman, *Governing Ungovernable City*, p. 81.

34. Ibid., pp. 200–202.

35. Ibid., pp. 202–205.

36. John P. Kotter and Paul R. Lawrence, *Mayors in Action* (New York: Wiley, 1974), p. 61.

37. There is formal control over the manager, but that is shared with the entire council.

38. Wikstrom, "Mayor as Policy Leader."

39. Boynton and Wright, "Mayor-Manager Relations."

40. Paul R. Eberts and Janet M. Kelly, "How Mayors Get Things Done: Community Politics and Mayors' Initiatives," *Research in Urban Policy* 1 (1985): 41–42.

41. Terry N. Clark and Lorna C. Ferguson, *City Money* (New York: Columbia University Press, 1983), pp. 187–203, distinguish between Jane Byrne's moving into public housing in Chicago in order to dramatize a problem and Pete Flaherty's combining symbolic actions with substantial alteration of Pittsburg's city government.

42. Eberts and Kelly, "How Mayors Get Things Done," pp. 53–55, report strong correlations among the mayor's local and national networking, the perception of higher number of active groups, the number of policy areas the mayor considered to be important, and the number of proposals submitted by the city to the federal government.

43. Charles H. Levine, *Racial Conflict and the American Mayor* (Lexington, Mass.: Lexington Books, 1974), has reservations but accepts the performance criterion; Ferman, *Governing Ungovernable City*, is opposed and prefers instead to examine variation in political skill. Ultimately, however, it seems that

the demonstration of effective political skills depends on some measure of performance.

44. For studies of the implementation process, see Jeffrey L. Pressman and Aaron B. Wildavsky, *Implementation* (Berkeley: University of California Press, 1973); Eugene Bardach, *The Implementation Game* (Cambridge, Mass.: MIT Press, 1977).

45. Yates, *Ungovernable City*, p. 147, who calls this type the broker, cites Mayors Beame and Wagner as examples.

46. Edward C. Banfield, *Political Influence* (New York: Free Press, 1965), pp. 250–253; Cunningham, *Urban Leadership*, pp. 44–46, 78.

47. Ferman, *Governing Ungovernable City*, pp. 137–138.

48. Henry W. Maier, *Challenge to the Cities* (New York: Random House, 1966), p. 37.

49. James Q. Wilson, "The Mayors vs. the Cities," *Public Interest* 16 (Summer, 1968): 25–37.

50. The term "executive" is used by Kotter and Lawrence, *Mayors in Action;* "manager" by Stone, "Complexity and Leadership."

51. Stone, "Complexity and Leadership."

52. Weinberg, "Boston's Kevin White"; Clarence N. Stone, Robert K. Whelan, and William J. Murin, *Urban Politics in a Bureaucratic Age*, 2nd ed. (Englewood Cliffs, N.J.: Prentice-Hall, 1986).

53. Ferman, *Governing Ungovernable City*, p. 216.

54. Yates, *Ungovernable City*, pp. 152–153. I have used the terminology presented in Figure 4–2. Yates's own labels are broker (caretaker), boss (broker), and crusader (reformer).

55. James H. Svara and James W. Bohmbach, "The Mayoralty and Leadership in Council-Manager Cities," *Popular Government* 41 (Winter, 1976): 1–6.

56. See James H. Svara, "Mayoral Leadership in Council-Manager Cities: Preconditions Versus Preconceptions," *Journal of Politics* 49 (February, 1987): 207–227. The cities included in the study are Charlotte, Durham, Greensboro, Raleigh, and Winston-Salem, all cities over 100,000 in population. Open-ended interviews were conducted with the mayor; three or four council members; the manager, assistant manager for operations, and heads of the departments of planning and budget; leaders of the Chamber of Commerce, the League of Women Voters, and the NAACP; and the city hall reporter from the newspaper. Respondents were promised anonymity. Since there are several cases of unanimous response within a particular city, it is not possible to identify the cities by name without violating the promise of anonymity. The five mayors are all directly elected for two-year terms. They preside over the city council and vote on all matters, with the exception of Charlotte. There, the mayor has limited voting authority and has the power to veto certain actions of the city council.

57. Boynton and Wright, "Mayor-Manager Relations," pp. 32.

58. Wikstrom, "Mayor as Policy Leader," p. 274.
59. Ibid., p. 275.
60. Ibid.
61. The introduction of a committee system with consultants hired for each committee, "enabled the council to develop, independent of the city manager, its own information, to draft ordinances, and to undertake special studies" (Sparrow, "Emerging Chief Executive," p. 6). In addition, the budget was reviewed by a fiscal analyst in the mayor's office and committee staff.
62. Wikstrom, "Mayor as Policy Leader," p. 274.
63. Boynton and Wright, "Mayor-Manager Relations," p. 31.
64. Wikstrom, "Mayor as Policy Leader," p. 275.
65. George, "Emergence of the Strong Mayor."
66. Pressman, "Preconditions of Mayoral Leadership."
67. The leadership of the mayor in city B, according to a few respondents there, is eroding in the "middle." Although once proficient at team leadership, which provided the basis for policy guidance, he has tended to concentrate more on the latter than the former. There is the risk that mayors after some time in office will forget that the council's support is essential to their policy leadership.
68. Wikstrom, "Mayor as Policy Leader," p. 274.
69. Sparrow, "Emerging Chief Executive," p. 8.
70. Ferman, *Governing Ungovernable City*, chap. 9.

Chapter 5

1. David M. Olson, *The Legislative Process: A Comparative Approach* (New York: Harper & Row, 1981).
2. John S. Latcham and Howard D. Hamilton, in "Purposive Roles of City Councilmen," paper delivered at the 1974 Annual Meeting of the American Political Science Association, elaborate purposive, general-policy, representational, and interest-group roles, and note the existence of others. They draw on the research of John C. Wahlke et al., *The Legislative System* (New York: Wiley, 1962). Betty H. Zisk, *Local Interest Politics: A One-Way Street* (Indianapolis: Bobbs-Merrill, 1973) distinguishes among representational roles, purposive roles as interest aggregator and decision maker, and roles based on the conception of the job.
3. Heinz Eulau and Kenneth Prewitt, *Labyrinths of Democracy* (Indianapolis: Bobbs-Merrill, 1973), p. 12.
4. Wayne F. Anderson, Chester A. Newland, and Richard J. Stillman, *The Effective Local Government Manager* (Washington, D.C.: International City Management Association, 1983), p. 51.
5. National Municipal League, *Model City Charter*, 6th ed. (New York: National Municipal League, 1967), pp. 7–9.

6. National Municipal League, *Handbook for Council Members in Council-Manager Cities.* (New York: National Municipal League, 1976), pp. 39–40.

7. W. E. Lyons, "Making Judges Out of Legislators: Rezoning on a Quasi-Judicial Model," *Legislative Studies Quarterly* 8 (November, 1983): 675. The states are Colorado, Kansas, Kentucky, Maryland, Montana, Nebraska, Nevada, Virginia, and Washington.

8. Ibid., p. 681.

9. International City Management Association, *Elected Officials Handbooks,* 3rd ed., (Washington, D.C. ICMA, 1988), vol. 2, pp. 2–4.

10. The usual method for differentiating trustees and delegates is to describe the alternative orientations. The Bay Area study (Eulau and Prewitt, *Labyrinths of Democracy,* p. 665) used the following question: "There are two main points of view concerning how a representative *should* act when he has to make up his mind. One is that, having been elected, he should do what the voters want him to do, even if it isn't his own personal preference. The second is that he should use his own judgment, regardless of what others want him to do. Which of these views is closest to your own view?" Latcham and Hamilton, "Purposive Roles," p. 28, follows Wahlke et al., *The Legislative System,* in using wording that seems to make the delegate choice less palatable by substituting "judgment and principles" for "personal preference": the trustee "should always vote his own judgment or follow his own convictions and principles regardless of what others want him to do." The delegate "should always do what the voters want him to do, even if it is counter to his own judgment or principles."

11. Eulau and Prewitt, *Labyrinths of Democracy,* chap. 20.

12. Gary Halter, Political Scientist at Texas A&M University, and former mayor of College Station, has observed that political scientists have not attempted to investigate how council members determine public opinion, even though asking elected officials whether they depart from public opinion in their voting. In his opinion, council members must make inferences from parts of the public who purport to speak for the whole.

13. Zisk, *Local Interest Politics,* p. 99.

14. Ibid., p. 101.

15. Latcham and Hamilton, "Purposive Roles," p. 16.

16. David Mayhew, *Congress: The Electoral Connection* (New Haven: Yale University Press, 1974); Heinz Eulau and Paul D. Karps, "The Puzzle of Representation: Specifying Components of Responsiveness," *Legislative Studies Quarterly* 2 (August, 1977): 233–254; Bruce Cain, John Frerjohn, and Morris Fiorina, *The Personal Vote* (Cambridge, Mass.: Harvard University Press, 1987).

17. Cain et al., *Personal Vote,* p. 2.

18. Mayhew, *Congress,* p. 36.

19. Peggy Heilig and Robert J. Mundt, *Your Voice at City Hall* (Albany: State University of New York Press, 1984), pp. 17–18.

20. Ibid, p. 85.

21. Steven A. Peterson and William H. Dutton, "The Responsiveness of Local Legislators: A Case Study," *Urban Interest* 4 (Fall, 1982): 18–28.

22. Paul E. Petersen, *City Limits* (Chicago: University of Chicago Press, 1981) argues that city officials generally make development decisions in this way.

23. Terry N. Clark, *Cities Differ But How and Why?* (Washington, D.C.: U.S. Department of Housing and Urban Development, 1975).

24. Zisk, *Local Interest Politics*, p. 104.

25. Heilig and Mundt, *Your Voice at City Hall*, p. 152.

26. Eulau and Karps, "Puzzle of Representation," p. 247.

27. Charles R. Adrian, "A Typology for Nonpartisan Elections," *Western Political Quarterly* 12 (June, 1959): 449–458.

28. Tari Renner, "Municipal Election Processes: The Impact on Minority Representation," *Municipal Year Book 1988* (Washington, D.C.: International City Management Association, 1988), p. 17.

29. Ibid., p. 14.

30. Eugene C. Lee, *The Politics of Nonpartisanship* (Berkeley: University of California Press, 1960); Willis D. Hawley, *Nonpartisan Elections and the Case for Party Politics* (New York, Wiley, 1973); Chester Rogers and Harold Arman, "Nonpartisanship and Election to City Office," *Social Science Quarterly* 51 (March, 1971): 941–945.

31. Susan Welch and Timothy Bledsoe, *Urban Reform and Its Consequences: A Study in Representation* (Chicago: University of Chicago Press, 1988), pp. 42–46.

32. Furthermore, the smaller the district the lower the income and education level of council members. Ibid., p. 45. See also Edward C. Banfield and James Q. Wilson, *City Politics* (New York: Vintage Books, 1963), pp. 89–94.

33. Albert K. Karnig and Susan Welch, *Black Representation and Urban Policy* (Chicago: University of Chicago Press, 1980).

34. Joseph Zimmerman, *The Federated City* (New York: St. Martin's Press, 1972); Susan A. MacManus, "Mixed Electoral Systems: The Newest Reform Structure," *National Civic Review* 74 (November, 1985): 484–492; R. Darcy, Susan Welch, and Janet Clark, *Women, Elections, and Representation* (New York: Longman, 1987), pp. 40–41.

35. LBJ School of Public Affairs, "Local Government Elections Systems," *Policy Research Report No. 62* (Austin: University of Texas, 1984), pp. 46–55, 145–146.

36. Peggy Heilig and Robert J. Mundt, "Do Districts Make a Difference?" *Urban Interest* 3 (Spring, 1981): 62–75.

37. Welch and Bledsoe, *Urban Reform*, pp. 93, 105.

38. Heilig and Mundt, *Your Voice at City Hall*, p. 77.

39. LBJ School, "Local Election Systems," p. 146.

40. Welch and Bledsoe, *Urban Reform*, pp. 63–67, 73–77.

41. Heilig and Mundt, *Your Voice at City Hall*, pp. 85–86.

42. Peterson and Dutton, "Responsiveness of Local Legislators," also report a relationship between constituency characteristics and representational roles in the Buffalo metropolitan area. They find that service and allocation responsiveness—securing information, helping people with courts and other agencies, and working to get grants—is greater in jurisdictions with higher need.

43. Eugene C. Lee, "City Elections: A Statistical Profile," *Municipal Year Book 1963*. (Washington, D.C.: International City Management Association, 1963), pp. 83–92; Robert T. Alford and Eugene C. Lee, "Voting Turnout in American Cities," *American Political Science Review* 62 (September, 1968): 796–813.

44. Hawley, *Nonpartisan Elections*, pp. 28–33.

45. Welch and Bledsoe, *Urban Reform*, p. 52.

46. Ibid., p. 102.

47. Ibid., pp. 96–99.

48. Rufus P. Browning, Dale Rogers Marshall, and David H. Tabb, *Protest Is Not Enough* (Berkeley: University of California Press, 1984), pp. 32–34.

49. Eulau and Prewitt, *Labyrinths of Democracy*, p. 130.

50. Charles Gilbert and Christopher Claque, "Electoral Competition and Electoral Systems in Large Cities," *Journal of Politics* 24 (May, 1962): fn. 30, cite instances when the dominant party used the primary to purge council members opposed to the city administration.

51. Welch and Bledsoe, *Urban Reform*, pp. 65–66.

52. Gilbert and Claque, "Electoral Competition," pp. 323–349.

53. Welch and Bledsoe, *Urban Reform*, p. 66.

54. Larry Bennett, "In the Wake of Richard Daley: Chicago's Declining Politics of Party and the Shifting Politics of Development," paper delivered at the 1987 Annual Meeting of the American Political Science Association, argues that Daley secured party-based support from the city council for redevelopment plans opposed by neighborhood groups. This preference for party over constituency contributed to the erosion of the neighborhood base for the Democratic organization in Chicago.

55. Kenneth Prewitt, *The Recruitment of Political Leaders* (Indianapolis: Bobbs-Merrill, 1970), pp. 32–48. It does not follow, however, that the higher one's social status, the more likely one is to run for office or be successful. High-status persons may see running for, and serving in, office as unattractive, especially in partisan contests, and the sacrifices required may interfere with private pursuits (Robert A. Dahl, *Who Governs?* [New Haven: Yale University Press, 1961], pp. 282–293). Furthermore, the social characteristics of the district may exert a check on the success of candidates from the elite. In a working-class city, for example, union officials, school teachers or craftsmen might be elected, whereas the wealthiest and best-educated citizens do not hold office "because they are social isolates" (Prewitt, p. 40).

56. Prewitt, *Recruitment of Political Leaders*, p. 86.

57. Alvin D. Sokolow, "Legislators Without Ambition: Recruiting Citizens to Small Town Office," paper delivered at the 1987 Annual Meeting of the American Political Science Association.

58. Prewitt, *Recruitment of Political Leaders*, pp. 100–101.

59. Ibid., pp. 130–131.

60. Albert K. Karnig and B. Oliver Walter, "Municipal Elections: Registration, Incumbent Success, and Voter Participation," *Municipal Year Book 1977* (Washington, D.C.: International City Management Association, 1977).

61. Prewitt, *Recruitment of Political Leaders*, p. 137.

62. Zisk, *Local Interest Politics*, p. 57.

63. Joseph A. Schlesinger, *Ambition and Politics* (Chicago: Rand McNally, 1966). Anthony Catanese, *Planners and Politicians* (Beverly Hills: Sage, 1974), disagrees that ambition is a positive force. Rather, he sees the reelection impulse as the cause of shortsightedness and expediency.

64. Cortus T. Koehler, "Policy Development and Legislative Oversight in Council-Manager Cities: An Information and Communication Analysis," *Public Administration Review* 33 (September/October, 1973): 440.

65. Prewitt, *Recruitment of Political Leaders*, p. 176.

66. Peterson and Dutton, "Responsiveness of Local Legislators," p. 28. Some of these may have gotten caught up in the drama of holding public office and try to continue in their position as "spectators." See James David Barber, *The Lawmakers* (New Haven: Yale University Press, 1965), chaps. 2 and 4.

67. Frank Levy, Arnold Meltsner, and Aaron Wildavsky, *Urban Outcomes* (Berkeley: University of California, 1974), pp. 12–14.

68. Catanese, *Planners and Politicians*, has a negative view of council characteristics on each of these dimensions.

69. Heilig and Mundt, *Your Voice at City Hall*, p. 92.

70. Eulau and Prewitt, *Labyrinths of Democracy*, p. 119.

71. Hervey L. Sweetwood, *Tools for Leadership: A Handbook for Elected Officials* (Washington, D.C.: National League of Cities, 1980); ICMA, *Elected Officials Handbooks*.

72. Sweetwood, *Tools for Leadership*, pp. 8–10.

73. ICMA, *Elected Officials Handbooks*, vol. 1, p. 6; vol. 2, chap. 5; vol. 5, chap. 1. The third edition provides considerably more discussion than the second of the representational aspects of the council position.

74. Jeptha A. Carrell, "The City Manager and His Council: Sources of Conflict," *Public Administration Review* 22 (December, 1962): 203–208, attributed this dissatisfaction to a sense that the council lacked power. There is no difference, however, in the formal power possessed by the North Carolina councils with a positive and those with a negative self-assessment.

75. Anderson et al., *Effective Local Government Manager*, p. 61.

76. Eulau and Prewitt, *Labyrinths of Democracy*, pp. 157–163.

77. Browning et al., *Protest is Not Enough*, chap. 4.

78. This trait is often attributed to the reelection impulse, but there are other

factors that orient council members to the near term. They wish to see concrete evidence of their accomplishments in office. There are numerous immediate claims on resources that are difficult to deny in favor of projects that may materialize at an unknown time in the future.

79. Laurence E. Lynn, Jr., *Managing Public Policy* (Boston: Little, Brown, 1987), p. 17.

80. Glenn Abney and Thomas P. Lauth, "Councilmanic Intervention in Municipal Administration," *Administration & Society* 13 (February, 1982): 435–456.

81. Heilig and Mundt, *Your Voice at City Hall*, p. 94.

82. Kenneth R. Greene, "Municipal Administrators' Receptivity to Citizens' and Elected Officials' Contacts," *Public Administration Review*, 42 (July/August, 1982): 347.

83. In my twelve-city survey, the council respondents indicated a preferred level of involvement of 3.4 versus the actual involvement of 2.7. Department heads were supportive of a larger council role in evaluation.

84. James H. Svara, "The Complementary Roles of Officials in Council Manager Government," *Municipal Year Book 1988* (Washington, D.C.: International City Management Association, 1988), p. 29.

85. Stephen W. Burks and James F. Wolf, Eds., *Building City Council Leadership Skills: A Casebook of Models and Methods* (Washington: National League of Cities, 1981), pp. 151–155.

86. Richard A. Hughes. "The Role of the City Council," *Public Management* 54 (June, 1972): 5.

87. The ground rules in ICMA, *Elected Officials Handbooks*, vol. 1, pp. 44–48, for evaluating the manager reflect the overall emphasis on rationality and cooperation between elected officials and the executive. An evaluation should (1) have a defined purpose, (2) begin with mutual agreement and acceptance, (3) be regularly scheduled, (4) be open and constructive, (5) use objective criteria, (6) specify goals and action steps. Assessment of the manager potentially leads the council into an examination of a broad range of concerns related to policy, administration, management, and interpersonal relations within government and between the manager and the public.

88. Ibid., vol. 4, chap. 2.

89. David N. Ammons, *Municipal Productivity* (New York: Praeger, 1984), p. 198.

90. Heilig and Mundt, *Your Voice at City Hall*, p. 118.

91. Burks and Wolf, *Council Leadership Skills*, p. 8.

92. Robert D. Thomas, "The Search for Legitimacy and Competency in Mayor-Council Relations: The Case of Houston," paper delivered at the 1987 Meeting of the Southern Political Science Association, shows how the mayors severely restricted the council's involvement (McConn) or countered the council's efforts to expand its role (Whitmire).

93. Glenn Abney and Thomas P. Lauth, *The Politics of State and City*

Administration (Albany: State University of New York Press, 1986) p. 183, report that council members in council-manager cities were much less likely to seek projects or services for their districts or jobs for constituents than were council members in mayor-council cities.

94. Cain et al., *The Personal Vote*, p. 229.

Chapter 6

1. Theodore Lowi, "Machine Politics—Old and New," *Public Interest* No. 9 (Fall, 1967): 83–92.

2. Even Woodrow Wilson ("The Study of Administration," *Political Science Quarterly* 2 [June, 1887]: 197–220) who is associated with the dichotomy between policy and administration favored broad latitude for administrators. He felt that "large powers and unhampered discretion seem to me to be indispensable conditions of responsibility" for administrators.

3. Charles F. Goodsell, *The Case for Bureaucracy* (Chatham, N.J.: Chatham House, 1983), chap. 1.

4. Eugene P. Dvorin and Robert H. Simmons, *From Amoral to Humane Bureaucracy* (San Francisco: Canfield Press, 1972), chap. 3.

5. Richard J. Stillman II, *The Rise of the City Manager* (Albuquerque: University of New Mexico Press, 1974).

6. Marini, Frank, Ed., *Toward a New Public Administration*. New York: Chandler, 1971); Martin L. Needleman and Carolyn Emerson, *Guerrillas in the Bureaucracy* (New York: Wiley, 1974).

7. For a recent review of the literature of professionalism and whether public administrators match the characteristics of professionals, see Richard C. Kearney and Chandan Sinha, "Professionalism and Bureaucratic Responsiveness: Conflict or Compatibility?" *Public Administration Review* 48 (January/February, 1988): 571–579.

8. Michael Lipsky, *Street-Level Bureaucracy* (New York: Sage, 1980), p. 203; Judith E. Gruber, *Controlling Bureaucracies* (Berkeley: University of California Press, 1987), pp. 23–24; Harmon Zeigler, Ellen Kehoe, and Jane Reisman, *City Managers and School Superintendents* (New York: Praeger, 1985), pp. 50–51.

9. Gruber, *Controlling Bureaucracies,* chap. 4.

10. The link may be weaker for other professionals who work in government but are part of a group consisting of potentially independent practitioners. A physician employed in a public clinic would presumably distinguish between those aspects of his job that were subject to nonprofessional review (e.g., selection of patients or ordering supplies and equipment) and those that were not (e.g., decisions regarding diagnosis and treatment). Ibid., chap. 5, finds that teachers resist control of their professional actions as educators.

11. Lipsky, *Street-Level Bureaucracy,* p. 202.

12. Frank Levy, Arnold Meltsner, and Aaron Wildavsky, *Urban Outcomes* (Berkeley: University of California, 1974), p. 227. Bryan D. Jones, *Service Delivery in the City* (New York: Longman, 1980), pp. 20–21, also views distribution as an unintended byproduct but one that results in part from pursuing *organizational* goals. These goals typically lack explicit distributional criteria. For example, reducing crime or maintaining the quality of housing refer to overall service goals rather than patterns of distribution.

13. Levy et al., *Urban Outcomes*, pp. 231–232.

14. Michael Lipsky, "Toward a Theory of Street-Level Bureaucracy," in Willis D. Hawley and Michael Lipsky, Eds., *Theoretical Perspectives in Urban Politics* (Englewood, Cliffs, N.J.: Prentice-Hall, 1976), pp. 196–213.

15. Ibid., pp. 201–207. The coping mechanisms include depersonalizing the citizen, classifying clients with stereotypes rather than dealing with them as individuals, handling citizens on a mass basis using routinized procedures, and responding harshly to any challenge to the authority of the *position* even if the citizen is only questioning the actions of the *person* with whom he is dealing.

16. Bryan D. Jones, *Governing Buildings and Building Government* (University, Ala.: University of Alabama Press, 1985).

17. Glen Sparrow, "The Emerging Chief Executive: The San Diego Experience," *Urban Resources* 2 (Fall, 1984): 3–8.

18. Barbara Ferman, *Governing the Ungovernable City: Political Skill, Leadership, and the Modern Mayor* (Philadelphia: Temple University Press, 1985), pp. 210–211.

19. Glenn Abney and Thomas P. Lauth, *The Politics of State and City Administration* (Albany: State University of New York Press, 1986), p. 224.

20. Ibid., p. 152.

21. Kearney and Sinha, "Professionalism and Bureaucratic Responsiveness," p. 575.

22. Joseph P. Viteritti, "Bureaucratic Environments, Efficiency, and Equity in Urban-Service-Delivery Systems," in Richard C. Rich, Ed., *The Politics of Urban Public Services* (Lexington, Mass.: Lexington Books, 1982) pp. 58–59. Italics in original.

23. Ibid., p. 65. Viteritti concludes from his research in New York City that these conditions may be produced by the nature of service and clientele, for example, a necessary service provided to the entire population is less subject to political pressures than an "optional" program provided only to selected groups.

24. Jones, *Service Delivery* and *Governing Buildings*.

25. Jones, *Service Delivery*, p. 77, also demonstrates that demand itself is much more highly affected by need than standard explanations of other forms of political participation recognize. In Chicago, however, the presence of large numbers of party workers in certain wards expands the level of demands.

26. Jones, *Service Delivery*, p. 227.

27. Jones, *Governing Buildings*, p. 124.

260 / Notes

260 / Notes

260 / Notes

28. Jones, *Service Delivery*, p. 225; Jones, *Governing Buildings*, p. 66.
29. Jones, *Governing Buildings*, p. 101. He argues, p. 151, that the bureaucratic impulse is so strong that without special effort there is a reversion to standard decision rules.
30. Ibid., p. 166.
31. Gordon Chase and Elizabeth C. Reveal, *How to Manage in the Public Sector* (Reading, Mass.: Addison-Wesley, 1983), p. 18.
32. Levy et al., *Urban Outcomes*, Appendix B.
33. John Clayton Thomas, *Between Citizen and City* (Lawrence: University of Kansas Press, 1986), pp. 101–102.
34. Levy *et al.*, *Urban Outcomes*, p. 233.
35. Zeigler *et al.*, *Managers and Superintendents*, p. 51, indicate that autonomy is not an obsession with city managers as it is with superintendents.
36. See the ICMA codes of ethics in Stillman, *Rise of the City Manager*, Appendix D. The manager's contributions to democratic governance are discussed in John Nalbandian, "The Evolution of Local Governance: A New Democracy," *Public Management* 69 (June, 1987): 2–5.
37. Richard J. Stillman II, "The City Manager: Professional Helping Hand, or Political Hired Hand? *Public Administration Review* 37 (November/December, 1977): 659–670.
38. Gladys M. Kammerer, Charles D. Farris, John M. DeGrove, and Alfred B. Clubok, *City Managers in Politics* (Gainesville: University of Florida Press, 1962), pp. 81–82.
39. Ferman, *Governing the Ungovernable City*, chap. 5. The term "shrinking violets" is from Anthony Downs, *Inside Bureaucracy* (Boston: Little, Brown, 1967).
40. Jones, *Governing Buildings*, p. 138.
41. James B. Hogan, *The Chief Administrative Officer* (Tucson: University of Arizona Press, 1976), p. 51.
42. Zeigler et al., *Managers and Superintendents*.
43. Gruber, *Controlling Bureaucracies*, pp. 23–24. It is harder to accept the conclusion that control is absent when administrators who are acting at their own behest "act in a way consonant with citizen preferences." This is virtually indistinguishable from anticipated reactions of what citizens want which Gruber classifies as controlled behavior, p. 13. We shall treat behavior that is consistent with public preferences and needs as an indicator of responsibility despite the contention of Zeigler et al. (*Managers and Superintendents*, p. 72) that acting on future needs as opposed to existing demands is a new form of authoritarianism.
44. For example, Howard D. Tipton, "Promoting the C-M Plan," *Public Management* 67 (July, 1985): 10, lists as a feature of mayor-council government that "the mayor is responsible for hiring and firing the bureaucracy" and "may not separate political from merit considerations."
45. Stillman, *Rise of the City Manager*, pp. 81–82.

46. Ibid.; Raymond E. Wolfinger, *The Politics of Progress* (Englewood Cliffs, N.J.: Prentice-Hall, 1974), pp. 402–404.

47. Hogan, *Chief Administrative Officer*, p. 47. All the additional data on CAOs in this paragraph are from Hogan's Appendix C.

48. Stillman, *Rise of the City Manager*, p. 10.

49. Mary A. Schellinger. "Local Government Managers: Profile of the Professionals in a Maturing Profession," *Municipal Year Book 1985* (Washington, D.C.: International City Management Association, 1985), p. 187.

50. Ibid. Computed from data given there.

51. Zeigler et al., *Managers and Superintendents*, pp. 53–55. Managers are not as upwardly mobile as superintendents, but they move more frequently.

52. Abney and Lauth, *Politics of Administration*, p. 137.

53. Karl Bosworth, "The Manager Is a Politician," *Public Administration Review* 18 (Summer, 1958): 216–222.

54. Deil Wright, "The Manager as a Development Administrator," in Robert Daland, Ed., *Comparative Urban Research* (Beverly Hills: Sage, 1969), pp. 203–248.

55. Charles R. Adrian, "Leadership and Decision-Making in Manager Cities," *Public Administration Review* 18 (Summer, 1958): 208–213; and William Browne, "Municipal Managers and Policy: A Partial Test of the Svara Dichotomy–Duality Model," *Public Administration Review* 45 (September-October, 1985): 620–622.

56. Charldean Newell and David N. Ammons, "Role Emphasis of City Managers and Other Municipal Executives," *Public Administration Review* 47 (May/June, 1987): 246–252. The breakdown of time for executive mayors is similar for management but manifests a different split between the other two roles: policy, 26 percent; political, 30 percent; and management, 44 percent.

57. Richard J. Stillman II, "Local Public Management in Transition: A Report on the Current State of the Profession," *Municipal Year Book 1982* (Washington, D.C.: International City Management Association, 1982), p. 172.

58. Browne, "Municipal Managers," pp. 620–622.

59. Stillman, *Rise of the City Manager*, p. 112.

60. International City Management Association, *New Worlds of Service* (Washington, D.C.: ICMA, 1979).

61. Newell and Ammons, "Role Emphasis of City Managers," p. 252.

62. Stillman, "Local Public Management," p. 169.

63. Chase and Reveal, *How to Manage*, p. 19.

64. Ibid., p. 33.

65. Jones, *Governing Buildings*, p. 134.

66. Chase and Reveal, *How to Manage*, p. 49.

67. Levy et al., *Urban Outcomes*, pp. 126–128.

68. The findings in this paragraph and the next are from Abney and Lauth, *Politics of Administration*, Tables 7.3–7.5. Because of the way their scale is

constructed, we can only be certain about form of government in the "extreme" categories. A council-manager government with district elections and party activity would be moderately "nonreformed" whereas a mayor-council with at-large elections and little or no party activity would be moderately "reformed."

69. Gruber, *Controlling Bureaucracies*, p. 92.

70. Ibid., pp. 109–110.

71. Jones, *Governing Buildings*, observes that the bureaucracy controls implementation and the party produces deviations from established policy.

72. Robert F. Nardulli and Jeffrey M. Stonecash, *Politics, Professionalism, and Urban Services* (Cambridge, Mass.: Oelgeschlager, Gunn & Hain, 1981), pp. 33–34.

73. Gruber, *Controlling Bureaucracies*, pp. 205–214.

74. Nardulli and Stonecash, *Politics, Professionalism, and Urban Services*, p. 24.

75. For a comprehensive discussion of administrative roles and management practices, see Wayne F. Anderson, Chester A. Newland, and Richard J. Stillman, *The Effective Local Government Manager* (Washington, D.C.: International City Management Association, 1983); and David R. Morgan, *Managing Urban America*, 2nd ed. (Monterey: Brooks/Cole, 1984).

76. Anthony Catanese, *Planners and Politicians* (Beverly Hills: Sage, 1974).

77. John Nalbandian and J. Terry Edwards, "The Values of Public Administrators: A Comparison with Lawyers, Social Workers, and Business Administrators," *Review of Public Personnel Administration* 4 (Fall, 1983): 114–127.

78. Thomas, *Between Citizen and City*, p. 88.

79. Roy E. Green, "Local Government Managers: Styles and Challenges," *Baseline Data Report*, 19 (March/April, 1987): 3.

80. Ronald O. Loveridge, *City Managers in Legislative Politics* (Indianapolis: Bobbs-Merrill, 1971), pp. 42–43.

81. Stillman, "Local Public Management," p. 172.

82. Greene, "Local Government Managers," p. 3.

83. Loveridge, *City Managers*, pp. 93–95.

84. Hogan, *Chief Administrative Officer*, p. 51.

85. In Table 6–1 and analysis of divergence in policy orientation, Loveridge, *City Managers*, omits the latter item that supports convergence.

86. The extreme opposition to this activity by council members in the Bay Area may be attributable to the wording of the question. Although Loveridge observes that his Table 6–1 contains responses to "identical questions," the question for council members refers to the manager's "working through the most powerful members of the community to achieve his policy goals" (Table 5–3, p. 86), whereas the manager's question omits the word "his" (Table 4–2, p. 49). The council version implies that the manager is seeking outside leverage to advance his own policy agenda independently of the council.

87. Hogan, *Chief Administrative Officer*, p. 51.

88. Abney and Lauth, *Politics of Administration,* chap. 7.

89. Jones, *Governing Buildings,* describes a situation in which there is coexistence between professional and party perspectives and a civil service personnel system and patronage. Two other examples of the incorporation of professionalism into mayor-council settings may be noted. Larry Bennett, "In the Wake of Richard Daley: Chicago's Declining Politics of Party and the Shifting Politics of Development," paper delivered at the 1987 Annual Meeting of the American Political Science Association, emphasizes Mayor Daley's commitment to good management as part of his political appeal in Chicago. Martin Shefter, *Political Crisis/Fiscal Crisis* (New York: Basic Books, 1985), p. 150, points out that the management information system created in New York after the fiscal crisis is the best among cities and comparable to that found in well-managed private firms.

90. Terry L. Cooper, *The Responsible Administrator* (Port Washington, N.Y.: Associated Faculty Press, 1982).

91. Richard T. Mayer and Michael M. Harmon, "Teaching Moral Education in Public Administration," *Southern Review of Public Administration* 6 (Summer, 1982): 223.

92. For analysis of the statements, see James H. Svara, "The Responsible Manager: Building on the Code and the Declaration," *Public Management* 69 (August, 1987): 14–19.

93. In addition to Anderson et al., *Effective Local Government Manager,* see Harry P. Hatry, et al., *How Effective Are Your Community Services?* (Washington, D.C.: Urban Institute, 1979); Elizabeth J. Kellar, Ed., *Managing with Less* (Washington, D.C.: International City Management Association, 1981); John Greiner et al., *Productivity and Motivation: A Review of State and Local Initiatives* (Washington, D.C.: Urban Institute, 1981).

94. James S. Bowman, "Ethical Issues for the Public Manager," in William B. Eddy, Ed., *Handbook of Organization Management* (New York: Dekker, 1983), pp. 69–102.

95. Cooper, *Responsible Administrator,* p. 127.

96. Mayer and Harmon, "Teaching Moral Education," p. 223.

97. John A. Rohr, *Ethics for Bureaucrats* (New York: Dekker, 1978), p. 2.

98. David K. Hart, "The Honorable Bureaucrat among Philistines," *Administration & Society* 15 (May, 1983): 45.

99. H. George Frederickson and David K. Hart, "The Public Service and the Benevolence of Patriotism," *Public Administration Review* 45 (September/October, 1985): 549.

100. Ralph C. Chandler, "The Problem of Moral Reasoning in American Public Administration: The Case for a Code of Ethics," *Public Administration Review* 43 (January/February, 1983): 33.

101. Hart, "Honorable Bureaucrat," p. 45.

102. The prologue to "City Management Declaration of Ideals" states that the ICMA *as an association* works to achieve equity, social justice, human

dignity, and the quality of life, but these are not related to the behavior of individual managers (*Public Management* 66 [August, 1984]: 2). Ralph C. Chandler, "The Problem of Moral Illiteracy in Professional Discourse: The Case of the Statement of Principles of the American Society for Public Administration," *Dialogue* 4 (Summer, 1982): 9, states that ASPA in a 1981 proposed code of ethics would have committed itself to "energetic promotion of public policies to enhance freedom, equality, justice, economic well-being, and the celebration of life," but this clause did not survive in the final version.

103. Douglas Yates, "Hard Choices: Justifying Bureaucratic Decisions," in Joel Fleischman et al., *Public Duties*. (Cambridge, Mass.: Harvard University Press, 1981), pp. 32–51.

104. Clifford J. Wirth and Michael L. Vasu, "Ideology and Decisionmaking for American City Managers," paper presented at the 1984 meeting of the American Political Science Association.

105. Elizabeth Howe and Jerome Kaufman, "The Ethics of Contemporary American Planners," *APA Journal* (July, 1979): 243–255.

106. Ibid., pp. 247–248.

107. Frank Marini, Ed., *Toward a New Public Administration* (New York: Chandler, 1971); Rohr, *Ethics for Bureaucrats*.

108. Lipsky, *Street Level Bureaucracy*, pp. 195–196.

109. Anderson et al., *Effective Local Government Manager*, p. 56, suggests devoting one meeting a month to assessing a different program or service delivery area.

110. Walter L. Balk, "Toward a Government Productivity Ethic," *Public Administration Review* 37 (January/February, 1978): 46–50.

111. The emphasis on the manager and the management dimension should not slight the importance of developing and administering programs in a way that is conducive to productivity. Peter F. Drucker, *Innovation and Entrepreneurship* (New York: Harper & Row, 1985) argues that a clear sense of purpose is the first step to increased innovation in the public sector. Balk, "Productivity Ethic," p. 49, observes that productivity improvement requires a setting in which mission and policy are consistent with organizational performance objectives. Too often competing interests produce unclear purpose in program definition that impedes effective administration and efficient management. In some cities, managers have taken the lead in improving productivity, only to have elected officials block change.

112. David N. Ammons, *Municipal Productivity* (New York: Praeger, 1984), p. 212. See also Martin Landau and Russell Stout, Jr., "To Manage Is Not to Control: Or the Folly of Type II Errors," *Public Administration Review* 39 (March/April, 1979): 148–156.

113. Karma Ruder, "The Debates Underpinning the ICMA Code of Ethics," *Public Management* 69 (August, 1987): 11. The previous guidelines adopted in 1972 offered no elaboration of the "resist encroachment" tenet.

114. Debra Stewart, "Ethics and the Profession of Public Administration:

The Moral Responsibility of Individuals in Public Sector Organizations," *Public Administration Quarterly* 10 (Winter, 1985): 487–495; Dennis F. Thompson, "The Possibility of Administrative Ethics," *Public Administration Review* 45 (September/October, 1985): 555–561.

115. Gary L. Wamsley, Charles T. Goodsell, John A. Rohr, Camilla M. Stevers, Orion F. White, and James F. Wolf, "The Public Administration and the Governance Process: Refocusing the American Dialogue," in Ralph C. Chandler, Ed., *A Centennial History of the American Administrative State.* (New York: Free Press, 1987), pp. 291–343.

116. Chase and Reveal, *How to Manage,* p. 60.

117. Jones, *Governing Buildings,* pp. 137–138.

118. Thompson, "The Possibility of Administrative Ethics."

119. Chase and Reveal, *How to Manage,* p. 113.

120. Ibid., pp. 114–115.

121. A group excluded by one department may be the "constituency" for another, for example, minorities had difficulty influencing the New York School System in the 1960s but were supporters of and empowered by the antipoverty agencies (see Shefter, *Political Crisis,* pp. 67–71).

122. Jones, *Governing Buildings,* p. 183.

123. Chase and Reveal, *How to Manage,* pp. 112–113.

124. Ibid., pp. 56–57.

125. Jones, *Governing Buildings,* p. 134.

126. Ibid., 149–150. In Chicago in 1974—the only year for which data are available—the proportion of positions that were likely patronage appointments ranged from 3 percent or less in police and fire to almost 50 percent in public works and streets and sanitation.

127. Donald A. Blubaugh, "The Changing Role of the Public Administrator," *Public Management* 69 (June, 1987): 7–10.

Chapter 7

1. Heinz Eulau and Kenneth Prewitt, *Labyrinths of Democracy* (Indianapolis: Bobbs-Merrill, 1973), p. 121. Italics in original.

2. Robert Axelrod, *The Evolution of Cooperation* (New York: Basic Books, 1984), pp. 110–123.

3. Ibid., p. 123.

4. Douglas Yates, *The Politics of Management* (San Francisco: Josey-Bass, 1985), chap. 6.

5. International City Management Association, *Elected Officials Handbooks,* 3rd ed., (Washington: ICMA, 1988), vol. 1, chap. 2; vol. 2, chap. 4.

6. For example, "Greensboro Visions" is a community strategic planning process being undertaken by the city government in conjunction with Guilford County and the Chamber of Commerce in which citizen task forces are develop-

ing long-range plans in the areas of economic development, public education, low-income housing, land-use planning, and transportation. For a review of approaches, see Ronald K. Vogel and Bert E. Swanson, "Setting Agenda for Community Change: The Community Goal-Setting Strategy," *Journal of Urban Affairs* 10 (No. 1, 1988): 41–61.

7. John Parr, "The Council-Manager Form and the Future," *Public Management* 69 (February, 1987): 4–6.

8. Mike Royko, "No Gray Areas in City Politics," *The Chapel Hill Newspaper* (September 19, 1984): 4A.

9. Charles E. Lindblom, "The Science of Muddling Through," *Public Administration Review* 19 (Spring, 1959): 79–88, and "Still Muddling, Not Yet Through" *Public Administration Review* 39 (November/December, 1979): 517–526.

10. Douglas Yates, *Bureaucratic Democracy* (Cambridge, Mass.: Harvard University Press, 1982).

11. Eulau and Prewitt, *Labyrinths of Democracy*, p. 423, suggest that favoring particular clienteles is more likely when there is a "placid political relationship between the council and the public."

12. Barbara Ferman, *Governing the Ungovernable City: Political Skill, Leadership, and the Modern Mayor* (Philadelphia: Temple University Press, 1985).

13. Yates, *Bureaucratic Democracy*.

14. Willis D. Hawley, *Nonpartisan Elections and the Case for Party Politics* (New York: Wiley, 1973); Bryan D. Jones, *Governing Buildings and Building Government* (University, Ala.: University of Alabama Press, 1985); Judith E. Gruber, *Controlling Bureaucracies* (Berkeley: University of California Press, 1987).

15. Susan Welch and Timothy Bledsoe, *Urban Reform and Its Consequences: A Study in Representation* (Chicago: University of Chicago Press, 1988), p. 120.

16. Terrell Blodgett and William N. Cassella, Jr., "The Model Charter Revision Project: Process and Outcomes," paper presented at the 1987 Southeastern Conference on Public Administration (SECOPA).

17. Glenn Abney and Thomas P. Lauth, *The Politics of State and City Administration* (Albany: State University of New York Press, 1986), p. 194.

18. Charles R. Adrian, "Forms of City Government in American History," *Municipal Year Book 1988* (Washington, D.C.: International City Management Association, 1988), pp. 9–10.

References

Abney, Glenn, and Thomas P. Lauth. 1982a. Councilmanic Intervention in Municipal Administration. *Administration & Society* 13 (February): 435–456.

―――. 1982b. Influence of the Chief Executive on City Line Agencies. *Public Administration Review* 42 (March/April): 135–143.

―――. 1986. *The Politics of State and City Administration*. Albany: State University of New York Press.

Adrian, Charles R. 1958. Leadership and Decision-Making in Manager Cities. *Public Administration Review* 18 (Summer): 208–213.

―――. 1959. A Typology for Nonpartisan Elections. *Western Political Quarterly* 12 (June): 449–458.

―――. 1988. Forms of City Government in American History. *Municipal Year Book 1988*. Washington, D.C.: International City Management Association: 3–12.

Adrian, Charles R., and Charles Press. 1977. *Governing Urban America*, 5th ed. New York: McGraw-Hill.

Alford, Robert T., and Eugene C. Lee. 1968. Voting Turnout in American Cities. *American Political Science Review* 62 (September): 796–813.

Allison, Graham T., Jr. 1971. *Essence of Decision*. Boston: Little, Brown.

―――. 1984. Public and Private Management: Are They Fundamentally Alike in All Unimportant Respects?, in Barry Bozeman and Jeffrey Strassman, Eds., *New Directions in Public Administration*. Monterey: Brooks/Cole: 32–45.

Ammons, David N. 1984. *Municipal Productivity*. New York: Praeger.

Anderson, Wayne F., Chester A. Newland, and Richard J. Stillman. 1983. *The*

Effective Local Government Manager. Washington, D.C.: International City Management Association.

Astley, W. Graham, and Andrew H. Van de Ven. 1983. Central Perspectives and Debates in Organization Theory. *Administrative Science Quarterly* 28 (June): 245–273.

Axelrod, Robert. 1984. *The Evolution of Cooperation*. New York: Basic Books.

Bachrach, Peter, and Morton S. Baratz. 1963. Decisions and Nondecisions. *American Political Science Review* 57 (September): 632–642.

Balk, Walter L. 1978. Toward a Government Productivity Ethic. *Public Administration Review* 37 (January/February): 46–50.

Banfield, Edward C. 1965. *Political Influence*. New York: Free Press.

Banfield, Edward C., and James Q. Wilson. 1963. *City Politics*. New York: Vintage Books.

Barber, James David. 1965. *The Lawmakers*. New Haven: Yale University Press.

———. 1972. *The Presidential Character*. Englewood Cliffs, N.J.: Prentice-Hall.

Bardach, Eugene. 1977. *The Implementation Game*. Cambridge, Mass.: MIT Press.

Barnard, Chester I. 1938. *The Functions of the Executive*. Cambridge, Mass.: Harvard University Press.

Bennett, Larry. 1987. In the Wake of Richard Daley: Chicago's Declining Politics of Party and the Shifting Politics of Development. Paper presented at the Annual Meeting of the American Political Science Association, Chicago, Ill.

Bernard, Richard M., and Bradley R. Rice. 1975. Political Environment and the Adoption of Progressive Municipal Reform. *Journal of Urban History* 1 (February): 149–175.

Blodgett, Terrell, and William N. Cassella, Jr. 1987. The Model Charter Revision Project: Process and Outcomes. Paper presented at the Southeastern Conference on Public Administration, New Orleans, La.

Blubaugh, Donald A. 1987. The Changing Role of the Public Administrator. *Public Management* 69 (June): 7–10.

Bolotin, Frederick N., and David L. Cingranelli. 1983. Equity and Urban Policy: The Underclass Hypothesis Revisited. *Journal of Politics* 45 (February): 209–219.

Bosworth, Karl. 1958. The Manager Is a Politician. *Public Administration Review* 18 (Summer): 216–222.

Bower, Joseph L. 1977. Effective Public Management. *Harvard Business Review* 55 (March/April): 131–140.

Bowman, James S. 1983. Ethical Issues for the Public Manager, in William B. Eddy, Ed., *Handbook of Organization Management*. New York: Dekker: 69–102.

Boyle, John, and David Jacobs. 1982. The Intracity Distribution of Services: A Multivariate Analysis. *American Political Science Review* 76 (June): 371–397.

Boynton, Robert Paul, and Deil S. Wright. 1971. Mayor-Manager Relationships in Large Council-Manager Cities: A Reinterpretation. *Public Administration Review* 31 (January/February): 28–36.

Browne, William. 1985. Municipal Managers and Policy: A Partial Test of the Svara Dichotomy–Duality Model. *Public Administration Review* 45 (September-October): 620–622.

Browning, Rufus P., Dale Rogers Marshall, and David H. Tabb. 1984. *Protest Is Not Enough*. Berkeley: University of California Press.

Burgess, Phillip M. 1975. Capacity Building and the Elements of Public Management. *Public Administration Review* 35 (December): 705–716.

Burks, Stephen W., and James F. Wolf, Eds. 1981. *Building City Council Leadership Skills: A Casebook of Models and Methods*. Washington: National League of Cities.

Cain, Bruce, John Frerjohn, and Morris Fiorina. 1987. *The Personal Vote*. Cambridge, Mass.: Harvard University Press.

Caro, Robert A. 1974. *The Power Broker*. New York: Random House.

Carrell, Jeptha A. 1962. The City Manager and His Council: Sources of Conflict. *Public Administration Review* 22 (December): 203–208.

Catanese, Anthony. 1974. *Planners and Politicians*. Beverly Hills: Sage.

Chandler, Ralph C. 1982. The Problem of Moral Illiteracy in Professional Discourse: The Case of the Statement of Principles of the American Society for Public Administration. *Dialogue* 4 (Summer): 2–14.

———. 1983. The Problem of Moral Reasoning in American Public Administration: The Case for a Code of Ethics. *Public Administration Review* 43 (January/February): 32–39.

Chase, Gordon, and Elizabeth C. Reveal. 1983. *How to Manage in the Public Sector*. Reading, Mass.: Addison-Wesley.

Cisneros, Henry G. 1985. The Quality of C-M Government. *Public Management* 67 (January): 3–5.

Clark, Terry N. 1971. Community Structure, Decision-Making, Budget Expenditure, and Urban Renewal, in 51 American Communities, in Charles M. Bonjean, Terry N. Clark, and Robert L. Lineberry, Eds., *Community Politics*. New York: Free Press: 293–313.

———. 1975. Cities Differ But How and Why? Washington, D.C.: U.S. Department of Housing and Urban Development.

Clark, Terry N., and Lorna C. Ferguson. 1983. *City Money*. New York: Columbia University Press.

Cooper, Terry L. 1982. *The Responsible Administrator*. Port Washington, N.Y.: Associated Faculty Press.

Costello, Timothy W. 1971. Change in Municipal Government: A View from the Inside. *Journal of Applied Behavioral Science* 7 (May/April): 131–145.

Crain, Robert L., and James H. Vanecko. 1968. Elite Influence in School Desegregation, in James Q. Wilson, Ed., *City Politics and Public Policy*. New York: Wiley. 127–148.

Crecine, John P. 1969. *Governmental Problem-Solving*. Chicago: Rand McNally.

Cunningham, James V. 1970. *Urban Leadership in the Sixties*. Cambridge, Mass.: Schenkman.

Cyert, Richard M., and James G. March. 1963. *A Behavioral Theory of the Firm*. Englewood Cliffs, N.J.: Prentice-Hall.

Dahl, Robert A. 1956. *A Preface to Democratic Theory*. Chicago: University of Chicago Press.

———. 1961. *Who Governs?* New Haven: Yale University Press.

Darcy, R., Susan Welch, and Janet Clark. 1987. *Women, Elections, and Representation*. New York: Longman.

Downs, Anthony. 1967. *Inside Bureaucracy*. Boston: Little, Brown.

Drucker, Peter F. 1985. *Innovation and Entrepreneurship*. New York: Harper & Row.

Dutton, William H., and Alana Northrop. 1978. Municipal Reform and the Changing Pattern of Urban Party Politics. *American Politics Quarterly* 6 (October): 429–452.

Dvorin, Eugene P., and Robert H. Simmons. 1972. *From Amoral to Humane Bureaucracy*. San Francisco: Canfield Press.

Dye, Thomas R., and John A. Garcia. 1978. Structure, Function, and Policy in American Cities. *Urban Affairs Quarterly* 14 (September): 103–122.

Dye, Thomas R., and Susan MacManus. 1976. Predicting City Government Structure. *American Journal of Political Science* 20 (May): 257–272.

East, John P. 1965. *Council-Manager Government*. Chapel Hill: University of North Carolina Press.

Easton, David. 1963. *The Political System*. Chicago: University of Chicago Press.

Eberts, Paul R., and Janet M. Kelly. 1985. How Mayors Get Things Done: Community Politics and Mayors' Initiatives. *Research in Urban Policy* 1: 39–70.

Eisinger, Peter K. 1982a. Black Employment in Municipal Jobs: The Impact of Black Political Power. *American Political Science Review* 76 (June): 380–392.

———. 1982b. Economic Conditions of Black Employment in Municipal Bureaucracies. *American Journal of Political Science* 26 (November): 754–771.

Engstrom, Richard L., and Michael D. McDonald. 1981. The Election of Blacks to City Councils: Clarifying the Impact of Electoral Arrangements on the Seats/Population Relationship. *American Political Science Review* 75 (June): 344–354.

Eulau, Heinz, and Paul D. Karps. 1977. The Puzzle of Representation: Specifying Components of Responsiveness. *Legislative Studies Quarterly* 2 (August): 233–254.

Eulau, Heinz, and Kenneth Prewitt. 1973. *Labyrinths of Democracy.* Indianapolis: Bobbs-Merrill.

Feiock, Richard C., and James Clingermayer. 1986. Municipal Representation, Executive Power, and Economic Development Policy Activity. *Policy Studies Journal* 15 (December): 211–229.

Ferman, Barbara. 1985. *Governing the Ungovernable City: Political Skill, Leadership, and the Modern Mayor.* Philadelphia: Temple University Press.

Flentje, Edward H., and Wendla Counihan. 1984. Running a Reformed City. *Urban Resources* 2 (Fall): 9–14.

Frederickson, H. George, and David K. Hart. 1985. The Public Service and the Benevolence of Patriotism. *Public Administration Review* 45 (September/October): 547–553.

Fulton, William. 1985. Henry Cisneros: Mayor as Entrepreneur. *Planning* 51 (February): 4–9.

George, Alexander L. 1968. Political Leadership in American Cities. *Daedalus* 97 (Fall): 1194–1217.

George, Billy. 1984. The Emergence of the Strong-Mayor, Council-Manager City: A Response to the Times. *Urban Resources* 2 (Fall): A1–A2.

Gilbert, Charles, and Christopher Claque. 1962. Electoral Competition and Electoral Systems in Large Cities. *Journal of Politics* 24 (May): 323–349.

Goodnow, Frank J. 1914. *Politics and Administration.* New York: MacMillan.

Goodsell, Charles F. 1983. *The Case for Bureaucracy.* Chatham, N.J.: Chatham House.

Green, Roy E. 1987. Local Government Managers: Styles and Challenges. *Baseline Data Report* 19 (March/April): 1–11.

Greene, Kenneth R. 1982. Municipal Administrators' Receptivity to Citizens' and Elected Officials' Contacts. *Public Administration Review* 42 (July/August): 346–353.

Greenstone, J. David, and Paul E. Peterson. 1973. *Race and Authority in Urban Politics.* New York: Sage.

Greer, Ann. 1974. *The Mayor's Mandate.* Cambridge, Mass.: Schenkman.

Greiner, John, Harry P. Hatry, Margo P. Koss, Annie P. Millar, and Jane P. Woodward. 1981. *Productivity and Motivation: A Review of State and Local Initiatives.* Washington, D.C.: Urban Institute.

Gruber, Judith E. 1987. *Controlling Bureaucracies.* Berkeley: University of California Press.

Hart, David K. 1983. The Honorable Bureaucrat among Philistines. *Administration & Society* 15 (May): 43–48.

Hatry, Harry P., Louis P. Blair, Donald M. Fisk, John M. Greiner, John R. Hall, Jr., and Philip S. Schaeman. 1979. *How Effective Are Your Community Services?* Washington, D.C.: Urban Institute.

Hawley, Willis D. 1973. *Nonpartisan Elections and the Case for Party Politics.* New York: Wiley.

Hays, Samuel P. 1964. The Politics of Reform in Municipal Government in the Progressive Era. *Pacific Northwest Quarterly* 55 (October): 157–169.

———. 1967. Political Parties and the Community-Society Continuum, in William N. Chambers and Walter D. Burnham, Eds., *The American Party System.* New York: Oxford University Press: 152–181.

Heilig, Peggy, and Robert J. Mundt. 1981. Do Districts Make a Difference? *Urban Interest* 3 (Spring): 62–75.

———. 1984. *Your Voice at City Hall.* Albany: State University of New York Press.

Higham, John. 1966. *Strangers in the Land: Patterns of American Nativism 1860–1925.* New York: Atheneum.

Hirlinger, Michael W., and Robert E. England. 1986. *City Managers and the Legislative Process: The Case of Oklahoma.* Tulsa: University of Oklahoma, Bureau of Governmental Research.

Hirschman, Aibert O. 1970. *Exit, Voice, and Loyalty.* Cambridge, Mass.: Harvard University Press.

Hogan, James B. 1976. *The Chief Administrative Officer.* Tucson: University of Arizona Press.

Holli, Melvin G. 1969. *Reform in Detroit: Hazen S. Pingree and Urban Politics.* New York: Oxford University Press.

Howe, Elizabeth, and Jerome Kaufman. 1979. The Ethics of Contemporary American Planners. *APA Journal* (July): 243–255.

Hughes, Richard A. 1972. The Role of the City Council. *Public Management* 54 (June): 3–5.

International City Management Association. 1977. *Make Policy—Who Me?* Washington, D.C.: ICMA.

———. 1979. *New Worlds of Service.* Washington, D.C.: ICMA.

———. 1984a. ICMA Code of Ethics with Guidelines. *Public Management* 66 (February): 10–11.

———. 1984b. City Management Declaration of Ideals. *Public Management* 66 (August): 2.

———. 1988. *Elected Officials Handbooks,* 3rd ed. Washington: ICMA.

Johnson, Karl F., and C. J. Hein. 1985. Assessment of the Council-Manager Form of Government Today: Managers Meet the Challenge Through Balance. *Public Management* 67 (July): 4–6.

Jones, Bryan D. 1980. *Service Delivery in the City.* New York: Longman.

———. 1983. *Governing Urban America.* Boston: Little, Brown.

———. 1985. *Governing Buildings and Building Governments.* University, Ala.: University of Alabama Press.

Judd, Dennis R. 1984. *The Politics of American Cities,* 2nd ed. Boston: Little, Brown.

Kammerer, Gladys M., Charles D. Farris, John M. DeGrove, and Alfred B. Clubok. 1962. *City Managers in Politics.* Gainesville: University of Florida Press.

Karnig, Albert K. 1975. Private Regarding Policy, Civil Rights Groups, and the Mediating Impact of Municipal Reforms. *American Journal of Political Science* 19 (February): 91–106.

Karnig, Albert K., and B. Oliver Walter. 1977. Municipal Elections: Registration, Incumbent Success, and Voter Participation. *Municipal Year Book 1977.* Washington, D.C.: International City Management Association.

Karnig, Albert K., and Susan Welch. 1980. *Black Representation and Urban Policy.* Chicago: University of Chicago Press.

Kaufman, Herbert. 1969. Administrative Decentralization and Political Power. *Public Administration Review* 29: 3–15.

————. 1981. Fear of Bureaucracy: A Raging Pandemic. *Public Administration Review* 41 (January/February): 1–9.

Kearney, Richard C., and Chandan Sinha. 1988. Professionalism and Bureaucratic Responsiveness: Conflict or Compatibility? *Public Administration Review* 48 (January/February): 571–579.

Kellar, Elizabeth J., Ed. 1981. *Managing with Less.* Washington, D.C.: International City Management Association.

Kingdon, John W. 1984. *Agendas, Alternatives, and Public Policies.* Boston: Little, Brown.

Koehler, Cortus T. 1973. Policy Development and Legislative Oversight in Council Manager Cities: An Information and Communication Analysis. *Public Administration Review* 33 (September/October): 433–441.

Kotter, John P., and Paul R. Lawrence. 1974. *Mayors in Action.* New York: Wiley.

Landau, Martin, and Russell Stout, Jr. 1979. To Manage Is Not to Control: Or the Folly of Type II Errors. *Public Administration Review* 39 (March/April): 148–156.

Latcham, John S., and Howard D. Hamilton. 1974. Purposive Roles of City Councilmen. Paper presented at the Annual Meeting of the American Political Science Association, Chicago, Ill.

LBJ School of Public Affairs. 1984. Local Government Elections Systems. *Policy Research Report No. 62.* Austin: University of Texas.

Lee, Eugene C. 1960. *The Politics of Nonpartisanship.* Berkeley: University of California Press.

————. 1963. City Elections: A Statistical Profile. *Municipal Year Book 1963.* Washington, D.C.: International City Management Association, 83–92.

Levine, Charles H. 1974. *Racial Conflict and the American Mayor.* Lexington, Mass.: Lexington Books.

Levine, Charles H., Irene S. Rubin, and George G. Wolohojian. 1981. *The Politics of Retrenchment*. Beverly Hills: Sage.

Levy, Frank, Arnold Meltsner, and Aaron Wildavsky. 1974. *Urban Outcomes*. Berkeley: University of California.

Liebert, R. J. 1974. Municipal Functions, Structure, and Expenditures. *Social Science Quarterly* 54 (March): 765–783.

Likert, Rensis. 1961. *New Patterns of Management*. New York: McGraw-Hill.

Lindblom, Charles E. 1959. The Science of Muddling Through. *Public Administration Review* 19 (Spring): 79–88.

————. 1965. *The Intelligence of Democracy*. New York: Free Press.

————. 1979. Still Muddling, Not Yet Through. *Public Administration Review* 39 (November/December): 517–526.

Lineberry, Robert L. 1977. *Equality and Urban Policy*. Beverly Hills: Sage.

Lineberry, Robert L., and Edmund P. Fowler. 1967. Reformism and Public Policies in American Cities. *American Political Science Review* 61 (September): 701–716.

Lineberry, Robert L., and Ira Sharkansky. 1974. *Urban Politics and Public Policy*, 2nd ed. New York: Harper & Row.

————. 1978. *Urban Politics and Public Policy*, 3rd ed. New York: Harper & Row.

Lipsky, Michael. 1976. Toward a Theory of Street-Level Bureaucracy, in Willis D. Hawley and Michael Lipsky, Eds., *Theoretical Perspectives in Urban Politics*. Englewood Cliffs, N.J.: Prentice-Hall.

————. 1980. *Street-Level Bureaucracy*. New York: Sage.

Loveridge, Ronald O. 1971. *City Managers in Legislative Politics*. Indianapolis: Bobbs-Merrill.

Lowi, Theodore. 1967. Machine Politics—Old and New. *Public Interest* No. 9 (Fall): 83–92.

Lupsha, Peter. 1974. Constraints on Urban Leadership, or Why Cities Cannot Be Creatively Governed, in Willis D. Hawley and David Rogers, Eds., *Improving the Quality of Urban Management*. *Urban Affairs Annual Reviews*, vol. 8: 607–623.

Lynn, Laurence E., Jr. 1981. *Managing the Public's Business*. New York: Basic Books.

————. 1987. *Managing Public Policy*. Boston: Little, Brown.

Lyons, William. 1978. Reform and Response in American Cities: Structure and Policy Reconsidered. *Social Science Quarterly* 59 (June): 118–132.

Lyons, W. E. 1983. Making Judges Out of Legislators: Rezoning on a Quasi-Judicial Model. *Legislative Studies Quarterly* 8 (November): 673–689.

McClelland, David C. 1970. Two Faces of Power. *Journal of International Affairs*. 24 (No. 1): 29–47.

MacManus, Susan A. 1978. City Council Election Procedures and Minority Representation: Are They Related? *Social Science Quarterly* 59 (June): 153–161.

_____. 1985. Mixed Electoral Systems: The Newest Reform Structure. *National Civic Review* 74 (November): 484–492.

Maier, Henry W. 1966. *Challenge to the Cities.* New York: Random House.

March, James G., and Johan P. Olsen. 1976. *Ambiguity and Choice in Complex Organizations.* Bergen, Norway: Universitetsforlaget.

March, James G., and Herbert A. Simon. 1958. *Organizations.* New York: Wiley.

Marini, Frank, Ed. 1971. *Toward a New Public Administration.* New York: Chandler.

Marwell, Gerald, and David R. Schmitt. 1975. *Cooperation: An Experimental Analysis.* New York: Academic Press.

Mayer, Richard T., and Michael M. Harmon. 1982. Teaching Moral Education in Public Administration. *Southern Review of Public Administration* 6 (Summer): 217–226.

Mayhew, David. 1974. *Congress: The Electoral Connection.* New Haven: Yale University Press.

Meier, Kenneth J. 1979. *Politics and the Bureaucracy.* North Scituate, Mass.: Duxbury Press.

Mintzberg, H. 1983. *Power In and Around Organizations.* Englewood Cliffs, N.J.: Prentice-Hall.

Mladenka, Kenneth R. 1980. The Urban Bureaucracy and the Chicago Political Machine: Who Gets What and the Limits to Political Control. *American Political Science Review* 74 (December): 991–998.

Mladenka, Kenneth R., and Kim Hill, 1978. The Delivery of Urban Police Services. *Journal of Politics* 40 (February): 112–133.

Morgan, David R. 1984. *Managing Urban America,* 2nd ed. Monterey: Brooks/Cole.

Morgan, David R., and Jeffrey L. Brudney. 1985. Urban Policy and City Government Structure: Testing the Mediating Effects of Reform. Paper presented at the Annual Meeting of the American Political Science Association, New Orleans, La.

Morgan, David R., and John P. Pellissero. 1980. Urban Policy: Does Political Structure Matter? *American Political Science Review* 74: 999–1006.

Murphy, Russell D. 1986. The Mayoralty and the Democratic Creed: The Evolution of an Ideology and an Institution. *Urban Affairs Quarterly* 22 (September): 3–23.

Nalbandian, John. 1987. The Evolution of Local Governance: A New Democracy. *Public Management* 69 (June): 2–5.

Nalbandian, John, and J. Terry Edwards. 1983. The Values of Public Administrators: A Comparison with Lawyers, Social Workers, and Business Administrators. *Review of Public Personnel Administration* 4 (Fall): 114–127.

Nardulli, Peter F., and Jeffrey M. Stonecash. 1981. *Politics, Professionalism, and Urban Services.* Cambridge, Mass.: Oelgeschlager, Gunn & Hain.

National League of Cities. 1980. *A National Survey of City Council Members: Issues in Council Leadership*. Washington, D.C.: NLC.

National Municipal League. 1967. *Model City Charter*, 6th ed. New York: National Municipal League.

———. 1976. *Handbook for Council Members in Council-Manager Cities*. New York: National Municipal League.

Needleman, Martin L., and Carolyn Emerson. 1974. *Guerrillas in the Bureaucracy*. New York: Wiley.

Newell, Charldean, and David N. Ammons. 1987. Role Emphasis of City Managers and Other Municipal Executives. *Public Administration Review* 47 (May/June): 246–252.

Newland, Chester A. 1985. Council-Manager Governance: Positive Alternative to Separation of Powers. *Public Management* 67 (July): 7–9.

———. 1987. Public Executives: Imperium, Sacerdotium, Collegium? Bicentennial Leadership Challenges. *Public Administration Review* 47 (January/February): 45–56.

Northrop, Alana, and William H. Dutton. 1978. Municipal Reform and Group Influence. *American Journal of Political Science* 22 (August): 691–711.

Olson, David M. 1981. *The Legislative Process: A Comparative Approach*. New York: Harper & Row.

Orbell, John, and Tory Uno. 1972. A Theory of Neighborhood Problem Solving. *American Political Science Review* 64 (June): 471–489.

Ouchi, William G. 1981. *Theory Z*. New York: Avon.

PA Times. 1985. Guidelines Proposed for Code of Ethics. *PA Times* (January 15): 5–6,10.

Parker, John K. 1971. Administrative Planning, in James M. Banovetz, Ed., *Managing the Modern City*. Washington, D.C.: International City Management Association, chap. 10.

Parr, John. 1987. The Council-Manager Form and the Future. *Public Management* 69 (February): 4–6.

Pease, Otis A. 1971. Urban Reformers in the Progressive Era, *Pacific Northwest Quarterly* 62 (April): 49–58.

Perrow, Charles. 1979. *Complex Organizations: A Critical Essay*, 2nd ed. Glenview, Ill.: Scott, Foresman.

Peters, Thomas J., and Robert H. Waterman. 1982. *In Search of Excellence*. New York: Warner Books.

Petersen, Paul E. 1981. *City Limits*. Chicago: University of Chicago Press.

Peterson, Steven A., and William H. Dutton. 1982. The Responsiveness of Local Legislators: A Case Study. *Urban Interest* 4 (Fall): 18–28.

Pfeffer, Jeffrey. 1981. *Power in Organizations*. Marshfield, Mass.: Pitman.

Pfiffner, James P. 1985. Political Public Administration. *Public Administration Review* 45 (March/April): 353–356.

Pressman, Jeffrey L. 1972. Preconditions of Mayoral Leadership. *American Political Science Review* 66 (June): 511–524.

Pressman, Jeffrey L., and Aaron B. Wildavsky. 1973. *Implementation.* Berkeley: University of California Press.

Prewitt, Kenneth. 1970. *The Recruitment of Political Leaders.* Indianapolis: Bobbs-Merrill.

Redford, Emmette S. 1969. *Democracy in the Administrative State.* New York: Oxford University Press.

Renner, Tari. 1988. Municipal Election Processes: The Impact on Minority Representation. *Municipal Year Book 1988.* Washington, D.C.: International City Management Association: 13–22.

Rich, Richard C. Ed. 1982. *The Politics of Urban Public Services.* Lexington, Mass.: Lexington Books.

Ripley, Randall B., and Grace A. Franklin. 1982. *Bureaucracy and Policy Implementation.* Homewood, Ill.: Dorsey Press.

Robinson, Theodore P., and Thomas R. Dye. 1978. Reformism and Black Representation on City Councils. *Social Science Quarterly* 59 (June): 133–141.

Rodgers, Daniel T. 1982. In Search of Progressivism. *Reviews in American History* 10 (December): 113–132.

Rogers, Chester, and Harold Arman. 1971. Nonpartisanship and Election to City Office. *Social Science Quarterly* 51 (March): 941–945.

Rogers, David. 1970. The Failure of Inner City Schools: A Crisis of Management and Service Delivery. *Educational Technology* 10 (September): 27–32.

———. 1971. *The Management of Big Cities.* New York: Sage.

Rohr, John A. 1976. The Study of Ethics in the P.A. Curriculum. *Public Administration Review* 36 (July/August): 398–406.

———. 1978. *Ethics for Bureaucrats.* New York: Dekker.

———. 1986. *To Run a Constitution.* Lawrence: University Press of Kansas.

Rosenthal, Donald D., and Robert L. Crain. 1968. Structure and Values in Local Political Systems: The Case of Fluoridation Decisions, in James Q. Wilson, Ed., *City Politics and Public Policy.* New York: Wiley: 217–242.

Royko, Mike. 1984. No Gray Areas in City Politics. *The Chapel Hill Newspaper* (September 19): 4A.

Ruder, Karma. 1987. The Debates Underpinning the ICMA Code of Ethics. *Public Management* 69 (August): 9–11.

Russell, Christine H., and Robert L. Crain. 1982. The Importance of Political Factors in Explaining Northern School Desegregation. *American Journal of Political Science* 26 (November): 772–796.

Sanders, Haywood T. 1979. Governmental Structure in American Cities. *Municipal Year Book 1979.* Washington, D.C.: International City Management Association.

———. 1982. The Government of American Cities: Continuity and Change in Structure. *Municipal Year Book 1982.* Washington, D.C.: International City Management Association.

Sanera, Michael. 1985. Implementing the Mandate, in *Mandate for Leadership II*. Washington: Heritage Foundation: Part 4.

Savas, E. S. 1979. How Much Do Government Services Really Cost? *Urban Affairs Quarterly* 15 (September): 23–41.

———. 1987. *Privatization: The Key to Better Government*. New York: Chatham House.

Sayre, Wallace S., and Herbert Kaufman. 1960. *Governing New York City*. New York: Sage.

Schellinger, Mary A. 1985. Local Government Managers: Profile of the Professionals in a Maturing Profession. *Municipal Year Book 1985*. Washington, D.C.: International City Management Association.

Schick, Allen. 1976. Congress and the "Details" of Administration. *Public Administration Review* 36 (September/October): 516–528.

Schiesl, Martin J. 1977. *The Politics of Efficiency*. Berkeley: University of California Press.

Schlesinger, Joseph A. 1966. *Ambition and Politics*. Chicago: Rand McNally.

Shank, Alan, and Ralph W. Conant. 1975. *Urban Perspectives*. Boston: Holbrook Press.

Shannon, John. 1987. The Return to Fend-for-Yourself Federalism: The Reagan Mark. *Intergovernmental Perspective* 13 (Summer/Fall): 34–37.

Shefter, Martin. 1985. *Political Crisis/Fiscal Crisis*. New York: Basic Books.

Sokolow, Alvin D. 1987. Legislators Without Ambition: Recruiting Citizens to Small Town Office. Paper presented at the Annual Meeting of the American Political Science Association, Chicago, Ill.

Sparrow, Glen. 1984. The Emerging Chief Executive: The San Diego Experience. *Urban Resources* 2 (Fall): 3–8.

Stanford, Melvin J. 1983. *Management Policy*, 2nd ed. Englewood Cliffs, N.J.: Prentice-Hall.

Stewart, Debra. 1985. Ethics and the Profession of Public Administration: The Moral Responsibility of Individuals in Public Sector Organizations. *Public Administration Quarterly* 10 (Winter): 487–495.

Stewart, Frank Mann. 1950. *A Half Century of Municipal Reform*. Berkeley: University of California Press.

Stillman, Richard J., II. 1974. *The Rise of the City Manager*. Albuquerque: University of New Mexico Press.

———. 1977. The City Manager: Professional Helping Hand, or Political Hired Hand? *Public Administration Review* 37 (November/December): 659–670.

———. 1982. Local Public Management in Transition: A Report on the Current State of the Profession. *Municipal Year Book 1982*. Washington, D.C.: International City Management Association.

Stone, Clarence N. 1982. Complexity and the Changing Character of Executive Leadership: An Interpretation of the Lindsay Administration in New York City. *Urban Interest* 4 (Fall): 29–50.

Stone, Clarence N., Robert K. Whelan, and William J. Murin. 1986. *Urban Politics in a Bureaucratic Age*, 2nd ed. Englewood Cliffs, N.J.: Prentice-Hall.

Stone, Harold A., Don K. Price, and Kathryn H. Stone. 1940. *City Management Government in the United States*. Chicago: Public Administration Service.

Svara, James H. 1977. Unwrapping Institutional Packages in Urban Government: The Combination of Election Institutions in American Cities. *Journal of Politics* 39 (February): 166–175.

———. 1985a. Dichotomy and Duality: Reconceptualizing the Relationship Between Policy and Administration in Council-Manager Cities. *Public Administration Review* 45 (January/February): 221–232.

———. 1985b. Political Supremacy and Administrative Expertise. *Management Science and Policy Analysis* 3 (Summer): 3–7.

———. 1986a. Contributions of the City Council to Effective Governance. *Popular Government* 51 (Spring): 1–8.

———. 1986b. Mayors in Council-Manager Cities: Recognizing the Leadership Potential. *National Civic Review* 75 (September/October): 271–283, 305.

———. 1986c. The Responsible Administrator. *Popular Government* 51 (Fall): 18–24, 27.

———. 1987a. Mayoral Leadership in Council-Manager Cities: Preconditions Versus Preconceptions. *Journal of Politics* 49 (February): 207–227.

———. 1987b. The Responsible Manager: Building on the Code and the Declaration. *Public Management* 69 (August): 14–19.

———. 1988a. The Complementary Roles of Officials in Council Manager Government. *Municipal Year Book 1988*. Washington, D.C.: International City Management Association: 23–34.

———. 1988b. Conflict, Cooperation, and Separation of Powers in City Government. *Journal of Urban Affairs* 10 (No. 4): 357–372.

Svara, James H., and James W. Bohmbach. 1976. The Mayoralty and Leadership in Council-Manager Cities. *Popular Government* 41 (Winter): 1–6.

Sweetwood, Hervey L. 1980. *Tools for Leadership: A Handbook for Elected Officials*. Washington, D.C.: National League of Cities.

Talbot, Allan. 1967. *The Mayor's Game*. New York: Harper & Row.

Thelen, David P. 1979. Urban Politics: Beyond Bosses and Reformers. *Reviews in American History* 7 (September): 406–412.

Thomas, John Clayton. 1986. *Between Citizen and City*. Lawrence: University of Kansas Press.

Thomas, Kenneth W., and Ralph H. Kilmann. 1974. *Conflict Mode Instrument*. Tuxedo, N.Y.: Xicom.

Thomas, Robert D. 1987. The Search for Legitimacy and Competency in Mayor-Council Relations: The Case of Houston. Paper presented at the

Annual Meeting of the Southern Political Science Association, Charlotte, N.C.

Thompson, Arthur A., Jr., and A. J. Strickland III. 1981. *Strategy and Policy: Concepts and Cases.* Plano, Tex.: Business Publications.

Thompson, Dennis F. 1985. The Possibility of Administrative Ethics. *Public Administration Review* 45 (September/October): 555–561.

Tipton, Howard D. 1985. Promoting the C-M Plan. *Public Management* 67 (July): 10.

Viteritti, Joseph P. 1982. Bureaucratic Environments, Efficiency, and Equity in Urban-Service-Delivery Systems, in Richard C. Rich, Ed., *The Politics of Urban Public Services.* Lexington, Mass.: Lexington Books: 53–68.

Vogel, Ronald K., and Bert E. Swanson. 1988. Setting Agenda for Community Change: The Community Goal-Setting Strategy. *Journal of Urban Affairs* 10 (No. 1): 41–61.

Wahlke, John C., Heinz Eulau, William Buchanan, and LeRoy C. Ferguson. 1962. *The Legislative System.* New York: Wiley.

Wamsley, Gary L., Charles T. Goodsell, John A. Rohr, Camilla M. Stevers, Orion F. White, and James F. Wolf. 1987. The Public Administration and the Governance Process: Refocusing the American Dialogue, in Ralph C. Chandler, Ed. *A Centennial History of the American Administrative State.* New York: Free Press: 291–343.

Weinberg, Martha Wagner. 1981. Boston's Kevin White: A Mayor Who Survives. *Political Science Quarterly* 96 (Spring): 87–106.

Weinstein, James. 1962. Organized Business and the City Commission and Manager Movements. *Journal of Southern History* 28 (May): 166–182.

Weick, K. E. 1976. Educational Organizations as Loosely Coupled Systems. *Administrative Science Quarterly* 21 (March): 1–19.

Welch, Susan, and Timothy Bledsoe. 1988. *Urban Reform and Its Consequences: A Study in Representation.* Chicago: University of Chicago Press.

Whitaker, Gordon, and Larry W. Davis. 1986. Politics, Policy, and County Managers. Paper presented at the Annual Meeting of the Southern Political Science Association, Atlanta, Ga.

Wikstrom, Nelson. 1979. The Mayor as a Policy Leader in the Council-Manager Form of Government: A View from the Field. *Public Administration Review* 39 (May/June): 270–276.

Wildavsky, Aaron. 1984. *The Politics of the Budgetary Process,* 4th ed. Boston: Little, Brown.

Wilson, James Q. 1968. The Mayors vs. the Cities. *Public Interest* No. 16 (Summer): 25–37.

Wilson, Woodrow. 1887. The Study of Administration. *Political Science Quarterly* 2 (June): 197–220.

Wirt, Frederick M. 1974. *Power in the City.* Berkeley: University of California Press.

Wirth, Clifford J., and Michael L. Vasu. 1984. Ideology and Decisionmaking for American City Managers. Paper presented at the Annual Meeting of the American Political Science Association, Washington, D.C.

Wish, Naomi Bailin. 1986. The Cost and Quality of Urban Life: A Matter of Governmental Structure or Regional Variation? *Municipal Year Book 1986.* Washington, D.C.: International City Management Association: 17–23.

Wolfinger, Raymond E. 1974. *The Politics of Progress.* Englewood Cliffs, N.J.: Prentice-Hall.

Wright, Deil. 1969. The Manager as a Development Administrator, in Robert Daland, Ed., *Comparative Urban Research.* Beverly Hills: Sage: 203–248.

Wuffle, A. 1986. Reflections on Academia. *PS* 29 (Winter): 57–61.

Yates, Douglas. 1977. *The Ungovernable City.* Cambridge, Mass.: MIT Press.

———. 1981. Hard Choices: Justifying Bureaucratic Decisions, in Joel Fleischman, Lance Leibman, and Mark H. Moore, Eds., *Public Duties.* Cambridge, Mass.: Harvard University Press: 32–51.

———. 1982. *Bureaucratic Democracy.* Cambridge, Mass.: Harvard University Press.

———. 1985. *The Politics of Management.* San Francisco: Josey-Bass.

Zeigler, Harmon, Ellen Kehoe, and Jane Reisman. 1985. *City Managers and School Superintendents.* New York: Praeger.

Zimmerman, Joseph. 1972. *The Federated City.* New York: St. Martin's Press.

Zisk, Betty H. 1973. *Local Interest Politics: A One-Way Street.* Indianapolis: Bobbs-Merrill.

Index

Governors, council members as, 123,
125, 153, 157
Green, Roy E., 191
Greensboro, North Carolina, 107, 144,
149, *230,* 243 n. 80, 25. n. 56,
265 n. 6
Greenstone, J. David, 235 n. 17
Greer, Ann, 93
Growth
administrator's commitmen: to, 85,
172, 243
as characteristic of council-manager
cities, 54
as factor contributing to cooperation,
243 n. 79
and mission, 15–16
Gruber, Judith E., 186, 187, 227, 233
n. 4, 238 n. 6, 258 n. 10, 260 n.
43
Guidebooks for officials, 147, 156
Guiding force, facilitative mayor as,
82, 115, 121

Halter, Gary, 253 n. 12
Hamilton, Howard, 127
Handbooks for elected officials, 147,
152
Hart, David K., 200
Hartford, Connecticut, 139, *230,* 243
n. 80
Hawley, Willis D., 137, 138 227
Heads. *See* Department heads
Heeler, Ward, 140
Heilig, Peggy, 61, 128, 131, 132, 137,
146, 152
Hein, C. J., 65
Hiring the manager
and council's supervisory role, 147
and determination of mission, 53
and executive role for mayor, 116
Hogan, James B., 176, 182, 183, 192,
195, 196
Homeowners, percentage of as indicator
of community characteristics, 66
Housing services, 69
Houston, Texas, 136, 257 n. 2
Howe, Elizabeth, 201
Hughes, Richard A., 155
Hyperpluralism, 41

ICMA. *See* International City Management Association
Ideals, ICMA Declaration of, 198,
204, 263
Ideological differences in city councils,
137–38, 140
Ideology as mayoral characteristic, 99–
100
Immigrants, attitudes of reformers regarding, 12
Implementation
and administration, *14,* 16, 21–22
and opportunities to influence policy, 49
Inclusiveness and cooperative pattern,
225
Income level
of council members, 135
of districts and council member attitudes, 137–38
Incumbency and reelection to council,
142
Incursions by council into administrative realm, 77, 182, 208
Influentials' control of manager, 85
Informal resources, 28, 41, 47, 49,
92–94, 99
Innovator type of mayoral leadership,
83, 103–6, *118*
Input/output (systems) model, 5, 6
Institutions. *See* Formal structure;
Forms of government
Insulation
as effect of strong parties, 67
in council-manager government, 41,
43, 52, 67–68, 79
International City Management Association (ICMA), 10, 14, 147,
155, 181, 198, 202, 203, 204,
209, 240 n. 43
Investigations by councils, 122, 124,
207
Isolate, organizational, 174, 176

Jacobs, David, 69
Johnson, Karl F., 65
Jones, Bryan, 38, 51, 69, 173, 205,
227, 233 n. 4, 235 n. 17, 237 n.
42, 238 n. 3, 241 n. 54, 259 n.

Jones, Bryan (*continued*)
25, 260 n. 29, 262 n. 71, 263 n. 89, 265 n. 126
Judicial role of council, 122, 123, 125, 145

Kansas, 253 n. 7
Karnig, Albert K., 66
Karps, Paul D., 132
Kaufman, Jerome, 201
Kearney, Richard C., 172
Kehoe, Ellen, 28
Kelly, Janet M., 97
Kentucky, 253 n. 7
Knave as type of administrator, 170, 174–76, *177*
Knoxville, Tennessee, 91, 92, 124, 243 n. 80
Koehler, Cortus T., 142
Kotter, John P., 94, 96, 99

Labor unions, 63, 64, 137, 138, 245 n. 15
Latcham, John S., 127, 252 n. 2, 253 n. 10
Lauth, Thomas P., 71, 151, 172, 180, 185, 187, 228
Lawmaking function of councils, 122
Lawrence, Paul R., 94, 96, 99
LBJ School, 136, 158
Leadership. *See also* Administrators; Council Members; Mayors
forms of, 221–22
level of mayors and council presidents, *163*, 164
in policy by managers, 181–82
responsibilities, 18–22
League of Women Voters, 251 n. 56
Lee, Richard C., 47, 88
Legislative. *See also* Council, city
acts, 125
function, 122–24
Levine, Charles H., 35, 99, 100, 244 n. 1, 250 n. 43
Levy, Frank, 170, 259 n. 12
Liaison channel
council president as, 164
mayor as, 108–9, 114, 116

Liberals as force in city elections, 138
Library in Oakland as administrative isolate, 171, 174
Likert, Rensis, 42
Lincoln, Nebraska, 243 n. 80
Lindsay, John, 50, 89, 106, 250 n. 25
Lineberry, Robert L., 38, 65, 66, 70, 84, 99
Lipsky, Michael, 171, 202, 259 n. 15
Locals as managers and CAOs, 175, 180
Loveridge, Ronald O., 52, 190, 192, 195, 196, 262 nn. 85–86
Lynn, Laurence E., 151
Lyons, W. E., 125
Lyons, William, 65

Machines
administrative agencies as new, 40, 70, 167
political party, 11
MacManus, Susan A., 46, 62
Madison, James, and separation of power, 44, 223
Maier, Henry, 104
Majority, shifting ideological on councils, 138
Management
council role in, 22, 144, 148, *149*, *154*, 155, 161–62
defined, 17
as dimension in governmental process, *14*, 16–17, *20*
responsibilities of city manager in, *199*, 202–3
responsibilities of department heads in, 207–8
Managers, city. *See also* Administrators
appointment, 51–53
characteristics, 178–80
educational background, *179*
future role, 227
as power in governmental process, 84–86
as prototypical administrator, 197
relationship with council, 55–58
relationship with mayor, 109–11

Marshall, Dale Rogers, 138
Maryland, 253 n. 7
Maverick type of mayor, 105, 114
Mayer, Richard T., 197
Mayhew, David, 247 n. 34
Mayor-centered governance ir council-
manager cities, 120
Mayor-council government, 45–46.
See also Forms of government
and executive mayors, 88–95
and factors producing conflict, 34–
36, 49–51
strong, 47–49
weak, 47
Mayors. *See also* Executive mayor;
Facilitative mayor; Form; of
government
relations with CAO, 182–84, *183*
relations with council, 55–57
relations with manager, 109–11
summary of types of leadership,
118
typical view of role in governmental
process, 28
McClelland, David C., 249 r. 24
Media, 5, 49
coverage and investigations, 207
coverage and symbolic representation, 132
mayor's relations with, 94–95
Meltsner, Arnold, 170
Memphis, Tennessee, 91, 92, *230*, 243
n. 80
Mencken, H. L., 3
Merit
commitment of council members to,
153
as criterion in selecting manager and
staff, 52, 202, 208
as reform principle, 11
Michigan, 181
Milwaukee, Wisconsin, 104
Minimal leadership by mayor, 100
Minneapolis, Minnesota, 89, 90, 92,
123, 182, *230*, 243 n. 80
Minorities. *See also* Blacks
representation on council, 135, 138
service delivery to, 68–69

Mission
council role in, 20–21, 144, 149–
50, *149*, 153, *154*
as dimension in governmental process, 13–15, *14*, 16–17, *20*
responsibilities of city manager in,
198–200, *199*
responsibilities of department heads
in, 205–6
Mladenka, Kenneth R., 69
Mobility, career of administrators, 180,
261 n. 51
Model. *See also* Dichotomy model;
Dichotomy-duality model
Ferman's of mayoral leadership, 93
Jones's of service distribution, 238
n. 3
Model City charter, 61, 124, 226, 235
n. 16, 249 n. 2
Models
of consensus, 86
of governmental process, 38
Monitoring
of governmental performance by
mayor, 111, 115
of staff performance by council,
155
Montana, 253 n. 7
Montgomery, Alabama, 157
Moody's bond ratings, *230*
Morale, council impact on staff, 152
Morgan, David R., 65, 66
Moscone, George, 93
Motivation to serve on council, 141
Mundt, Robert, 61, 128, 131, 132,
137, 146, 152
Municipal reform movement. *See*
Reform movement
Mutual adjustment, 27, 32, 33, 223–
24
Mutuality of interests in cooperative
pattern, 32
Mutually exclusive conceptions of
manager's policy role, 192, 195

NAACP, 251 n. 56
Nalbandian, John, 188
Nardulli, Peter F., 187

Printed in the United States
3541

9 780195 057621